Romans

Personal Theology for Every Woman's Heart

By

Christine E. Wyrtzen

PRESS

Romans
Personal Theology for Every Woman's Heart
by Christine E. Wyrtzen

Printed in the United States of America

ISBN 9781625098054

www.xulonpress.com

.

ACKNOWLEDGMENTS

*J*ohn Piper does not know me, to my knowledge, and has no idea how his book and national conference called, **THINK,** impacted me in 2010. I was convicted, then challenged, to go deeper and take the women I teach deeper through my ministry, *Daughters of Promise*. This study of Romans was the result. Thank you, sir, for always causing me to love Jesus more through your ministry. I am but one life you have touched and this is but one book, I'm sure, that is the direct result of God using you through *Desiring God Ministries.*

In no lesser way, I am so grateful to my daughter, Jaime, for the months of editing on this project. You did what would have bogged me down for a good year had I done it alone. And, I wouldn't have done it well! While I know you love to edit, it is still tedious work. You saw it through to the end, on time, with enthusiasm, and all with our young grandchildren in tow. My daughter, I can't tell you what it means to work with you in this ministry and to share Jesus together. Thank you for this labor of love!

INTRODUCTION

Studying Romans is a daunting adventure. There are three reasons for that.

1. Romans has been studied by more brilliant individuals than probably any piece of biblical literature in history. This book has been one of profound interest over the centuries to wherever Christianity has spread. To study this book is to travel the similar journey of Martin Luther and many other spiritual giants like him.

2. While I do not hold a seminary degree, I am a serious Bible student and have been for many years. I pray I can handle this book with the integrity and respect it deserves.

3. I suspect that Romans will deeply change me. Martin Luther was profoundly changed; so much so that he put his life on the line for the truth he discovered there. Change can be scary. Am I willing to be so moved as to risk everything for Jesus Christ? Can this book do that to me? I already know the answer is 'yes.'

Change is what I need most. As long as I live here on earth, there are places of spiritual death in my soul that need to be touched by Jesus Christ. I need spiritual life in places I'm not yet aware. I long as I study: to be moved, instructed, challenged, and deeply stirred; then just maybe, there will be the likes of a new personal reformation. In whatever ways the Gospel is shallow to me, I pray it expands to a broader depth.

Will you join me in asking God to open your heart wide to Paul's letter and the Holy Spirit's teaching? How open we are will determine how much the journey will affect us. If we want change at all cost, God will be faithful to answer our prayers. He loves seekers; the ones who search for Him with their whole hearts.

I'm on the edge, ready to jump into Romans with my whole heart. Oh God, change me. Amen

CHAPTER 1

SERVANTS AND MASTERS

Paul, a servant of Christ Jesus. Romans 1:1a

*T*here was once a master of a great kingdom. He was wealthy beyond measure and needed to hire servants to take care of his estate. He sent a foreman to the streets to hire whomever was needed to keep his house in order. He would never get to know them personally however. Most of them would long for their freedom. They would know that their master's only interest in them would be in their ability to take care of what he owned. They would strain under the workload and despise their lowly status.

There was once a Master of a different kingdom. He was also wealthy beyond measure and needed no one to maintain His kingdom. He was all-sufficient. He loved to create though and, over the course of seven days, made the world, made man and woman, and gave them the privilege of ruling this paradise. They rebelled against their Creator though, declared mutiny, and were banished from His lovely estate but He forgave them and made a way for them to come home.

How? This kind Creator sent His Son to live among the fallen for a while. He assumed the role of a servant and taught people many things; that His Father loved them dearly, longed to forgive and restore them, and give them back their role in his kingdom. To turn things upside down, the Son even served the fallen ones by giving them the ultimate gift; His life. Love fueled this unthinkable sacrifice and since then, the desire to become a servant like this crucified Son has spread like wildfire. Radical love calls for a radical response.

The Apostle Paul met Jesus on the road to Damascus and ever since that encounter, he walked in the Son's footsteps. He identified himself as His servant, a bond-slave of the very One he once thought a fraud.

To be a servant of an earthly master is to labor, often in anonymity. To be a servant of Christ is to whisper 'Savior' and 'Friend' and enjoy an intimacy that is not of this world. Martyrdom has been the portion of many servants, even the Apostle Paul, who went to his death feeling that such an end was his privilege, not twisted fate.

Never could I serve a Master such as You. I am Your servant and I love my calling. Amen

THE AUTHOR

Paul, a servant of Christ Jesus. Romans 1:1

Most historians say that Paul was born around the time that Jesus was a toddler. When Jesus was two, Paul was being rocked to sleep in his mother's arms. His birth into the very era of the time of Christ was not to be significant to him for several more decades. Though he couldn't know it, he was created to live in a time of history that framed his calling perfectly.

I have heard some say, *"I was born before my time."* Or, *"I should have been born a hundred years ago."* What they mean by that is this; they believe their lives are ill fitted for this present time. They feel out of step and truly believe that they would more fully thrive in another era. Perhaps you feel that way today.

None of us can fully know the plans of God. Our vision of the role we play in the kingdom is short sighted. We push one domino over and are often blind to the many dominoes that fall over way down the line because we lived to give the first one its push. Paul, who spent his childhood unaware that he was a contemporary of the Messiah, studied the Torah like so many Jewish boys before him. The routines of his life did not reveal the powerful storylines that lay ahead of him; his persecution of Christ followers, his conversion, and his passionate witness to the Gentiles that would eventually cost him his life and change the world.

There is no such thing as having an insignificant part in history. A divine strategist has planned our births for a specific purpose on the kingdom's timeline. Each child of God should sit up straight and grow wide-eyed at the realization that life is precious, and ordered, and prolonged by a God who plans for Apostle Paul-sized destinies.

Just because we can't see the breadth of our calling doesn't mean it doesn't exist. For many of us, only history will pull back the curtain wide.

I was chosen by You to live in these perilous times, the possible end of days before You come for Your bride. That is no mistake. By your mercy, reveal my role so that I don't waste time. Amen

EDUCATION AND EXPERIENCE

Paul, a servant of Christ Jesus. Romans 1:1

Paul grew up in Tarsus to a well-to-do family. He was privileged to be tutored under the Rabbi Gamaliel, the President-Patriarch of the Sanhedrin. Gamaliel was the Pharisee doctor of Jewish law. No young student of the Torah could have wished for a better teacher. This brilliant and well-respected Rabbi shaped Paul's life and gave him a coveted education.

However, Paul but didn't recognize Jesus. His education served to make him a zealot whose passion was to protect the sanctity of the Jewish faith by annihilating Christians. He was there in person to support the stoning of the Apostle Stephen. Though he was only feet away from this eloquent witness, Paul failed to see the glory of Jesus in a martyr's face. He was absolutely blind in spite of his brilliant education. Paul lacked experience with Christ, which he eventually got on his way to Damascus.

Education, by itself, does not a Christian make. Many are raised in the church, have all the doctrine down pat, but because they lack experience with Jesus, their lives have no power. Their knowledge lacks context. Education without experience is a dangerous thing.

So is experience without education. If one has encountered Jesus but then fails to get to know Him through His revealed Word, he will be equally as reckless with the truth.

I have attended meetings over the years where the speaker was introduced as 'one of the foremost Christian thinkers of our times.' His mind held the audience in awe. His grasp of history and Christian ethics, though brilliant, did not reveal to us that he had been with Jesus. I have also talked with people who have had life-changing encounters with Christ but did not follow it up with path of discipleship. They went on to form their theology with their own interpretations of their experiences.

May God save us today. For those who are educated and enjoy the prestige of letters after their name, I would say this ~ You are a blind sheep without the entrance of the Spirit giving light to the Word. Humble yourself to see the glory of Christ. For those who see the Lord but are coasting on experience, I would say that form and context must be added to provide a foundation for your faith in Christ. Study and meditate in order to know "whom you have believed."

Show me Your glory ~ both in Your Word and on my Damascus road. Amen

SET APART FOR SOMETHING DIFFERENT

Paul, a servant of Christ Jesus, called to be an apostle, set apart for the Gospel of God. Romans 1:1

Before Paul met Christ on the road to Damascus, he was a Pharisee. He knew what it was to be 'set apart' for that is the very meaning of the word Pharisee. (A separated one) He was set apart to the Pharisaic traditions. Pharisees crossed the street rather than get near to someone they considered vile and a great sinner. The list of things they abstained from was long.

But when he met Jesus, he was set apart for something different. Instead of defining his life by what he was *against,* he was released to define his life with a declaration of what he was *for.* He was set apart for the Gospel of God. Pharisees were generally righteous, narrow, cruel, and obsessive. A disciple of Christ was gracious, merciful, and humble while truth telling. What a transformation Paul experienced. Only God could do that.

Christians today have been set apart by God to be pro-active, marked by joy. The list of things we are *for* is expansive. Yet, so many have failed to depart from the Pharisaical ways of legalism. They feel called to be the policemen of the church, pointing fingers and nit-picking. When presented with a visionary idea, they exclaim, *"I guess I don't have a problem with that."* The question is, *"What are they for, not against?"*

A bitter root of judgment plagues the church and some justify it by saying that they are just contending for the faith. However, it seems that these people are rarely happy. Their demeanor is angry, suspicious, narrow, and ever ready to pick a fight with other believers. A true contender for the faith is a passionate communicator of the Gospel, filled with grace and the power of the Spirit. Contending for the faith takes up the smallest portion of his time for the presentation of the Gospel is his ultimate goal and highest joy.

Jesus, I am joyfully for Your Gospel; seeing people turn from darkness to light. Amen

SENT TO DO WHAT?

Paul, a servant of Christ Jesus, called to an apostle. . .
Romans 1:1

Paul, a servant of the One who became a suffering servant to us, called Him to be an apostle. An apostle is someone who is sent out with a message. At his conversion, Paul was given this assignment that would define the rest of his life. He probably thought, before his conversion, that his duty was to protect the sanctity of the Jewish faith from Christian heresy. As it turned out, he was to encounter Christ and become what he had once hated.

What was Paul's calling straight out of the mouth of Jesus? And, is it similar to ours? The mandate out of heaven was a clear and beautiful one. Here it is in Paul's own words. *"But rise and stand upon your feet, for I have appeared to you for this purpose, to appoint you as a servant and witness to the things in which you have seen me and to those in which I will appear to you, delivering you from your people and from the Gentiles-to whom I am sending you to open their eyes, so that they may turn from darkness to light and from the power of Satan to God. . ."* (Acts 26:16-18)

Our understanding of the 'call' can get so muddied when we mix it in with the realm of spiritual gifts. *"I am called to teach, or encourage, or give to others, or show hospitality, or exhort."* But each gift is just a vehicle to the main event ~ *"Opening their eyes so that they may turn from darkness to light and from Satan to God."* That begs me to examine whether my understanding of my mission is clear enough. What do I say when I encourage? What do I teach when I open the scriptures? Do I pick and choose inspirational topics and a smattering of scriptures that will make someone feel good *or* do I speak a Word that fashions a sharp arrow of conviction? The answer to that question is whether or not my audience, large and small, personal and impersonal, is motivated to make a choice between darkness and Light.

Ah, yes, Paul grasped it. Perhaps he had an advantage because he saw the light, fell to his knees, and heard the voice of his Lord. But that excuse won't grant me, or anyone else living today, any pardons. God speaks even more powerfully now through the Spirit of the One who also spoke to Paul because that Voice is not without, it is within. He speaks each time I open His Word. If my perception of what I was born to do is diluted and fuzzy, I cry out today with a full voice and with an intensity of my heart ~

Let me hear your call again, Lord. Wake me up. Make my crooked path straight. Amen

PROPHETS AND THE PRESENT

Paul, a servant of Christ Jesus, called to be an Apostle, set apart for the Gospel of God, which he promised beforehand through his prophets in the holy scriptures.
Romans 1:1

Nearly every time Paul gave a defense for the Gospel, he didn't start with the birth of Jesus in Bethlehem. Since most of his accusers were Jewish leaders, he was intent on showing them that Jesus was connected to their scriptures, the fulfillment of their law. The Torah, which they embraced and knew front to back, had predicted his coming. God was not only the Alpha and Omega, but also the God of the in-between. Nothing was random, nothing was haphazard, but each event in history a meticulously conceived plan according to the wisdom of a Sovereign God.

Why was this important to the Jews? Because it's hard for any of us to completely leave everything familiar and embark on something new. And it wasn't necessary where the Jews were concerned. They had the Torah and the writings of the prophets in their hands, the complete revelation of Jesus Christ. To believe on Him was to complete their faith, to be as Abraham looking ahead for the Lamb of God and finding Him in Jesus.

God is the consummate storyteller. The revelation of Jesus in Bethlehem was connected to the plotline in Eden when Adam and Eve sinned. Everything in between followed the storyline.

He is also the consummate storyteller of my life. Not one thing has happened to me that isn't an integral part of God's plotline for me. I didn't always believe that; taking a handful of painful events and putting them in the "useless" category. God just couldn't use those, could He?

I had a dream many years ago where I was sitting with Jesus for a day in a secluded place. We had nothing but time because the clock on the wall had stopped. Relieved that there were no time constraints, I began to talk and tell Him my story. He gently interrupted and made this surprising suggestion. ***"Tell you what, Christine. Let me tell you your story."***

As he did, and it seemed that the dream took all night, He wove together the events of my life, starting with my place in His heart before the world was created, down through the ancestral lines of my family, to the behaviors of my parents, teachers, and pivotal people in my life. His version was much longer than mine and reminded me that He was not only the God of the past and future, but everything in the middle.

In God's plot line, there is no such thing as 'wasted'. Not even our mistakes. Though we know the end of the story revealed in Scripture, the redemptive twists and turns take us by surprise and delight. May I not be like the Jews who failed to recognize Jesus when He stood in front of them. As He orders the events of my day, I ask for the eyesight to see His fingerprints.

After all these years, I am beginning to love my storyline. It is interwoven with Yours, with the cross. Amen

<u>A SAVIOR OR A KING?</u>

..And was declared to be the Son of God in power according to the Spirit of holiness by his resurrection from the dead, Jesus Christ our Lord. . . Romans 1:3-4

Jesus had always been God and He had always been powerful. But when He came as a babe, flesh veiled that power. It wasn't until the resurrection that the earth was reminded again of the power of the One who had lived for three decades and then died a criminal's death on a cross. Through the empty tomb, the "Son of God in power" was again on full display.

What I have to remember is this; life in the flesh just veiled His power; it didn't erase it. He held it in check, by choice, through His obedience to His Father's greater plan. Jesus didn't come to earth to set up His kingdom; He came to take care of our sin problem. We needed a Savior first, then a King.

The Jews who were being crushed under the Roman government so desired a King to deliver them from their oppressors that they couldn't appreciate the gift this Savior was giving them. Pain obscures my vision too. What I often need the most is not what I think I need. That which crushes my heart today can so fill my field of vision that deliverance from it is all that I pray for. When God doesn't cooperate by removing my version of the 'Roman boot of oppression,' I can easily become disillusioned, just like the people of Jesus' day.

One day, Jesus will set up His kingdom. He won't wear a crown of thorns but a royal crown. His robe won't be torn to pieces and sold as souvenirs. The trail of His robe will fill the temple. In the meantime, I must trust my Savior and King to give me what I need most, especially as I understand that my flesh obscures my vision. When I'm frustrated, my eyes filled with the tears of misunderstanding, Jesus knows. He experienced the limitations and temptations of the flesh and knows the difficult path of faith and trust inside these mortal bodies.

You are my Savior and my King. I reaffirm my trust in the places where it is weak. Amen

FAITH AND ITS OUTCOME

..Jesus Christ our Lord, through whom we have received grace and apostleship to bring about the obedience of faith. . . Romans 1:5

Obedience is a word that makes the natural heart twist. Just hearing it makes any man or woman long for another subject matter more pleasant. I think that most of us believe that the faith that led to our salvation was one thing and the faith of obedience is yet another. One got us in the kingdom but the other is some rigorous, complicated lifestyle that no one wants to really think about.

The Gospel was designed to be simple; simple enough for a child. So is the subject of faith and obedience. The smallest child knows what it is to obey or disobey. They don't even have to have language skills to know whether or not what they are doing pleases or displeases those around them.

Faith is the connector between the Gospel of our salvation and the lifestyle of obedience. Here's how:

To be saved, I had to have faith to believe that God was telling me the truth about my spiritual condition. He said I was lost. He said that my sin had separated us. He said that Jesus was sent to die for my sin. He said I had to repent. He said I had to accept Jesus' sacrifice for me, personally, and follow Him for the rest of my life in order to be His child. I never witnessed any of these events personally but I chose to believe God. Because God said it, I repented, trusted in His death and resurrection, and asked to be His child.

To be sanctified, set apart to live a life of obedience, I continue to believe the 'rest of what God says.' He tells me what will bring me internal wellbeing. I believe Him and act upon His advice. He tells me what kind of people I should make as friends. I believe Him and obey. He tells me what kind church I should make my home. I obey by looking for one with sound theology and disciple-making priorities. He tells me how to use my mind and guard my heart. I follow His instructions to the letter.

Following Jesus is possible, whether the disciple is a child, an adolescent, or an adult. Each one embarks on the same path. They listen to God, they believe and are saved, and then they act upon what He says. Obedience of faith is hearing and choosing to obey by virtue of Who said it. I defer by my obedient response.

Help me teach Your Word with simplicity. We're all children and need understanding. My day is planned, Lord. I follow what You say to the letter – by faith. Amen

HOW A CHURCH GOT STARTED

To all those in Rome who are loved by God and called to be saints. Romans 1:7

Have you ever been on a life-changing trip? Perhaps it was a mission trip and what you saw and experienced changed you to the core. You returned back home with pictures and stories and couldn't wait to share your experiences with others. Your undying passion was evidence that cataclysmic events had occurred while you were away.

After the resurrection, a group of believers gathered to worship and pray. Acts 2 describes them as being of "one accord." That means that what they shared in common was a passionate love for Jesus, the One who had loved them, changed them, and now had ascended from them into heaven. Their fellowship was electric as they worshipped.

Among that group were a few believers from Rome. They were, I suspect, warmly included in that prayer meeting because believers are one in Christ regardless of nationality. As this group met, the Spirit of God came upon them all. They heard the sound of a rushing wind and God's power fell. They were all changed. Forever. These Roman guests went back home to Rome and it is suspected that the Roman church was born by these few who had been transformed on their trip to Jerusalem.

Those who have been touched powerfully by the Spirit of God start great works of God, both churches and ministries. However, leaders who are called by men often take the stage and put people to sleep. Their mission is academic and half-hearted. They lack the fire of a God-call.

Oh, but those who see the glory of God, who feel the hand of God on their shoulders, who are changed by time in His presence, who experience the power of God as they hear their call into ministry, bring a combustible power to whatever they do. Churches that are birthed in the sparks of a "Pentecost" may start in a godless, pagan place like Rome but they eventually change Rome and then the world. Though Paul had never been to Rome, he knew of their faith and he was vested to write his most important work to build doctrine into their foundation of their church. Education *plus* experience serves to make churches that can withstand the fires of Roman persecution.

I do not know the future. Will I be like my brothers and sisters in the Roman church who were strong enough to stand under fire? Only if I strengthen my foundation with sound teaching. Plant "Romans" in my spirit, Lord. Amen

RELIGIOUS REPUTATIONS

First, I thank my God through Jesus Christ for all of you, because your faith is proclaimed in all the world.
Romans 1:8

Rome was the center of the world in New Testament times. Whatever happened there became known. The happenings inside Rome were the daily newspaper the world read.

The Christians were known for their faith because they were visible, authentic, and active. Paul was thankful for their reputation that tells me that their faith was the real thing, rooted in Jesus Christ.

Religious reputations of many kinds abound, even in so-called Christianity. Our world today is a fish bowl because of current technology. If something tragic happens on any corner of the globe, it can be filmed and reported within hours. People are interviewed and many, in hard times, talk of the importance of their faith. They can be New Age, Buddhist, even Christians, but I often listen and hear them speak of 'faith' in vague terms. *"My faith is important to me and is getting me through this."* Hearers can be inspired, think well of them, but their testimony revealed little. They can have faith that whatever they are experiencing is a phase. They can have faith in themselves or in the goodness of people who extend charity during times of crisis. Be assured this is not the kind of faith Paul is praising the Roman Christians for.

Unless faith is well placed, it is meaningless. Anyone who places their faith in Joseph Smith, Mary Baker Eddy, L. Ron Hubbard, Mohammed or any other self-proclaimed deity, has an empty faith; one which will lead them to an eternity separated from God. Faith in Jesus Christ was what carved out the stories that circulated the Roman Empire, so much so that Claudius the Emperor expelled Jewish Christians from the city.

Rest assured that the world, at that time, was not regarding a Christian as a religious person. Religious people are pious, self-impressed, aloof, and seek to create a reputation that centers on being respected. Religion brings the smell of death. My faith in Christ is not about me, it is all about Him. I do not have faith because I am a good person. My faith is needed and active because I am **_not_**, and He is. If others speak well of me apart from Christ, I should be scrambling to correct them and give glory to Whom glory is due.

Faith in Jesus Christ creates humble spokesmen. They are meek, yet unmovable, willing to die for the reputation of their Savior if He is maligned in any way. Real faith is active, loving without reason, forgiving recklessly, and serving others because Jesus did. This spreads like wildfire and the church of Jesus Christ cannot be stopped.

For what am I known? Is it all about you, in me? Strip away all self-serving, Lord. Amen

PRAYERS FOR STRANGERS

For God is my witness, whom I serve with my spirit in the gospel of his Son, that without ceasing I mention you always in my prayers. . . Romans 1:9

Something amazing happens when we pour ourselves out daily at the feet of Christ. We press our heart to the surface, offer it to Him without any reservations, and ask Jesus to live large in us. At that point, His Spirit rises up strong in our spirits and we are in touch with His thoughts and affections. What He loves, we love. There is no other explanation for the complete reformation of our heart's desires.

This phenomenon has to be the reason for Paul's words. He has never been to Rome to meet the Christians there. Yet, in spite of the fact that they are strangers to him, he admits to praying without ceasing for them. Who prays non-stop for strangers? I don't. Family, friends, maybe. But strangers? I only do it if the power of Christ has taken over my heart and His burden for someone has become mine.

Can you imagine how long Paul's prayer list was? He had to be invested in so many churches, so many that he had started. Rome wasn't the only place on his mind yet he admits to offering up continual prayers for them.

If ever I needed just one verse to confirm that the Spirit, not the frenzy of a type-A personality, fueled Paul's spiritual work in the kingdom, this verse does it for me. So many gifted people who can make things happen without being led by God's Spirit carry on ministry work. Entrepreneurs know how to start things and grow them. Men and women with charisma are clever with words and can easily create a following. Is any of their work God's work? Let enough resistance come, enough personal suffering, and the wheat is separated from the chaff. The cost becomes too high and ministries fold.

Not so with Paul – which makes his letter to the Romans that much more valuable to me. He was the real deal. He suffered and yet his passion for seeing Christ embraced by the nations was not snuffed out. He prayed without ceasing whether in prison or out, whether hungry or fed, whether cold or warm, whether bone-weary or rested. May God's prayer list become mine today as I allow my heart to fuse with His heart. Praying for strangers will be inevitable.

Who are You concerned about today, Lord? What person or nation? Make me one with You so that I feel what You feel. Make unceasing prayer my reality regardless of personal cares. Amen

MUTUAL ENCOURAGEMENT

For I long to see you, that I may impart to you some spiritual gift to strengthen you ~ that is, that we may be mutually encouraged by each other's faith, both yours and mine.
Romans 1:11-12

I have found that mutual encouragement is a rare thing. Encouragement alone is hard enough to find, but it does usually exist in one-sided relationships. One person is spiritually strong; the other weak. The strong one gives of himself, speaks words of faith, and the weaker one takes it in like a thirsty sponge. The weak person has little to give in return except gratitude.

Mutual encouragement happens when both people live by the strength of their faith in Christ. Each has tasted self-sufficiency and forsaken it. Each has leaned with all their might on the resources of Christ and found Him, daily, to be enough. Their faith may be tenuous but by the mutual sharing of their journeys, they are strengthened to remain steadfast.

Perhaps you know what it is to be dragging, to be so low that you wonder if Jesus can, and will, sustain you. Yet, you pour your heart out in prayer, find a Word to stand on, and walk amidst great resistance. Think about this. There is another soul like you; one who knows what it is to press in for the spiritual grit necessary to endure suffering. The two of you could benefit from time together. As you both share your story, resolve will be doubled.

There was a time when Paul needed little encouragement. He was the law and wielded great power. He was cruel and unbending. What a transformation Christ wrought. Paul was laid to the ground on the Damascus road and learned humility. He became acquainted with physical and emotional limits. Softened, he reached out to the church for strength and a kind of fellowship that was rooted in vulnerability and mutuality. It became him. For each of us who are prone to be lone rangers, invulnerable to the expression of need for another, let us think twice about what we're missing.

Whom do I need today? Who needs me? Send me where it's mutual. Amen

UNANSWERED PRAYER

I want you to know, brothers, that I have often intended to come to you (but thus far have been prevented), in order that I might reap some harvest among you as well as among the rest of the Gentiles. Romans 1:13

Paul was prevented from going to Rome, the thing he repeatedly asked of God. We are not told all the possible reasons God said no but the list of reasons could be numerous.

Paul asked for a good thing, didn't he? It was noble. Visit Rome. Teach and encourage Christians. This is the prayer God loves to answer with a yes, right?

These are the mysteries of prayer that are hardest for God's children like me to understand. It takes so much spiritual growth to pray consistently for things that are kingdom centered. Then when I do, when my prayers are God-honoring, why wouldn't God answer them all with a yes? For example ~

- Praying for God to reach a prodigal child.
- Praying for an unsaved loved one to come to faith.
- Praying for ministry expansion for the sake of the Gospel.
- Praying for the healing of a disease for God's glory.

It is my experience that God says "no", or "wait", for many reasons. Perhaps I need to be changed as I wait on God for that long-awaited answer. I will learn endurance and the security of a child who asks without ceasing. Jesus was clear about the nature of persistent prayer when he told the parable of the widow who kept asking and asking for what she wanted. The point of the story in His own words (in Luke 18) was this ~ *"Ask and don't give up."* This kind of childlike trust that God's heart is bent 'for' me while I keep asking is only something learned in the school of prayer.

There are things I pray for this morning, ongoing requests that are deeply heartfelt, concerns that easily keep me up at night. I pray for His deliverance and while there are glimmers of it now and then, the mighty hand of God has not moved yet. I keep asking, tearfully, while checking my heart and the status of my relationship with God. Am I angry He hasn't answered yet? Do I feel entitled, by my 'performance', to a quicker answer? Do I begin to question what kind of Father withholds the answer when the pain threshold is high? Being honest on my knees and working out my feeble faith with prayer and the Word is a necessity or my faith can deteriorate under my limited perspective.

Paul finally did get to Rome. He kept asking but it took a while. In the meantime, God took him to geographical areas that needed the Gospel more, Asia for one. I keep asking too. If it's warfare, I fight on my knees. If it is God directly preventing it because there is something better for me, I stretch out my faith as I wait.

If you feel stuck where you are and the answer you're looking for in prayer has not come, don't assume it won't. Ask God to show you what you can do to be effective in the kingdom today, in small ways, right where you are. That starts and ends with persistent prayer.

I wait. I trust without sharp words on my tongue. Your grace makes it possible. Amen

BEING DIFFERENT

I am under obligation both to the Greeks and to barbarians, both to the wise and to the foolish. Romans 1:14

A barbarian referred to anyone who did not speak Greek. This language dominated all art, culture, and education. To be a barbarian was to be outside of the respected mainstream. A person who was not able to speak and read the language suffered a stigma.

To be outside the mainstream, whether in society at large or in a small group of local people, is to know the pain of exclusion. There are so many ways you and I can be different. Racially, we can be part of a minority and feel others' disgust. We can be the brunt of racial slurs and jokes. Educationally, we can fail to possess a degree others perceive we need to be taken seriously. Our opinions are dismissed. The rich can discount us because we came from humble beginnings. The poor can discount us because they believe we fail to understand what it means to be poor. The list of things is long that can keep us on the outside.

The Gospel is for everyone. Paul knew that he was called to bring the message of Christ across all barrier lines. Jesus didn't bring the Gospel to the wealthy or the wise first. He took it to poor villages and to the common people. The religious elite found that offensive.

Jesus is a stumbling block, to everyone, in every station of life. His message of sin and the need for repentance is not naturally palatable whether you are rich, poor, educated or uneducated, Jewish or Gentile. Once my eyes are open to His identity and my ears are open to His message, I am under the same obligation to bring His message of salvation to everyone regardless of who they are.

There are biases in most every family if we're careful to listen and pick up on attitudes. I've had to repent for some prejudices in my family that I inherited. I am learning to love as Jesus loves and I've got a long way to go. My love cannot be conditional. Jesus' call to sinners had no racial, educational, or financial qualifications. He said, *"Come!" "Red and yellow, black and white, we are precious in His sight."* Aren't you glad!

There is no one You don't love. There can be no one from whom I can withhold Your love if I have Your heart. Wake me up to the ways I discriminate. Amen

SHAME

For I am not ashamed of the Gospel, for it is the power of God for salvation to everyone who believes. Romans 1:16

I am poised on the two most important verses in all of Romans. I sat up straight as I read them and realized that men and women down through the centuries have lost their lives because they stood up for their truths. They refused to recant when a sword was held over their head. Today, I hold the Word in my hands, in my own language, because Martin Luther took on the practices and politics of the Catholic Church when it refused to adhere to the truth of Paul's words, inspired by the Spirit of God.

It's not easy to stand-alone. Shame is a powerful weapon. Perhaps you are the only Christian in your entire family. The ridicule you sustain because you believe God's Word is cruel, even crushing, at times. The one who stands against the tide of popular opinion, even against family ways, is rarely loved. Their freedom is too threatening.

I also realize that I am writing today to some Christian leaders who are fighting for truth in the midst of their own lukewarm congregations. Committee meetings get overheated quickly in Laodicean churches as truth becomes relative and the sword gets dull. The one who threatens the status quo is publicly lynched.

If I have a history of suffering from other kinds of shame, shame for the Gospel can feel like a trigger that I try to avoid at all costs. Though _this_ shame is not the same, Satan would have me believe that it is because of symptomatic familiarity. Once again, I wake up and declare that, this time, it's different. This is the hour I must not recant.

How do I sustain the shame others inflict? I set out to see how Jesus endured shaming. Mentally, what was his focus and shield? I find His answer in Hebrews 12:2. *"Looking to Jesus, the founder and perfecter of our faith, who for the joy that was set before him endured the cross, despising the shame, and is seated at the right hand of the throne of God."*

There was nothing more shaming than the cross. His whole world (except for the few standing at the foot of his cross) had turned against Him. While in agony, He heard taunting, even from royalty. Yet their words did not erode His mission, His trust, and His theology. He focused on the 'joy set before Him.'

Setting my affections entirely on the kingdom and my future life with Christ is hard work. Yet, it is critical for me if I am to have the strength to plant my feet in truth and do it lovingly in the face of my accusers. Being spit upon, repeatedly, without reacting with a sneer will only be possible as I think of kneeling at the feet of Jesus and hearing, *"Well done, my child."* I remember that, one day long ago, He was on a cross. On a day shortly thereafter, He returned to sit at the right hand of His Father. Shame is temporary. Glory is eternal.

I follow You. You are Truth. I follow You. I remember that You put all accusers into the hands of your Father, whom You knew judged righteously. I, also, do not take revenge but bear their reproach patiently, by the power of Your Spirit. Amen

THE GREAT EXCHANGE

For in it the righteousness of God is revealed from faith for faith. Romans 1:17a

When God's holiness, His righteousness, is revealed, sin is exposed. A crisis becomes immediately evident. I realize that I cannot stand before a righteous God. No matter how much good I've done, my sin cannot be erased. I want peace with God, want to belong to Him, want to talk with Him as Adam and Eve did before the fall, but sin keeps us separated. How do I become righteous so that God can be mine and I can live forever in His presence?

Only one way.

A great exchange needed to take place. Someone needed to pay for my sin. Someone righteous; a Savior who would invite me to place all my sin upon Him – marking Him for death. Having been emptied of my sin, this Savior would give me His righteousness. He gets my sin. I get His holiness. Such an unfair exchange and I'm forever aware of my debt.

This is weighty doctrine. But best of all, it is a story that makes my heart leap for joy. No longer do I need to be separated from God. I am dressed in His Son's righteous perfection for all eternity but only because Jesus was willing to exchange what *He* had for what *I* didn't have.

Who dies for an enemy, pays for His worst sins, and offers the best of Himself? Only a Savior whose love is outrageous. The Gospel is such extravagant good news that every person who has experienced this great exchange struggles to find a language that tells the story adequately. The best I can do is say, *"Jesus loves me and has changed my life forever."* Indeed! It's that but so much more than that.

The love that prompted this exchange cannot be grasped. The best poetry falls short so I tell the story with my life. I have a joy that cannot be snuffed out by trials. I have a steely commitment to serve this Savior upon threat of death. I am the grateful recipient of a righteousness I did not have to earn, and could never have earned. The Lamb of God knew that and before the foundation of the world, saw me in my desperate sinful condition and made a way for me to come home. The Lamb would take my sin and dress me in the robes of His righteousness.

I often lose my words when something is too painful. I also lose words when I try to explain what Your love is like. Our great exchange changes me every day. Thank you! Amen

FAITH PLUS NOTHING

The righteous shall live by faith. Romans 1:17b

I write today with fear and trembling. Prayerfully, I seek God for the concepts and language to write about this critical and most important issue in all of Christianity. This is the verse Martin Luther stood on and why his life was on the line. Protestantism was born on the foundation of this theological truth.

If ever someone had the moral credentials to earn his salvation, it was Paul. He listed them elsewhere in Philippians. The humbling discovery he made on the road to Damascus was that his 'credentials' had actually **kept** him from saving faith. The very things he worked so hard to attain, that he thought were winning him eternal favor with God, were his own stumbling blocks. He came to understand that his attempts to act righteous were like presenting an offering of filthy rags.

The law was not given so that we could mimic it and please God. There is no brown-nosing the Teacher. Righteousness, through the Law, was revealed so that we would understand that we are completely *incapable* of attaining it, needing to reach out our arms to Christ for that divine exchange ~ He takes my sin, I take His righteousness.

Without Christ's atonement, I am utterly lost and condemned. There is no balance sheet keeping track of my good works and bad deeds. That is not the basis by which God accepts or condemns me. The question has always been, *"What will Christine do with Jesus and His death on Calvary?"* I can bring nothing to the table to contribute to my salvation.

Some would argue. *"But I bring my faith to the table. I choose to believe."* Even that isn't true. If I have the faith to believe, it is only because God opens my eyes. By His grace, He extends faith to me so that I can see the treasure of Jesus and believe.

I offer some closing questions as we often wrestle with our insecurity as God's children.

- If I did nothing to earn my salvation, then why do I work so hard to try to keep it?
- Do I believe that I must perform righteously to keep God happy with me?
- Do I really know how to rest in the finished work of the cross?
- Do I really believe that I received Christ's righteousness?
- Where is my deep joy over the gift of that evident?

Children of God are adopted by faith alone. We come empty handed; orphaned, filthy, emaciated and deeply scarred. God does not despise us for that. His compassion reaches out in the person of Jesus to do what we can't do for ourselves. We cry, *"Abba, Father!"* and are invited to embrace Him without any hint of reservation. How? By understanding that we are dressed in the robes of His Son, the One who took our sins, paid the debt we owed because of them, and then removed them from His sight forever. In that we rest. In that we heal. In that we worship.

You did it all. I did nothing. You loved me that much. Amen

A SUBJECT IGNORED

For the wrath of God is revealed from heaven against all ungodliness and unrighteousness of men, who by their unrighteousness suppress the truth. Romans 1:18

God's wrath is not a subject most churches address. And of the few that do, some exclude teaching on God's tender grace. Focusing on either one, while ignoring the other, distorts the Gospel and hurts any congregation. A right view of the character of God can only be attained when His wrath and grace are dually understood.

One of the reasons people prefer not to think about God's anger is because of their experience with angry people around them. God's anger is not of the human kind.

There are two New Testament words for wrath. One is *'thymos'*; meaning a panting rage. The other is *'orge'*; meaning something which simmers and ripens. *'Thymos'* is used in the book of Revelation to describe the wrath of God that will be poured out one day in all of its fury. However, in every other instance in the New Testament, *'orge'* is used. God wants us to know that He does not reach out to strike when He has been momentarily offended. He's not temperamental. Instead, He's longsuffering in nature, and while He waits, his anger simmers over a long period of time as He sees wickedness spread over the whole earth. His ripened anger will one day culminate in the eternal condemnation of all those who have not trusted Christ as their Savior.

This all sounds pretty academic. Where's the heart food in this for today?

Jesus' death provided a way of escape from God's wrath; both the panting rage and the simmering kind. My unrighteousness, the sin that deserved His full punishment and condemnation, went to Christ instead. He took God's wrath in my place. Dressed in His holiness, I get to live in a tender, intimate relationship with His Father. I don't have enough words to express what that privilege means to me.

Unrighteousness does suppress the truth. It encourages people to reject a God who tells them that they are sinners and need to repent. God's people however, dressed in His righteousness, love the Truth and are willing to listen to God regardless of how much it costs them personally. That small test is one way to tell whether or not I am God's child. Am I a truth lover or a truth hater? Will I love the truth even when God's wrath is the subject matter? May it be so.

Knowing that the full manifestation of Your wrath is still to come, I am compelled to tell the story of the cross to those still under the curse with even more urgency. Forgive my laziness, Father. Amen

A KNOWING OR TO KNOW

..who by their unrighteousness suppress the truth. For what can be known about God is plain to them, because God has shown it to them. Romans 1:18b-19

From Paul's words, it is clear that there is no excuse for an atheist. There is enough revelation of God in all of nature to dispel any doubt that He exists. One would have to choose *not* to see it. A person's sinful nature, no matter how brilliant their intellect, suppresses the truth.

World missions have gone a long way to reach the yet-unreached people groups. In the far reaches of the jungle however, before missionaries ever reach their borders, they already have proof of God's existence. The revelation of Him through nature should be enough to cause them to worship Him. So why send missionaries? An awareness of God is not the same as having a personal experience with Jesus Christ. Without someone to tell them of Jesus Christ, to open the scriptures and read it to them, they will not connect with a Savior who longs to forgive them and live inside of them. While they can know a lot *about* God by studying their natural habitat, it is a far cry from a personal 'knowing'.

The 'grid' God uses for who is a true Christian and who is not remains consistent whether God is regarding a person in a thatched hut in the jungles of Indonesia or a western world businessman who sits in a church pew every Sunday. Both can know a lot about God from their surroundings but the question is this ~ has each one acknowledged their need of a Savior?

As someone who has experienced the joys and liabilities of living life in the public eye for over 30 years, I have had first hand experience with the differences between others thinking they know you and really knowing you. For any person with a degree of fame, others can study their career. They can know their discography, every song on every recording, the years of a certain project's release, and even the words to every song. They can learn the names of their family members through studying Wikipedia, read their biography (if they have one) and come out feeling like they 'know' the person. But this is far different than having a personal relationship with the singer. For a fan that is obsessive, that difference is often ignored.

Could it be that you are one who considers yourself very knowledgeable about God, and because of that, you believe that this qualifies you to call yourself a Christian? You may have stood on the rim of the Grand Canyon and marveled at God's power but failed to know, firsthand, the power of the cross for your sin. You marveled at the Creator but still denied the One who wants to provide your atonement.

If the topic of God is just of interest to you, beware. If the person of God, in Jesus Christ, is precious to your soul, be encouraged. We are not to be like the Pharisees; well studied but full of dead men's bones.

Thank you for the day You pierced my heart with the truth of my sin and my need of You. Amen

THE FOUNDATION OF A FOOL

For although they knew God, they did not honor him as God or give thanks to him, but they became futile in their thinking, and their foolish hearts were darkened.
Romans 1:21

A fool, in scripture, is described as one who denies the existence of God. *"A fool hath said in his heart there is no God."* Void of the ability to know and speak truth, he sets out to become a philosopher; one who reasons things out in a way that makes sense to him. But according to Truth, defined by an all-knowing God, it makes no sense at all. According to James Boice, he has simply 'rearranged error.' Now, *that* is futility.

I can so easily act like a fool when I take the matters of my life into my own hands and figure out solutions by myself. Even though I may have pretty good common sense and average problem solving skills, my strategies are foolish. Given enough time, I will discover that I have traveled in circles or taken a wrong path, even though the path seemed so right at the time I made the choices. Only God knows everything. Like Adam and Eve, I am to live by revelation in relationship, not assuming I can eat of the tree of good and evil and figure things out on my own.

Honoring God means that I seek His wisdom about every single issue in my life. I start with the scriptures and see if they address, in specifics, the scenario I'm facing. Sometimes it will and other times it won't. At that point, I seek God in prayer, wait for Him to lead me to the answers. It may be scriptural principles that I can apply to my situation. I may never before have considered them in that context but the Spirit of God, ever my teacher, customized them for me to fashion a strategy.

My point is this. I don't have to be an unbeliever to dishonor God and have darkened thinking. Going off lone-ranger on any issue facing me is to disrespect and dishonor God. I should live asking, *"What should I do about this? What is your plan for me?"* Then, I dig in to find the answers in meditation and prayer. This is the way of wisdom; the way of the prosperous man and woman. Believe me, I've learned this the hard way.

I honor You with my dependence. Lead me as Your little child; kindly, deliberately, and with concepts You help me understand. Amen

WHY MAN MAKES SUBSTITUTE GODS

Claiming to be wise, they became fools, and exchanged the glory of the immortal God for images resembling

mortal man and birds and animals and creeping things.
Romans 1:22-23

Why would I want a substitute for God? Why would I turn my back on His incredible glory and prefer the graven images of dead things? I can only speak for myself and offer some reasons that have caused me to run, personally, from God's presence.

- God created me in His image. I know right from wrong because He gave me a conscience. I have violated it and have known what it is like to be racked with guilt. I have hated the feeling.
- God is holy. When in prayer, I have sensed His purity and have felt the depths of my sin. I have hated the feeling.
- God gave the Law and revealed His will. I have realized that it was impossible to live up to it and every time I did the opposite of what He commanded, I wanted to forget that I ever read it. I have hated the feeling.

So, I can understand idolatry. I've committed it so easily. But longevity with God tells me that there is another way. I don't need to be a fool, put my hands over my eyes and pretend that I don't see Him, hear Him, or sense Him.

God invites my worship, my focus, and a preoccupation with His glory because He loves me and invites me to receive the very thing that I overlooked for so many years. **_Grace_**. It was grace that caused Him to hang on a cross so that my sin could be forgiven. It was grace that caused Him to justify me and declare me 'pure'. It is grace that causes His Spirit, every day, to empower my obedience. If I have any thoughts that cause me to fear drawing closer to God, I can be sure that I believe the lies of the enemy.

His glory stuns my soul with wonder, then joy. All those years, I protected myself from the very thing that would have saved my life. And that is the lie of idolatry. *"You don't want God. He won't satisfy. Come and make yourself another god."* Never again!

I've been a fool and worshipped at other altars. They had no glory. Give me the grace to walk wisely and feast on Your beauty. Amen

A FATHER WHO LETS US EXPERIENCE CONSEQUENCES

Therefore God gave them up in the lusts of their hearts to impurity. Romans 1:24a

When we see our children make bad choices, we usually want to rush in and prevent them from experiencing the consequences. What we try to protect them *from* might have saved them. Instead of facing the consequences, they grew to feel entitled to our interventions. They continued to sin recklessly.

This dynamic doesn't just exist between parents and children either. Anyone who loves another can try to spare them from pain. While feelings of love may motivate our actions, prudence is absent. The truth is – we all need the pain of our consequences to bring us to God.

At first glance, this verse, and the way it is worded, can seem like it describes a bad parent. i.e. When God's child sins, He dusts His hands, shrugs in disgust, and then leaves them to their folly. That is *not* the meaning here. This *'giving them up'* is a judicial act where God allows His child to reap what he sows. All the while He watches, grieves, beckons, longs, and weeps over the pain His child will feel when sin bears its consequential fruit.

So, are you a rescuer? Perhaps that has been your role in the family. Raised in the midst of strife, you sought to smooth the turbulence by taking on others' pain so they could return to a peaceful state. You spent your life fixing things, by default. Whatever the angst, and no matter if another's sin caused it, you absorbed the consequences and tried to return order to your surroundings. You were willing endure the many risks that accompany instability.

Depending on the situation, and whether innocent children are involved, it's best to let things just fall apart. People only learn to make different choices by eating the fruit of their own deeds; the good and the bad. I know. I was a peacemaker. I wallpapered the Titanic when I should have been preparing to board the lifeboat.

I bless Your Fathering, for the many times You allow Your children to come to the end of themselves. You are the Father who waits on the porch with the light on. I release others to Your care today and will not interfere. Amen

PREDISPOSED TO WHAT?

For this reason, God gave them up to dishonorable passions. For their women exchanged natural relations for those that are contrary to nature; and the men likewise gave up natural relations with women and were consumed with passion for one another. . . Romans 1:26-27

Simplistic evangelical thinking believes that a homosexual identity is birthed environmentally. Flawed parenting, early childhood experiences, these are some of the things we believe solely shape sexual orientation. However, what about members of the gay community who protest that they were indeed born this way? We are prone to dismiss their claims because how can we defend God's Word if a true genetic component exists? Does this erase guilt and provide a loophole for God's commandments?

I do admit that those who have proclaimed a genetic pre-disposition toward homosexuality have, in the past, left me stumbling for words. However, John Piper suggests in a sermon from this very passage in Romans that if homosexuality *is* a bent, determined by genetics as well as environment, that we should not be surprised. At the fall of Adam and Eve, the whole world was disordered. Genetic pulls went askew for *every* person, across the board.

The truth is ~ each one of us has genetic pre-dispositions toward sinful behaviors and unhealthy bents. The one who struggles with a generational pull toward alcoholism must deal with his 'bent' at the foot of the cross. So must the one who struggles with unhealthy sexual orientations. No matter the sinful pull, the remedy is the same. We come to Christ, plead for mercy, take hold of undeserved grace, and stand in the victory of Calvary when we battle our respective thorns in the flesh. Christ promises victory, one battle at a time.

Once we know our Achilles' heel, we must protect ourselves from situations that would invite temptation, lest we fall. For the person who struggles with homosexual desires, he must do what every one of us must do when we're in the battle of our lives. We immerse ourselves in scripture. We flee temptation. We invite accountability. We rely on the prayers and support of our Christian family. We hold on to the hope that, in heaven, our battle will be over. The effects of the fall will be a thing of the past for all of us, regardless of how our genetic wiring went awry. The sons of God will be revealed and the groaning of earth will be silent.

You are more of a treasure than the sin that beckons me to indulge and momentarily feel better. I guard my relationship with You and focus on Your beauty. Amen

HOW POWERFUL IS THE CROSS FOR ME?

And since they did not see fit to acknowledge God, God gave them up to a debased mind to do what ought not to be done. Romans 1:28

Paul writes to the Christians in Rome who were in no way naïve and sheltered from their culture. They were first century Romans. Life was barbaric, sexually deviant, and politically cut throat. One could see about anything in broad daylight, even in the so-called temples of the day. The blood of people and animals ran down walls like water.

What happened to a person when God gave them up to do whatever their hearts desired was on full display. One didn't have to go to the bad side of town to see it. There were no corners of Rome where life was provincial, where behavior looked righteous but sin was under the surface. A God-ward conscience was a rare thing. Paul described the behavior of the majority of the people. They were a people *"filled with all manner of unrighteousness, evil, covetousness, malice, envy, murder, strife, deceit, maliciousness."*

If you were rich in ancient Rome, you were privileged to live on a large piece of land outside the stench of the city. Opulence reigned but the danger of political alliances plagued you day and night. If you were poor and lived inside the city, gangs ruled and life was physically dangerous. Whether rich or poor, sin – the likes of what we can only begin to imagine, was encouraged and displayed. Talks of being impaled on a pole for petty crimes were commonplace around dinner tables.

It was out of this that Paul was converted. It was out of this that the Roman church was born. The power of the cross to change lives from such debauchery to godliness was the Christian's witness. Each one, treasuring Jesus, lived in such a way as to provide a stark contrast between one who worshipped Roman gods and one who followed Christ.

The implications for me are staggering. As I tend to become discouraged over the places where sin still has a hold over me, I remind myself of Calvary. Christ died for my sins, died to make me a daughter in a new kingdom, and powerful life change will be the result when I treasure Jesus today more than I treasure doing the things which come so easily for me but dishonor my Savior.

I pray that You will let my heart and mind live in first century Rome as I read Paul's words. Don't let me get used to 'cross' talk without being profoundly moved. Amen

"I DON'T WANT YOU, GOD!"

Though they know God's decree that those who practice such things deserve to die, they not only do them but give approval to those who practice them. Romans 1:32

There are many reasons a person can reject God. I know some who have proclaimed themselves an atheist because they suffered a personal tragedy and couldn't reconcile that with the presence of a loving God. Most push God away because His Spirit convicts them of sin. Wanting their own way, they are too uncomfortable in God's presence. Since sin's pull is so strong, God gets pushed out.

It is a sad thing when God leaves us to treasure what we want. If an unbeliever rejects the truth of God and embraces intellectual freedom, he will slide into the abyss of moral uncertainty. The mind of this kind of aged person is a frightening thing to witness. Deception has infiltrated most of his mind, often to the point of complete delusion.

If someone else rejects God because they treasure their sin, their lives can appear to hold together for a while. But, a divergent path from God is just that. The two roads slowly lead further away from each other and the consequences are more severe with time. The sin they originally embraced conceives more and more sin until there appears to be a wasted life. This person may even assume an immoral leadership to condone and promote the similar sins of others.

You may not be reading this today in an emotionally detached way. And believe me, I am not writing it that way! The people I'm describing may be your son, or daughter, or parent. The searing pain you feel over their condition is real and the reality of these biblical truths is all too personal. Is there hope for one who has fallen so far from God? Oh yes. As much as one can fall, he can also rise to heights to glory as he embraces Christ, turns from his sin, and is driven to become like the One who now fills His vision. We all emulate the One we worship.

How do I pray for one so lost? *"God, Satan has blinded their mind. I speak Your scriptures over them, that their deception will be torn down with violence by the power of Your Word. 2 Cor.10:4 Only the grace of Your Spirit and the preaching of the Gospel over their own souls (even just done out loud in prayer), will cause Your light to shine in their darkened minds. Let them see Your glory today."*

You've said that no one is a hopeless cause. The lowest sinner can be Your righteous son and daughter. I stand in hope and use my mouth to speak Your Word in prayer over their darkened soul. Amen

CHAPTER 2

JUDGING

Therefore you have no excuse, O man, every one of you who judges. For in passing judgment on another you condemn yourself, because you, the judge, practice the very same things. Romans 2:1

$\mathcal{P}$assing judgment and being discerning are two different things. Paul is addressing the first here. He is talking to the audience he wrote to in chapter one; those who see another person exchange the value of God's beauty for the sins they want to commit. God has given them over to deception and the consequences of their choices. In so doing, it would be easy for those who _know_ the truth to feel morally superior to them, and then judge them.

To judge ~ is to set others apart and cast them aside. It is to feel, *"That is disgusting. I'd never do that."* Paul is pretty forthright that if this is my thinking toward anyone in sin today, then I am sinning when I put myself above them. If my life resembles the life of Jesus in _any_ respect, it is only by the grace of God that fuels my ability to make some righteous choices.

What is my attitude toward those who live in blatant sin? I often feel disgusted when I should be saddened that they live under the bondage of sin. Disgust separates me from compassion, and then, prayer. How will they hear without prayer and a preacher, one who speaks the word of God with heartfelt compassion?

If someone close to me is living in the bondage of sin, I am one who suffers at their hands. My anger turns to self-righteousness. Only a lot of time with God, in the Word and in prayer, preserves humility and creates in me a willingness to pray for those who hurt me. The arrows may fly, even land in the soil of my soil, but I resolve to remember that I don't fight against flesh and blood, but against the kingdom of Satan. He speaks through, and works through, the strongholds of deception. The one whose words cut like a knife is being used to serve up evil. Even so, God hates his sin but loves him. I am to cry out for the mercy to be like God.

I don't love like you. I'm so glad your judgment against me didn't win. You acted out of compassion by sending Jesus. The least I can do is pray for others to see their sin, see You, and receive Your forgiveness. I want to love like You love. Amen

FAST TALKING

Do you suppose, O man – you who judge those who practice such things and yet do them yourself – that you will escape the judgment of God? Romans 2:3

The first obstacle humanity faces is for man to recognize his own guilt. The second challenge is, once recognized, to own it both personally and publicly. Rarely do we encounter others who quickly admit to being wrong. Even when backed into a corner and guilt is obvious, they can still feign innocence. Without Jesus, rarely have I admitted wrong. If my sense of self is fragile, I will feel I can't afford to be wrong.

If we are addicted to other's respect and acceptance, being wrong is not an option. At all costs, we must talk our way out of situations lest those around us come to the conclusion that we're guilty. Self-defense can be developed into a cunning art form. We can do it so much that acquitting ourselves with the greatest confidence is like breathing.

If I am one who has trouble admitting I'm wrong, I must bring my shaky self to the arms of Christ. I have not yet understood my sin, the power of the cross, and Christ's love for me. I am holding on to a faulty self-righteousness that needs to be surrendered at Calvary. Admitting guilt does not diminish me as it frees me to enjoy God's mercy. Never am I more attractive to others than when humble.

If I am in close relationship with someone who cannot admit they are wrong, this is a painful stumbling block to intimacy. Reconciliation and closure are non-existent.

I am also aware that heinous crimes have been committed against many of us. Those who sinned so greatly against us (or someone we love) may not have admitted wrongdoing, or worse yet, they owned it but have shown no remorse whatsoever. Evil appears to have won but it is just an illusion. The ones who sin so recklessly and talk their way out of earthly courts will one day stand before God. The One who sees the heart of a man plays no political games. His judgments are rock solid and there is no escaping the day when perfect justice prevails. Until then, we live in a lifestyle of forgiveness, we pray for our enemies, and we rest in the coming Kingship of Jesus upon the earth.

On day, every knee shall bow. All pride will be smashed. I choose to start now. Amen

TAKING ADVANTAGE OF KINDNESS

Or do you presume on the riches of his kindness and forbearance and patience, not knowing that God's kindness is meant to lead you to repentance? Romans 2:4

I'm not sure I've ever thought about kindness being a stumbling block in relationships before. How could someone's patient spirit trip me up? Yet, it obviously does because Paul asks his readers whether or not they presume upon God's kindness by their deeds of unrighteousness. Instead of their hearts growing more tender when they consider God's longsuffering nature toward them, they use His love as an excuse to keep sinning. Mankind will try to get away with as much as he can if there are no negative consequences. Repentance is usually the last thing on our minds.

So, this has gotten me thinking. Kindhearted people *can* often be disrespected. Children take advantage of a soft tempered parent, ignoring the rules, and presuming on their parent's mild disposition. Gracious hosts can be presumed upon as well. Guests push the limits by arriving late, making themselves too much at home, believing that if ever there were a time to be lazy about manners, it would fly with a patient host.

What does it say about my heart if I am willing to extort kindness for a license to do whatever I want? And in the process, I offend the one who extended it to me? When Peter was under pressure during the time of Jesus' arrest, he repeatedly denied he knew Jesus, when asked. The first two times were probably easier than the third. Jesus was not around when Peter was confronted. But the third time was different. Luke records the moments and tells us that when Peter spoke the words of denial, Jesus was standing across the courtyard to hear them and their eyes locked. The pain that caused Peter must have been brutal. He saw the effects of his sin upon the face of His Savior and friend.

I am asking God to write that story on my heart. God is only invisible to *me*. I am not invisible to *Him*. When I sin and presume that He will overlook it because of His longsuffering nature, his face wears a look.

You are so incredibly kind and thoughtful toward me. I do not want live carelessly and cause Your face to fall today over my choices. I nail all traces of treacherous love to the cross. Amen

WHERE DO I STAND ON THE WRATH ISSUE?

But because of your hard and impenitent heart, you are storing up wrath for yourself for the day of wrath when God's righteous judgment will be revealed. Romans 2:5

Wrath is not a palatable subject. No one likes to think of someone being angry with them. Children who have angry parents do everything in their power to over- perform in order to fix the relationship. When we hear that the One who is storing up wrath against us is God, that is enough to undo us. If we ignore the issue, it is to our peril.

God is absolutely pure. Our sin and rebellion must be judged. Down through the centuries, God's wrath was stored up as men and women perpetrated evil upon the earth. His judgment spilled out now and then on occasions like the destruction of Sodom and Gomorrah. But overall, His wrath accumulated, like a dam about to burst. The full measure of His wrath was poured out on Jesus.

The reason Jesus sweat drops of blood in the garden was not because He faced a death by crucifixion. It was because He was about to experience the full measure of God's wrath, poured out upon Him, for the sins of all mankind. The dam broke and the accumulated weight of God's fury fell on Jesus. This is the essence of the Gospel ~ that I can do nothing good to undo God's wrath against me. Only putting every ounce of trust in Christ, who bore all my punishment, will save me.

People alive must deal with the reality that their sin is recorded, and is accumulating, in heaven's bank, and with it; wrath is being stored up incrementally. Our future depends on how we deal with this issue. Accept Christ's substitutionary death and all God's wrath against _me_ goes to _Him_. Reject Christ and I will have to bear my own wrath.

Martin Luther said, *"The Last Day is called the day of wrath and of mercy, the day of trouble and of peace, the day of destruction and of glory."* If I open up my heart wide to Christ, painfully acknowledge my need of a Savior who bore all my wrath, then mercy, peace, and glory is mine. It's all because of Him. Nothing because of me. It's all because of what He did. Not because of anything good I do to compensate for my bad side. Unearned favor. This is the joy of my salvation.

Who bears the full wrath of God's fury for an enemy? No one I know. Only You. Don't let this story grow cold in my heart. Amen

WHAT DOES IT TAKE TO BREAK?

There will be tribulation and distress for every human being who does evil, the Jew first and also the Greek, but glory and honor and peace for everyone who does good, the Jew first and also the Greek. Romans 2:9-10

I can't communicate the impact of these verses in a way that matches the fire in my spirit. I am watching the truth of these concepts play out in people's lives and these realities are staggering when viewed off the written page and in the everyday lives of human beings.

Paul wants to make sure that we get the message that no one is exempt from the truth of these principles. His "Jew and Greek" references teach that that these verses target everyone. God is no respecter of persons. If I spurn God's ways, there will be tribulation and distress. If I live by the Spirit, I will know glory, honor, and peace. The contrast between both ends of these spectrums is stark and should serve to be a wake-up call to any who live in the distress of disobedience. Yet, most seem to persist and fight God.

As a Christian, I can take up a spot in the pew, sleep my way through the Sunday morning sermon, casually dismiss any of God's commands that ruffle the feathers of my pride, and resolve to live my life the way I want. The outcome though, will be tribulation and distress. There will be trouble in my house the likes of which no one may know on the outside. Torment will be my companion. I will indulge in things that distract me from it and numb out my conscience. The ability to function in the down slope of disobedience will continue to deteriorate. Tribulation and distress will escalate to the level of blinding pain.

Who can do good and live God's way on their own strength? No one. If I recognize that, come to the end of myself and rely on the power of the Spirit to change my heart, I will know three things according to Paul:

1.) Glory – God will transform me into someone who resembles Jesus. By the power of the Word and His Spirit, with time, I will cease to recognize the old me.

2.) Honor – God will show me His favor. I will experience what it's like to live my life with a God who blesses my every encounter and appointment. His hand prepares the path for my feet and I feel completely taken care of.

3.) Peace – I love solitude. I am not afraid to hear God's voice in my spirit because I am at peace with Him. Even when I am in other's storms, I know a calm deep in my soul. I don't even fear death. I know that on the other side of death's sting, the greatest peace awaits me as I am finally delivered from ALL the distress and tribulation of this world.

Why would I ever run from God in light of these realities? Yet I have, and now I watch others as they wage their war with God. Oh, how long it takes for pride to break and men to submit to God's ways over their own. For every one in our path today who walks in disaster and yet continues to fight God's wooing, we pray that God's corrective work will be swift, merciful, and the results, permanent.

Come, Lord Jesus, with power and conviction upon your disobedient children. I long to see them know glory, honor, and peace. Amen

LOOPHOLES

For all who have sinned without the law will also perish without the law, and all who have sinned under the law will be judged by the law. Romans 2:12

Unbelievers are stuck on issue of whether or not God is fair. Is He capable of sending someone who has never heard the Gospel to eternal condemnation because they failed to accept Jesus as their Savior? Wrestling with that issue, they are distracted from the reality that *they* have heard the Gospel and are without excuse. It's as if they look for a reason to discredit God so that their own rejection of Him is justified.

Paul gives the answer here to the question of God's ultimate fairness. Each man is judged according to the revelation of God he has received. Those who have lived without knowledge of the law are *still* without excuse. Those who have heard the Gospel are also without excuse. In the previous chapter, he explains that God has revealed himself in nature and in the moral code of mankind, no matter the culture, to cause man to worship Him and seek His face.

49

People, in every culture, have God's moral code written on their heart. They are warmed by love and appalled by hatred. They embrace honesty and feel violated when lied to. They punish treachery and applaud fairness. Even the most hardened atheist will cry out over the injustice of being wronged yet conveniently fail to explore why he has a strong internal opinion at all about the fact a wrong was committed. By whose standard was the 'wrong' considered wrong? Mankind was made in the image of God and we have enough conviction in us about right and wrong, even with a carnal conscience, to know that God exists.

Why does this issue matter to me today? God is not easily understood. He is full of mystery. Because of that, my faith can be threatened by seeming inconsistencies. I can be tempted to bend toward unbelief. Instead of looking for loopholes today that I believe might absolve me from putting all my trust in Him, I stand on what I do know. He is just, fair, loving, and longsuffering. If a particular mystery in scripture appears to put any part of His character in question, I know it is only because I have partial eyesight. He is King and He rules righteously.

Whatever I don't understand makes me move closer to You, by faith, instead of farther away. I guard my faith with a vengeance. Amen

FAKE RIGHTEOUSNESS

For it is not the hearers of the law who are righteous before God, but the doers of the law who will be justified. Romans 2:13

Paul needs to make it clear to the Jews that they cannot be secure about eternity just because they are, by birthright, God's chosen people. He was once like them; reciting pedigree, education, and his impressive generational line. He thought himself a notch above Gentiles. He belonged to the people who were given the Mosaic Law and he, like most Jews, spent vast amounts of time in the temple reading it, studying it, and memorizing it. This boosted his pride and gave him a false sense of security. It all came crashing down on the road to Damascus when Jesus revealed that Paul was actually persecuting *Him*, amidst such holy performances in the company of Pharisees.

None who just 'know' the Bible are secure. Christian education does not a Christian make. Extra credit cannot be earned with God for intellectually knowing His Word. The foundation of justification is an acknowledgment of sin and trusting in Jesus for salvation by faith alone. The 'doers' of the law Paul refers to are those who stopped performing; those whose behavior is an outgrowth of a heart change wrought by Calvary.

Performance has always plagued the church. We can fool men – and since men are the ones standing in front of us with skin on – the agenda of our perceived need for respect can dictate the need for one sterling performance after another. The only problem is this ~ God is King and Judge and his criterion is the only one that matters. He condemns the self-righteous. If men are fooled, the payoff is a short window of time where we are held in high esteem for our appearance of holiness. What a price is paid. At the end of a brief life, we hear God say, *"Depart from me. I never knew you."*

To abandon the need to impress others and God, I need to be humble. I agree to play by God's rules. He judges me by my heart, not by my deeds. He knows if what I do today is fueled by love for Him, by habit, or by my need to look good. He reads my thoughts, every one, and sees my cobweb of mixed motives. Daily, they are entangled. Daily, I cry out to God to help me sort them out so that I can deal with my sin and my love for Him, all at the same time. Searching my heart is what He does best and what He has promised to those who ask.

Nothing qualifies me to be yours except what Jesus did for me. I bring nothing to the table except my trust and my faith. It's all about You, Lord. Amen

I CAN RISK BEING KNOWN

On that day when, according to the Gospel, God judges the secrets of men by Christ Jesus. Romans 2:16

Have you ever felt studied? Perhaps you know the anxiety of feeling inadequate while in the company of one extremely perceptive. The fear of exposure can be crippling.

I have often played an internal game with myself. What if, for one day, my thoughts were an open book to the people around me? They would see not only what I do, but what I think. How frightening. Yet, that is what it is like to be in relationship with God. He sees what I do, how I feel, and what I think. My thoughts are an open book.

This is one of the reasons I believe people repress a knowledge of God. Their own sin condemns them to such a degree that they can't bear being known by a God who might also condemn them. They cannot imagine being laid bare before someone so powerful.

The picture is bleak unless there is more to the story. If I am known by one who loves me, not one who wants to judge me, then that makes all the difference in the world. The sad reality is that there are many who stay away from church because they fear being around God. And, there are children of God who study the Bible but fail to have a prayer life for the same reason. They fear hearing what God might say to them. In all of this, Satan dances in victory.

There is more to the story. The One who knows me so well is able to separate what I do from who I am. He hates my sin but loves me. As soon as God saw the spiritual condition of Adam and Eve, that they were separated from Him and cursed forever, He made a plan to restore them. Them, and me. Love overruled. Sin must be atoned for by a perfect sacrifice and since I am sinful and couldn't do it for myself, Jesus left heaven to come and die in my place.

To be known by God is to be known by the One who gave His most precious Son to die for me. He sees my sin but offers forgiveness. He sees what I want to hide but puts His robe around my shoulders in response. Only that kind of love can give me the courage to bare my soul to Him without fear. Perfect love casts out fear.

My soul is bare before You. But, You see me perfect, in
Jesus. No more hiding, ever. Amen

BETTER THAN

But if you call yourself a Jew and rely on the law and boast
in God. . . Romans 2:17

Up until this point in Romans, Paul has been talking about all people. All have ignored the revelation of God in nature. All have rejected Him and are in bondage to their sin. All have embarked on a journey of moral and spiritual decline. Now however, he is talking to the Jews. He knows that they believe they are not like everyone else. They are the kind who stand in the synagogue and thank God that they are not 'lost' like the rest of the world. They shake their heads over the desperate situation outside the church; not owning the truth that they are part of sin's problem.

Paul is about to talk straight to them about spiritual arrogance. His message will burn in the hearts of any of us who sit inside the safety of our churches and cluck our tongues over the decline of our society. *"Schools are breaking down. Crime rates are ever on the rise. Threats from abroad are inside our borders. Teen suicides are escalating off the charts. Pornography is now a female addiction as well as male."* We see it all, our hearts may even sink, but how many of us identify ourselves with the problem?

Sin, repentance, and the grace of forgiveness are the three most needed preaching topics <u>inside</u> the church. The family of God is often so incestuous that we never make friends with one unbeliever. We think of ourselves as 'us' and everyone else as 'them'. We support the evangelist and say under our breath, *"Preach it!"* We review our spiritual commitments and are self-impressed.

I want to hear what Paul is going to say to me. It's obvious already that I am bent to review my behavior and think myself better than I am but God looks at my heart. This is the recurring theme throughout all of scripture and yet the Spirit of God keeps prompting the writers of the Bible to accentuate the truth of it again.

In school, none of us liked the kid who buttered up the teacher, kept all the rules, only to earn himself the title of 'the teacher's pet'. Why? We knew he was conniving. His behavior was self-serving, in no way reflective of an inward goodness. I shouldn't be surprised that the church can be full of teacher's pets. We believe the rules aren't made for us and we hold up our charts full of green check marks to remind God how lucky He is to have us in His family. The sin of pride that prompts me to boast is the same sin of pride that keeps the unbeliever in bondage to his sin. The moment I own *that* is the moment I will love others and walk humbly with God.

Every day, help me see <u>my</u> sin and <u>Your</u> grace. Amen

MISSING THE POINT

But if you call yourself a Jew and rely on the law and boast in God and know his will and approve what is excellent, because you are instructed from the law; and if you are sure that you yourself are a guide to the blind, a light to those who are darkness, an instructor of the foolish, a teacher of children, having in the law the embodiment of knowledge and truth ~ you then who teach others, do you not teach yourself? While you preach against stealing, do you steal? You who say that one must not commit adultery, do you commit adultery? You who abhor idols, do you rob temples? You who boast in the law dishonor God by breaking the law. For, as it is written, "The name of God is blasphemed among the Gentiles because of you."
Romans 2:17

I tell others that I follow Jesus. I decline the invitation to do things that I know He wouldn't do. I engage in things others think foolish because Jesus *would* do them. Is God honored by my convictions? I can fool myself into thinking so if I am oblivious to the difference between external behavior and internal faith. The first without the latter begets spiritual arrogance.

The Jews were proud of their heritage and boasted in the fact that the Law was given to them through Moses. Many of them were teachers of the truth God had entrusted. But, just as we are, they were guilty of every point. There are many ways to steal, even with the heart. There are ways to commit adultery, even with the heart. There are ways to worship idols, even with the heart. Though people around us can't read our thoughts and see the individual sins, they can pick up self-exaltation and whether we convey that we are above breaking the law. The theme of my life must be the Gospel and my need for the cross.

- Every day, I break God's law.
- Every day, because of Jesus sacrifice, I am forgiven.
- Every day, I realize I do not have the ability to keep from sinning.
- Every day, I pray for daily bread so that the Spirit can bring heart change.
- Recognition of my dependence on God serves humility and smashes pride.

When others are repelled by my good behavior because it feels hollow, seems arrogant, and is void of love, it is time to ask myself if God's name is being blasphemed among unbelievers. I can discredit what I think I am promoting. The very things I teach, I need to continue to learn.

Wake me up if my life is a walking contradiction! Keep me heart centered, Lord. Amen

WHAT I TEACH BEST

[You] who teach others, do you not teach yourself?
Romans 2:21

Rick Warren, giving an address to an audience of which I was a part, said ***"You only believe the part of the Bible that you actually*** *do."* I realized that I know far more than I practice. The only thing that counts with God is obedience.

For the first two decades of ministry, I was mainly a concert artist. To be able to progress from one song to the next, I often had to make remarks. Often, I told the story of how I came to choose a particular song. But mostly, I considered the lyrical content of the song I was going to comment on and then did a short study of its theme. I was a 'quick study' of the subject and might very well have come across as a know-it-all while failing to have an experiential wisdom of the topic.

God has been teaching me these past 12 years to teach only what I know firsthand. My most effective messages are the ones that reveal what I, currently, am learning. The Spirit of God is most powerful when I am willing to tell the stories of His grace in my own life; when I'm not afraid to tell others where I'm most broken. The power of this ministry lies in the healing of my deepest wounds. If I am moved by what I teach, challenged in my deepest parts, then women are moved.

In the past, I looked at the best parts of myself and believed that *these* were what qualified me to be in full time ministry. I stuffed the dark side out of view because I believed that anything in the shadows would disqualify me. I couldn't see that God's touch on *that* would be the catalyst for God's Spirit to do His greatest work through me. Passion is born when I see God touch the impossible. When I stretch out before God as an open book, then I can begin to take hold His promise for transformation. The greatest miracles I behold should not be external, but internal. *This* is the breeding ground for my greatest sermons.

Every place I falter, where I churn, where my faith fails, these are the messages of tomorrow. Transform my darkness in the presence of Your glory. Amen

CUTTING OF THE HEART

For no one is a Jew who is merely one outwardly, nor is circumcision outward and physical. But a Jew is one inwardly, and circumcision is a matter of the heart, by the Spirit, not by the letter. His praise is not from man but from God. Romans 2:28-29

A Jew believed that anyone who had been circumcised would never go to hell. His circumcision secured his salvation. Paul removes this last prop from their belief system. He emphasizes that, once again, God does not look at externals but internals. Circumcision of the heart, not the body, was what mattered to God.

And the Lord your God will circumcise your heart. . . Deut. 30:6 God wants to do surgery on my soul, to *cut out* or *cut away* sin; the sin that prevents Him from writing His law on my heart. I am to be a clean slate and accept whatever He writes. Fighting him by putting my hands over my ears, shielding my eyes, even being stiff-necked, prevents this internal circumcision from taking place. So much for respecting the privilege of this holy appointment.

It is no wonder that the Jewish leaders were enraged with Jesus and His apostles. The message of the Gospel erased what they believe qualified them to inherit salvation. To learn that all their rituals and external performances were as nothing to God must have been devastating. Perhaps it was too threatening a truth to own.

The Spirit of God is the great surgeon of my soul. When I interact with the Word and meditate on it, He takes truth to the part of my soul that needs attention. When His Word cuts like a sword through my strongholds of deception, it feels frightening and emotionally excruciating. I can hang on to a particular lie, or way of life, for many decades. The longer I resist Him, the more protective and defensive I am of what is really killing me. I need to be broken like a wild horse. Yielding to the Spirit is what will take me down, and then, save me.

My heart bears the scars of much surgery. It was painful but the results turned joyful with time. I trust You with this holy process. Make my heart totally pleasing to you. Amen

CHAPTER 3

TALK ABOUT PRIVILEGED

*Then what advantage has the Jew? Or what is the value of
circumcision? Much in every way. To begin with, the Jews
were entrusted with the oracles of God. Romans 3:1-2*

*T*he first story is really unthinkable. The Jews, the ones who were
given the Ten Commandments, the ones who were chosen by
God to hear Him speak and hold His revelation in their hands, were
the ones who twisted the message. Instead of walking humbly and
reflecting the heart of the God who had spoken to them, they grew
arrogant and self-righteous. The ones who had memorized such vast
portions of the Torah, the Torah that prophesied the coming of Jesus,
failed to even recognize Christ when He stood in front of them.

Yet, they were still Jews. They were still God's chosen people.
They were still precious to the heart of their Bridegroom and He did
not disown them because of their unbelief. Once chosen, God's love
never wavers.

The second story is really unthinkable as well. Chosen to be
included in God's Jewish storyline, I was also given the oracles of
God. Once I became His child, I even received a personalized inter-
preter of the scriptures in the form of the Holy Spirit. I didn't have to
go to a temple, to a priest, to the Holy of Holies, in hopes that God
would speak to me. I had His holy presence inside of me. He lived
in me to interpret God's oracles so that I would follow the cloud by
day and the pillar of fire by night.

Yet, in spite of knowing so much scripture, I took His presence
for granted. He waited patiently for me to take the oracles seriously,
to open them and ask for His insight. I waited four decades. The
Messiah was right in front of me yet I failed to engage Him in a way
that would turn my life upside down. In my mid-forties, that ended
when I experienced him at my own Red Sea. He parted the waters
and I embraced His oracles to my heart and haven't looked back.

Since the age of seven, I was God's child. I remained precious
to the heart of my Bridegroom in spite of my indifference. He did
not disown me because of my unbelief. He waited. He called. He
allowed me to experience just enough pain to make the fires of my

life refining, not consuming. The heat drove me to His Word and the oracles made my hands tremble.

They still do, Lord. Don't let me take my spiritual heritage for granted. Ever. Amen

WHEN TRUTH IS CORNERED

What if some were unfaithful? Does their faithlessness nullify the faithfulness of God? Romans 3:3

Paul has just spent many verses explaining that Jews and Gentiles must both come to a faith in Christ to be saved. The ground at the foot of the cross is level. The Jews do not have an advantage because of their generational bloodline or the fact that the men have been circumcised. This was hard for them to hear, so hard, that Paul heard many argue ~ *"If Jews are unfaithful, as you say, and God condemns them because of their sin, doesn't that make God unfaithful? After all, He made an everlasting covenant with them and called them 'His people'. What happened to God's promise?"*

Paul thinks this question is so important that he will spend all of chapter nine answering it.

To the Jew, and perhaps to us as we wrestle with certain scriptures, it can appear as if truth has cornered God. We believe there can only be two options for answering. The first would give all Jews guaranteed salvation because of who they are. The second would have them saved by faith alone, and since most did not acknowledge Jesus, God's faithfulness to His covenant with them is in question.

I have seven more chapters to prepare to understand Paul's answers to this question. I'm relieved about that! But what struck me this morning is this ~ what do I believe when God seems to appear guilty? When there is circumstantial evidence that might point to the possibility that God isn't good, or loving, or faithful, what does that do to my faith? If I'm one who has to put God in a box of my own understanding, I will be in trouble. If I'm willing to admit that the kingdom holds many mysteries and I am not capable of understanding them all, then I can more easily exercise my faith.

When God appears to break a promise, I know that the problem is me. God is a promise keeper. When God appears to be absent, the problem is me. God is ever near. When God appears to be lax in His judgment, the problem is me. God rules righteously.

Paul readily admits that these arguments are difficult for the Jews but they wrestle in the cobwebs of spiritual darkness. Instead of standing on the bedrock of God's character, they put God on the witness stand and rely on their own clever arguments to condemn Him. Such is the downfall of man when we risk our lives on the shifting sand of human reasoning.

A child can stand on the truth of your character and remain unshaken. I vow to trust you like that, to not be moved by the appearance of an inconsistency. You character is unchanging. Amen

BAD NEWS – GOOD NEWS

"None is righteous, no, not one; no one understands; no one seeks for God." Romans 3:10-11

I cannot be fully moved by the Gospel and the power of the cross until I admit to myself that I am not good at the core of me. Left to myself, I would not even want God. My desire to come to Jesus was fueled by a gift of grace, something I couldn't conjure up on my own. It's hard to admit that I would be capable of any sin. Instead, I want to make one horizontal comparison after another. *"But God, I didn't do what that person did."*

During a meal they shared, just before Jesus was arrested and brought to trial, Jesus revealed to Peter that in the next few hours, Peter would betray Him. He explained that, when pressured, Peter would deny even knowing Him. Peter's face fell at the news. I can't help but wonder if he thought, *"What?! I'm capable of that?"* That was the bad news. But what followed was the good news for any of us who are fixated on how much we are bent to sin. Jesus said to Peter, *"Don't be worried and upset."* There was mercy before the betrayal.

A few weeks ago, I had a short time to spend with a 13-year-old boy who is in trouble with the authorities for stealing. He is on the verge of going into permanent juvenile detention. He attended a day of my teaching while under house arrest and I saw him soak in the message. During a break, He came to talk with me about his life.

I asked him point-blank. *"Why are you stealing?"*

"Because I want the kids in school to be impressed by what I have. How do I stop?"

"You have to treasure Jesus more than you treasure the payoff you get from stealing." I explained that the only way that would happen was to meditate on the Word of God and fall in love with Christ. The payoff of being loved by Jesus would far outweigh the reward of how he felt when he held stolen goods in his hands.

As I think about this young kid, orphaned, trying to survive by grabbing what he can in this world, I realize that I am faced with similar choices as I am inclined to run from the truth of who I really am without the power of Christ in my life.

1.) I can live trying to pretend that I am better than I am but then I take the cross lightly.

2.) I can live overwhelmed by my sin, hate myself for failing, but then think that the cross is not for someone bad like me.

3.) I can embrace the bad news that, left to myself, I would not seek Christ. But His extravagant mercy reaches out to save me and entirely change my nature. The Gospel is for me, still, every day.

Bad news ~ I am a sinner. Good news ~ I am His, daily changed by His grace.

There aren't enough ways to praise You for what You do for me everyday. I boast in You. Amen

WHAT WORKS ITSELF OUT

"Their throat is an open grave; they use their tongues to deceive. The venom of asps is under their lips. Their mouth is full of curses and bitterness." Romans 3:13-14

Paul has spent all of Romans, so far, in describing how men turn away from God, how they reject God's presence in the revelation of nature. He's been plentiful with his own descriptive language but now reaches back into the Psalms to quote three different passages. He no longer explains *what* causes men to go astray; he uses O.T. quotes to paint a picture of how men act *when* they go astray.

Any man or woman who rejects God creates an inward reality that eventually works its way out. Heart breeds behavior. Thoughts breed speech. If anyone spurns Christ, how will anything they do or say resemble the Christ they have spurned? How will an unbeliever talk like Christ, bless others as Christ would bless them? It won't happen.

Instead, their inner life will be fraught with deception. What are curses? Untrue statements. Out of the graveyard of the unbeliever's dead heart come false statements about most everything. They do not provide sound advice when we lean on them. The feedback they give is self-generated wisdom, skewed by the world and their own soulish experiences. I'm not saying that nothing good is inside, nothing noteworthy, but they are certainly unpredictable friends, spouses, parents and business partners. Rely on them for some kind of stability and there will be frustration.

Without the Spirit inside, any of us are on a downward spiral. We accumulate opinions, judgments, and biases that are not of the kingdom and we are usually generous with our opinions, unaware that what proceeds out of the heart of an unbelieving man or woman is utter foolishness, leading others into harm's way.

I just turn on the TV to watch the slick orators of our political houses of Congress and I see these scriptures come alive. Oh God, fill Your church with Your Spirit, with the Word, so that we may be sound and true. Amen

FEAR

"There is no fear of God before their eyes." Romans 3:18

Our emotional lives are so twisted by sin. The things we should feel – we don't. What we shouldn't feel – we do. And all feelings are rooted in beliefs.

The One an unbeliever should fear is a holy and powerful God. Yet, that man or woman holds a position of bravado or casual indifference about Him. What they fear, instead, are far less important things that make no difference to their eternal destiny. Sadly, those fears even infect shallow believers inside the church.

What do I fear today? Being alone. Being rejected. Being poor. Being sick. My child's distress. A failed marriage. Being exposed. Failing in business. Getting old. The future repeating the past.

What I shouldn't fear, I do. What I should revere, I don't. The cure? Time with God and time in the Word. Only the transformation by God's Word and His Spirit will confront my faulty beliefs and, as I defer to the truth of what God is revealing, change my thinking *and* feelings.

Fear is the biggest tactic of Satan. But the power of fear to hold me captive can be history. God can do a work in me to re-wire the way I feel about the things which threaten to paralyze me. Simultaneously, I will begin to care about the only One I hold in awe: God. I won't fear being alone; God is with me. I won't fear being rejected; God accepts me. I won't fear being poor; God is my provider. I won't fear my child's distress; God is their Father.

Fear of God is what saved me. Continued awe of Him is what continues to transform the landscape of my fearful soul from one of terror to faith.

My God, may You get bigger in my soul so my fears will get smaller. I want to live fully in Your kingdom, starting now.
Amen

SILENCED BY GLORY

Now we know that whatever the law says it speaks to those who are under the law, so that every mouth may be stopped, and the whole world may be held accountable to God.
Romans 3:19

The radiance of God's glory is veiled even though so many of His children, including me, ask everyday, *"Show me your glory today."* I've seen enough of it to change my heart but the amount I have seen is a grain of sand in the vast ocean of glory. What happens when God shows His face and gives more than a small dose? Apparently, silence.

Job was silenced in his accusations when God became present and started asking him questions.

Isaiah was silenced when He saw God in all of His glory. Immediately, he pronounced himself unclean.

Habakkuk tried to speak and nothing came out.

John, as well as he knew Jesus, saw Him in His glorified state and fell as dead at His feet. Jesus had to touch him and bring life back to John's body.

One day, all of us will stand before God. We will see him in **all** of His glory. It won't be the same as standing before human judges. There, we are often acquitted, even though guilty. Our judges are fallen and we grow cynical of earthly laws and their consequences when we are tempted to discount those in higher authority.

The most eloquent will be silenced on the day they see God. He who has been self-impressed, insistent that his good deeds outweigh his bad deeds and are enough to earn him a place in heaven, will tremble and lose his voice in the presence of holiness. Even the most faithful of God's children will bow low in humility. God is more glorious than any human description; more holy than flawed people can even conceive.

As a fallen woman, I cannot imagine what perfection is like. For now, I see glimpses of Him and it stirs me to worship and defer my will to His. Since I was created to worship and to love God, this is the most exhilarating experience I will ever know in this lifetime. Any of Satan's counterfeits pale in comparison.

Let me see as much of Your glory as I can see and live. Please, Lord. Amen

WHO IS UNREASONABLE?

For by works of the law no human being will be justified in his sight. . . Romans 3:20

The one whom I offend is the one who has the right to tell me what it will take to make the relationship right. If I steal from my neighbor and he wants the stolen goods back along with a sincere apology, but I bring him gifts instead, he will still hold the offense in his heart. I have failed to make things right. *"But I was kind to him,"* I argue. *"You just can't make him happy no matter how nice you are to him!"* I complain. The problem is my rebellion against addressing the real issue.

God is the One whom we have offended. He addresses the problem of our sin, held up against His holiness, in all of scripture. He makes it plain that the only remedy is a Savior, which He lovingly provided. Yet, everyday men and women refuse to come to Him on His terms. They do kind things, join a church, contribute to philanthropic ventures, feel better about themselves in the process, and declare that God should be happy with them. When they hear the Gospel, they are offended by God's diagnosis of their sin and His provision of a Lamb on their behalf and call him 'impossible to please' and 'unloving.'

A study was done some time back on the life and lifestyles of the mob. Not surprisingly, there were many confirmations of brutal murders, extortion, gambling, etc. Surprisingly, it was discovered that within their extended families, there was tenderness, respect, consideration and kindness. They were loyal friends and defended one another admirably. But this way of life was only to preserve their well-being – and it was done at the expense of everyone else. Should their good deeds excuse them? We think not.

God is holy. God is eternal. God is the Creator of me, a sinner. He has the total right and authority to define sin, to define how life should work. My part is to squash my own rebellion against <u>any</u> of His words and defer to Him. He is not hard to please. He gave me His Spirit to enable joyful obedience. He is not unloving. He provided His only Son, as a Savior, to die for my rebellion. I have no ground whatsoever to name call. That is the ultimate offense against One who gave everything so that I could be delivered from the things I clutch with both hands, the things which bring death, not life. Is there any King so kind!

I play by Your rules. Your opinion is the only one that counts. And, whatever You say is the only thing that will be good for me in the long run anyway. I totally defer to You, humbly. Amen

BUT NOW

But now the righteousness of God has been manifested apart from the law, although the Law and the Prophets bear witness to it - the righteousness of God through faith in Jesus Christ for all who believe... Romans 3:21-22

What wonderful words and implication ~ "But now!" They separate one part of life from another. They provide a defining moment and one that is life changing. I think of the life stories that have used this expression.

- I was sick all my life *but now* I'm healthy.
- I was an orphan *but now* I'm part of a loving family.
- I was unemployed *but now* am doing what I've always dreamed I would.

Paul has painted a bleak, but truthful, picture of man's condition before God. It has spanned two whole chapters. He tells me that I can do nothing to earn God's favor. All my efforts get me nowhere. I am rebellious even though I may be impressed with the good things I do. I am headed for destruction without a Savior. I have spurned the many ways God has revealed Himself in nature and I am held accountable for that.

The emotional temperature of the book radically changes though with this verse as Paul announces that there is a *"but now"* available to my hopeless situation. Righteousness can be mine to embrace as a gift because there is a Savior named Jesus. It's mine if I place all of my hopes in Him. This is the foundation of every saint's testimony.

- I was once blind *but now* I see.
- I used to work frantically to please God, and couldn't, *but now* He draws close to me and sees me as someone pure, because of Jesus.
- I was once condemned, *but now* the judge has given me freedom.
- I once was poor, *but now* am rich, forever, in the kingdom.

There should be no such thing as a stoic Christian. Every promise of God is really a *'but now'* sentence. They change every bleak prediction of my life.

Thank you for changing my story. Amen

MEASURING THE ATONEMENT

For there is no distinction: For all have sinned and fall short of the glory of God and are justified by his grace as a gift. . . Romans 3:22b-24a

People who consider themselves 'good' believe on some level that they don't need as much grace to be saved. Do they need the cross? Yes, but not as much of it as the most degenerate of society.

It's as if they measure out the blood of the atonement and believe that they only need five percent or twenty percent to be forgiven.

As Christians, it's easy to still practice a horizontal kind of comparison with others. We can look at someone else's sin and say to God, *"But I didn't do that!"* The pride of not seeing ourselves as sinners continues.

The truth is this: I need the same amount of atonement for my sin as the man accused of triple homicide on death row. We are both completely lost without Christ; both in need of His complete work on Calvary to be justified. Until I see myself as having completely missed the mark of God's glory, in the company of every other sinner on this earth, I do not really know and understand the Gospel.

The spirit of revenge and bitterness holds God's family in bondage. So few follow Jesus in the lifestyle of forgiveness. One of the reasons I can hold onto the pain of offenses is because I haven't received the radical forgiveness Christ offers to me. If I think *I* only needed a small amount of the blood Jesus shed in order to be saved, then I will offer *others* stingy amounts of forgiveness to others. I can't give away what I haven't first received. I consider the words of Jesus about the woman who washed His feet with her tears. *"She loved much because she was forgiven much."*

All have sinned. All are completely lost and condemned. Jesus's blood flowed, all of it, for me. Until I see myself as lost, I will not dance for the joy of being found. A hopeless repentant makes a deliriously happy convert.

"I am a beggar showing other beggars where to find bread."
I am a justified sinner showing other sinners where to find forgiveness. Oh God, don't let me forget these truths. Amen

MOVED BY A WORD

..Christ Jesus, whom God put forward as propitiation by his blood, to be received by faith. Romans 3:24b-25a

'*Propitiation*' is a word we usually pass over quickly when reading through Romans. Someone once said that it means '*substitute*'. Knowing that, I pass over it quickly, thinking that I understand and don't need to linger on it. What a mistake.

Worshippers in the ancient world knew the world well. They would bring their sacrifices; animals, even newborn babies, and kill them at the altar, all for the purpose of appeasing angry gods. While their faith was misplaced, their conscience was right in knowing that a 'god' who bore wrath needed to be appeased. The One, true God sent Jesus to be the sacrifice. He bore our wrath so we could appear guiltless before Him.

William Cowper, a prolific poet and hymn writer, came to Christ through this verse. Orphaned at six years old, he was sent to a boarding school where he suffered extreme mistreatment at the hand of bullies. He was a frail child with an artistic temperament; an easy target for peers who abused power. In 1756, when he was just 25 years old, he was committed to an asylum to supposedly live out a life sentence. He is quoted to have said, *"My sin! My sin! Oh, for some fountain open for my cleansing!"* The torment, which fed his instability, was little more than recognition of His need for forgiveness.

God heard his cries. His doctor was a gentle old man, a follower of Christ, whom God used to bring William to faith. When he shared Romans 3:25 with him, the power of Christ's death washed over him and he understood the magnificent implications of the atonement. He embraced Christ and the powerful experience was captured with his pen.

There is a fountain filled with blood
Drawn from Immanuel's veins;
And sinners, plunged beneath that flood,
Lose all their guilty stains.

The dying thief rejoiced to see
That fountain in his day;
And there have I, as vile as he,
Washed all my sins away.

Many end their lives in suicide because they are overcome with guilt. Others live out a life sentence of depression and regret as they rehearse their failures like a favorite old movie. Their track record haunts them like a ghost. Some with obsessive-compulsive disorder scrub their hands till they bleed in order to find a kind of cleansing that brings relief. All is offered in Christ. Complete cleansing, one that lasts forever, is offered in the fountain of His blood. I'm invited to stand in the flow and, with tears, say *"thank you."*

If there's any part of me that has not really taken in what your death means for me, today, please open my eyes completely. Amen

GOD – SOFT ON SIN?

. . .In Christ Jesus, whom God put forward as a propitiation by his blood, to be received by faith. This was to show God's righteousness, because in his divine forbearance he had passed over former sins. It was to show his righteousness at the present time. . . Romans 3:24b-26b

When Nathan confronted David over his relationship with Bathsheba, and David acknowledged the gravity of his sin, Nathan said something that is related to these words from Paul. He said, *"The Lord has put away your sin."* Or, *passed over.* The world is outraged when any judge just passes over sin. Doesn't that diminish His glory and put His righteous standing at stake? Is God forever regarded as someone soft on sin, not to be taken seriously? If He passes over sin, doesn't that encourage us to pass over it too?

As Jesus bled to death (became our propitiation), He demonstrated God's holiness and what it took to satisfy it. *The message was this: I am righteous and holy. And because sin needs to be forgiven in order to make you holy, it will require the death of my Son. Mankind falls short of my glory in huge measure. I cannot just pass over sins forever without requiring a perfect sacrifice that will forgive sins. I can only wipe them out forever for someone who puts*

*their faith in Jesus. Sin is a big deal. My glory is a big deal. And
without Jesus, the sin has no remedy and must be condemned.*

God needed to save me in a way that showed that He is serious
about His own glory. There is no way I could have, by myself,
worked to make myself acceptable to God. My sin problem polluted
my chances forever. There was only one way to satisfy the require-
ments of a righteous God; through the sacrifice of a perfect Lamb.

On the very day tens of thousands of lambs were being brought
to Jerusalem to be sacrificed for the Passover, Jesus – the perfect
Lamb, was being sacrificed on the cross. That day, human lambs
died for nothing. Today, sacrifices are still made, still for naught.
Animals are dying needlessly. Humans are expending themselves
needlessly, trying to earn God's favor and eradicate their guilt. Oh,
look to the Lamb, O earth, and believe.

*I sin, everyday. I repent, everyday. And now, I repent for
all the times I took it lightly. I am silenced by Your glory.
Amen*

PERMISSIVE MIS-PERCEPTIONS

*. . .In Christ Jesus, whom God put forward as a propitia-
tion by his blood, to be received by faith. This was to show
God's righteousness, because in his divine forbearance he
had passed over former sins. It was to show his righteousness at the present time. . . Romans 3:24b-26b*

I've been pretty worked up emotionally since writing from the
previous verse. I realized that I didn't really grasp, nor convey, the
weight of this verse. So, I'm writing again on the same thing.

I think I've treated my sin, and God's holiness, casually. It's as
if I was adopted into a family with an overly permissive father. As a
new member of the family, I was told that, while he'd rather his children obey, when we sin, he'll always forgive us. Forgiveness was
cheap. Sinning was easy. The holiness of the father was immaterial
and not to be taken too seriously. He was really a pushover and his

longsuffering nature gave the illusion that forgiveness didn't cost him all that much. With a wave of his hand he cleared sin's debt.

If I had lived at the time of Jesus, and if I'd accompanied Him through the last twenty four-hours of His life, I'd have been horrified at what He suffered. I'd have been pleading with the soldiers to stop their mistreatment. *"Enough!"* I would have cried. Yet, Jesus would have silenced my objections, as He did with Peter, to remind me that the crucifixion He faced was what it would take to extend forgiveness any time I asked for it. My first hand knowledge and experience of His suffering would forever temper my desire to sin. His innocence, and my guilt, would haunt me.

Adam and Eve experienced the killing of the first sacrifice. An animal lost its life so that the skin could cover Adam and Eve's nakedness. Having never seen bloodshed, I wonder if they were traumatized by the act. I bet so. The world of Eden was forever shattered on that day. Sinning put in motion the need for bloodshed in order for repentant sinners to be covered, and then washed clean. The ultimate cost would be the blood of Jesus, which should ever be in my vision when I'm tempted to sin. What may look so desirable that causes me to cave is really the very thing that propelled the hammer that nailed the hands and feet of my Savior. Oh, what it cost Him every time He says so graciously, *"Christine, I forgive you."*

Help me hate sin the way You hate it and remember the cross. Amen

BOASTING

Then what becomes of our boasting? It is excluded. . .
Romans 3:27a

If Jesus took the entire wrath that I deserved upon Himself, then what is there for me to boast about? Only that *"I am a sinner and Christ is a great Savior."* (John Newton) I have nothing in myself to make God happy enough with me to earn a place in heaven. Lest I'm inclined to wallow in worthlessness, God turns around and offers love and redemption in the form of Jesus. My horrible condition is eclipsed by undeserved favor. I'm invited to live in joy rather than self-loathing. The One who has every reason to despise me doesn't. This is the good news of the Gospel.

Yet in spite of this, pride still nips at my heels. It is the most dangerous of all vices. C.S. Lewis described it this way.

"Boasting is essentially competitive. Pride gets no pleasure out of having something, only out of having more of it than the next man. We say that people are proud of being rich, or clever, or good-looking, but they are not. They are proud of being richer, or cleverer, or better-looking than others. If everyone else became equally rich, or clever, or good-looking there would be nothing to be proud about. It is the comparison that makes you proud: the pleasure of being above the rest."

So what does the Christian sometimes boast of? The size of our ministry. Church growth. How smart our children are. How much we've read, how much Bible we know, how many hours we pray, the list can be pretty long. We can be *really* clever and preface everything with, *"By God's grace. . ..this is true."* But in the human heart, only <u>we</u> know if it's a way to boast without apology because humility appears to be present.

Oh, how insidious pride is. The only way to stay on top of it is to stay in the scriptures and hold the glory of Christ up as a mirror to my soul. Everyday, I need the comparison. I need the counseling of the Holy Spirit to help me see myself as He sees me. He is the One who gently reveals the first inkling of pride and reminds me again how much the landscape of my soul needs the cleansing of the Word. Without it, I will be hungry for attention, greedy for praise, and act on my perceived need to be out in front so that I can soothe my ragged self-perception.

Satan declared that he would ascend to God's throne and take His seat. That pronouncement was the beginning of his downfall. Boasting in anything other than the glory of God is ruinous. It destroys my chances to share Christ with others. Jesus is beautiful.

Jesus is full of glory and what He has done *in* me must become the point of all my stories.

Show me how aggressive I need to be against any pride in my soul. Today, I want Your glory to be on full display. Amen

TOLERANT OR RIGID?

Or is God the God of Jews only? Is he not the God of Gentiles also? Yes, of Gentiles also, since God is one--who will justify the circumcised by faith and the uncircumcised through faith. Romans 3:29-30

The Jews believed that God was only *their* God. That made them moral elitists, believing themselves to be better than anyone outside their race.

The Gentiles believed that there were *many* gods. That made them tolerant, encouraging indulgences in all kinds of depravity. Their many gods permitted wickedness and Greece was a cesspool.

Paul addressed the tension one faced when choosing whether or not he would align with the Jew or the Gentile. Neither offered a righteous option. One group was prideful and monotheistic. The other practiced all forms of wickedness and was polytheistic. How did God solve the dilemma between the two extremes?

He sent His Son to die for all mankind; circumcised and uncircumcised. Each needed to come through faith in Christ. Each was unable to earn his salvation based on race and good works. Paul made it clear that faith alone qualified a Jew and faith alone qualified a Gentile.

Romans is a book that often appears to split hairs. It's cumbersome at times, I'll admit. Studying it is a workout and many mornings I face a writing crisis! God is helping me as I ask Him each day, *"Please show me what difference this issue makes in my relationship with You!"* All truth must connect with our hearts.

So, why do these verses today matter? Because without this solid rudder, I will lose my way. Let's face it. There are denominations that boast in being right. They believe they have a corner on truth and no one outside their box could possibly be saved. They are like the Jews; elitist and exclusionary.

Unbelievers who are moral relativists also surround us. They pride themselves in being tolerant. They are very willing to let us talk about our faith but we better not tell *them* what to believe. As soon as we do, we're seen as prideful and judgmental.

I stand in the truth of Paul's writing today that all people must come to the cross empty handed. Evangelicals, Charismatics, Mormons, Catholics, Muslims, Buddhists, Hindus. We come to God one way ~ through faith in Christ ~ plus nothing. I do not have any advantage over another man or woman. I must be firm but humble when sharing with others. I must not make them feel excluded not can I be tolerant for tolerance sake. Jesus is not discriminating. He calls all sinners to Himself and what each of us does with His invitation, Jew or Gentile, determines where we will spend eternity.

If I'm your child, it's only because of Your grace. If someone else is not yet your child, I invite them with urgency, conviction and humility. Amen

CHAPTER 4

ABRAHAM AND JESUS

What then shall we say was gained by Abraham, our fore-father according to the flesh? For if Abraham was justified by works, he has something to boast about, but not before God. For what does the scripture say? "Abraham believed God, and it was counted to him as righteousness."
Romans 4:1-3

$\mathcal{P}$aul's teaching rubbed against the grain of religious Jews so he spent three chapters in the beginning of Romans showing that justification is only through faith in Christ, not of works. As the Jews heard Paul speak, they probably thought of Abraham and raised one of the same questions we hear today. *"How could Abraham be justified (through Christ) if the death of Christ had not happened yet?"* They were thinking of Genesis 15:6. *"And he believed the Lord and it was credited to him as righteousness."* Jews believed that Abraham was good, that his salvation was because of his obedience in matters like circumcision. Based on that, they clung to their own good works and religious piety run rampant. Paul knew he needed to talk about Abraham to prove justification by faith alone.

If I believe that the Gospel of salvation is only as old as the cross, then I am shortsighted. Jesus was called *"The Lamb"* from before the foundation of the world. God revealed Himself, and Jesus, to Abraham! Abraham believed, looked ahead to the Lamb's sacrifice on Calvary, and *"it"*, *"Christ's righteousness"*, was credited to Abraham's account. The process of salvation was identical to mine.

Here are some astounding facts that support how Abraham came to faith. 1.) God preached the Gospel to Abraham. (Gal.3:8-9) Wow, what did that sermon sound like and look like? 2.) Jesus said that Abraham knew him. (John 8:56) So much more happened than what was recorded in scripture!

God is much bigger than I thought. God is never inconsistent. Salvation, even in Genesis, has always been about Jesus, the Lamb of God. God has been the creative communicator, working through time to make Jesus known. As a Christian woman in 2010, I have not placed my faith in a Savior, and a plan, that is only two thousand years old. My feet are standing in a salvation that was conceived before time, one that has not changed with history. Never am I more secure than when I trust the God of the ages.

Man thinks himself clever when he believes he has found a loophole, a seeming inconsistency in scripture. Ultimately, our need to be clever is a way to escape the reality of our sin and the need for Christ's atonement on our behalf. Today, I am aware more than ever that there are **_never_** legitimate loopholes with God and His Word. My faith is well placed. Abraham experienced the revelation of Jesus, just like me, and believed amidst a world of unbelief. God blessed that and He still does.

> *You are so big. I am so small. Jesus has always been 'the*
> *Lamb'. And, I have always been yours, chosen before time.*
> *Amen*

LET THEM TALK!

A lineup of O.T. characters speak up.

So, perhaps like me, you were astounded that God had preached about Jesus to Abraham, and that even Jesus admitted that Abraham knew Him. Is he the only Old Testament character who knew of Jesus? James Boice, a down to earth scholar, pieces together scriptures and uses some poetic license to help us understand their testimonies regarding a Savior they'd never seen, but One who justified them by faith. I hope you are as moved as I am by this piece and the history of our salvation.

Abraham is the focus of Paul's attention in this section of Romans. But it is worth saying that the same point can   made about any of the other Old Testament believers. They would all have explained the hope of their salvation in the same terms. Let's ask a number of them what they "discovered in this matter" (cf. Rom. 4:1).

Here is Adam. Let's start with him. *"Adam, you were the first man, and we should assume from this that what you believed in regard to salvation is of value for us. What did you believe in this matter? Did you believe that you could be saved by your works? Or did you have an anticipation of the coming of Jesus Christ and ground your faith in him?"*

Adam replies, *"You know my sad story, how I sinned by eating of the forbidden fruit and how I carried the human race into sin and death as a result of my transgression. But if you know that, you also know how God appeared to me after my fall and announced the coming of a Savior who would crush the head of Satan, though he would himself be wounded in the process. I did not know who he was at that time, but I believed in him. And I expressed that faith by naming my wife 'Eve,' because she would be the one through whom the gift of spiritual life would come. 'Eve' means 'life giver.' We thought she would give birth to the Messiah. So we named her first son 'Cain,' meaning 'Here he is!' We were wrong in that; it was many thousands of years before our line actually produced Jesus Christ. But we had the right idea, and we were credited with righteousness because of faith in Jesus."*

Let's ask Jacob what he *"discovered in this matter"*— *"Jacob, were you saved by your good works or by faith in the deliverer to come?"*

Jacob replies, *"I wasn't saved by my works—or by my ancestry either, even though I was the grandson of Abraham. I didn't have as much understanding as my grandfather. He was the spiritual giant in our family. But you will recall that as I lay dying I looked forward to the coming of the Savior and said, 'The scepter will not depart from Judah, nor the ruler's staff from between his feet, until he comes to whom it belongs and the obedience of the nations is his' [Gen. 49:10]. I was saved because I believed what God said about that Savior."*

Here is Moses. Let's ask him. *"Moses, how were you saved?"*

Moses replies that even he, the lawgiver, was saved by faith in Jesus Christ and not in any ability he might be supposed to have had to keep God's commandments. *"The Lord told me, 'I will raise up for them a prophet like you from among their brothers; I will put my words in his mouth, and he will tell them everything I command him' [Deut. 18:18]. I was saved because I believed that promise."*

Our next witness is King David. *"Tell us, David, you were called a man after God's own heart, weren't you?"*

"Yes," replies David.

"That means you tried to think and act as God does. Does that mean that you were saved by your own good works or obedience?"

David explains that he was an adulterer and murderer. *"If I had trusted my works, I wouldn't have had a chance. No, I was saved because I looked forward in faith to that one who God promised would sit upon my throne forever. I knew that a person who would rule forever was no mere man. He must be the Savior-God. I believed that and was saved by him."*

Lord Jesus, I see it. You can reveal Yourself to anyone, at any time. We don't need you here in the flesh to know You exist. You long to be known and if I seek for You, You delight in revealing Yourself. I am a seeker! Amen

WHEN I CAN'T LIFT MY HEAD UP

Blessed are those whose lawless deeds are forgiven, and whose sins are covered; blessed is the man against whom the Lord will not count his sin. Romans 4:7-8

When someone hurts me badly, seeing ***them*** can be a reminder of what they've done. The sin is attached to the person. Even after I forgive them, I can still remember it when I see them across the room.

In our justice system, when we punish a crime, we punish the person who committed it. That's all we can do in this world.

Ah, the kingdom is different! When God forgives, he separates my sin from ***me***. I no longer wear it when He looks at me. One of the words for 'forgive' is to 'send away'. This is what Peter meant when he said, ***"He himself bore our sins in his body on the tree, that we might die to sin and live to righteousness." I Pet.2:24*** God took that 'thing' for which I repented, took it off of me and put it on Jesus. Jesus died for it as if He was the One who committed it.

So why would I wallow in past failures? Why would I let my one huge mistake weigh down my spirit and cause me to walk with my head to the ground? Jesus took it from me and put it on Himself, forever. When He looks at me, He does not see the sin. He sees His own perfection. I am not defined, in heaven, by my past.

I echo David's words to himself in Psalm 42. *"Why are you so downcast, oh my soul?"* Satan is the author of a self-punishing life-style. He takes every failure, magnifies it by a thousand, records it like a movie and plays it over and over again in my head. He rejoices when I am hard on myself. He encourages payback and self-hatred. He offers a heavy robe of guilt as a part of my wardrobe and I often wear it because it appears to fit me perfectly. Right color. Right size. Right length.

When I can't hold my head up, I remember that I am **not** my sin! Christ wore my sin, once and for all, on a cross. Then He declared, *"It is finished."* Sin, forever removed.

So, who am I? A forgiven, justified, righteous, child of God. He is the lifter of my head to this new reality. I throw guilt into the depths of the sea.

Do I really understand justification yet, Lord? Write Romans on my heart, in every place. Amen

SACRAMENTS AND SALVATION

He received the sign of circumcision as a seal of the righteousness that he had by faith while he was still uncircumcised. Romans 4:11

Have you ever noticed that pride is insidious? Take someone who is insecure. What looks like weakness of character is really pride in disguise. Someone declares themselves to be unacceptable and outside of God's declaration of love. Take someone who can't forgive themselves for something they've done. Even that can be rooted in pride. God says that His blood washes away all sin yet, with veiled arrogance, they believe they are the exception and refuse His grace.

Pride kills the beautiful essence of the Gospel. God's extravagant grace toward sinners is diluted by pride as I try to believe that my salvation couldn't be *all* about what Jesus did and *nothing* about what I did. Does my family's spiritual history and stature mean nothing? Does my baptism give me no edge? Doesn't my church history contribute, even a little, to my qualifications for faith?

A Jew who trusts in Jesus is not saved because he is a Jew. He is saved the same way a Gentile is saved; through faith in Christ. A longstanding Baptist or Methodist is saved the way a hardened sinner living on the streets is saved. Each of us brings nothing to the table except our declared sinfulness and understanding of being under God's wrath. We put all our faith in Christ, the Wrath-bearer, the One who paid the penalty for us.

The Roman church was confused about Paul's teaching that a person is only saved by faith alone; that their Jewish-ness had absolutely nothing to do with it. They tried to prove their point by drawing attention to Abraham's circumcision. But there was a hole in their argument. Abraham was declared righteous (saved) by faith in Genesis 15. God did not tell him to be circumcised until Genesis 17, fourteen years later. It was critical for Jews to understand that circumcision was only a sign that Abraham had been set apart, a seal others could point to that would show that he was different.

My baptism is a sign, a seal, for my world as well. It identifies me as being one with Jesus. The sacraments are signs that point to faith, they don't replace it or add to it. They point backward to that moment when, by faith, I came empty-handed to the foot of the cross.

The next time I 'do anything holy' and momentarily feel puffed up, I take the Word and smash my pride against the rocks.

I just keep trying to make myself feel better about me. But anything good that I do, any good that is in me, You birthed and enabled. Exposed pride and self-centeredness. Amen

MY SPIRITUAL FATHER

The purpose was to make him the father of all who believe without being circumcised, so that righteousness would be counted to them as well, and to make him the father of the circumcised who are not merely circumcised but who also walk in the footsteps of the faith that our father Abraham had before he was circumcised. Romans 4:11b-12

If our father were a distinguished man, well-known and well-loved, we would tell everyone about him. Like the kid in grade school who brags to his friends, *"My daddy is stronger than your daddy,"* we would probably brag about whom we were related to.

I don't know how you feel about your family tree. Perhaps your line of descendants is the cause of much embarrassment. The good news for any of us who have come to God by faith is that we get a new ancestral line. Abraham becomes our father.

This father of faith made it clear that the way to God is by faith, not by works. I am glad that he didn't perform a long series of rigorous religious acts for a hundred years, and at the end, proclaim that this was the way to salvation. Actually, he did something far harder; he trusted God.

When he took the hand of his child, led him up the mountain, and laid him on the altar in obedience, he showed us the essence of faith. Isaac took his father's hand and trusted Abraham through the journey to the altar; Abraham took *his* Father's hand and trusted God on the journey as well. Believing God, by faith, and looking ahead for the Perfect Sacrifice became the template for our salvation.

For the Jew who recognizes Jesus as the Messiah and trusts Him to be his Savior, Abraham is his father. For the Gentile who recognizes Jesus as His Savior, he also calls Abraham his father.

Regardless of whom we are related do, regardless of what they've done to make us proud or bring us shame; we have a new ancestral line to give us reason to stand tall. Abraham is our father of faith. All of his descendants, including Jesus, are brothers. Family shame is a thing of the past if we walk in the truth of the Scriptures.

My journey with You is still about radical trust. I cling to Your promises in all the places where I am making my way up the mountain today. I walk in the footsteps of my father, Abraham. Amen

WAY TO WRECK A GIFT

For the promise to Abraham and his offspring that he would be heir of the world did not come through the law but through the righteousness of faith. For if it is the adherents of the law who are to be the heirs, faith is null and the promise is void. Romans 4:13-14

Talk about a gift. Because of Abraham's faith, God justified him and then made a covenant promise to him. He would be the father of many nations and through his seed the earth would be blessed. This promise was not made because Abraham had done anything to deserve it. It was a gift with no strings.

Many today are trying to earn their way to heaven. They believe they can generate enough moral goodness to get in God's good graces. If their good outweighs their bad, perhaps God will save them from the fires of hell. The story of Abraham, and Paul's review of his story in Romans, strongly reminds us of the error of this kind of belief. It's ludicrous (and arrogant) to believe that I can do anything good enough to appease the wrath of a holy God. I am sinful, by birth, by nature. Any good that I do does not wash away guilt. Only the blood of the atoning Savior can do that – and that blood offering is a gift. No strings attached other than fully casting my hope upon Him.

I got to thinking this morning about how I can easily wreck a gift. As one who has habitually over-performed so that people would not reject me, I couldn't accept their gifts easily. What complicated it was that there were people who gave gifts with strings attached. They gave in order to be praised. But there have also been many who gave because God's love prompted them to do so. Instead of accepting their love, I worked to prove to them that I really appreciated it, that they shouldn't be sorry that they gave what they gave. I spoiled the love gift.

It's hard to relax in God's gift of love as well. I'm sure I'm not the only one who has worked hard to keep God happy with me. I crashed in my forties, disillusioned. Fear that God's love was conditional kept me burning the candle at both ends.

God's love, expressed through Jesus, is free, no strings attached. Should I work hard for the kingdom? Oh yes. But not because I'm trying to show God I was worth saving. I work hard because I'm grateful for a love I didn't earn. Perfect love casts out the fear of rejection. Performance pressure is birthed out of fear and pride and is healed by humbly accepting the warm place God provides next to His heart. He will never turn me aside, not because I have earned His faithfulness, but because He *is* faithful.

If fear is running my life in any way, show me. Amen

LIFE WITHOUT A MIRROR

For the law brings wrath, but where there is no law there is no transgression. Romans 4:15

When I come into contact with the law, I become of aware of what sin is. I learn what is right and what is wrong. Without exposure to it, I am like a child who has had poor parenting. The neighbors say of his poor manners and bad behavior, *"Poor kid. He doesn't know any better."*

God said it another way. *"My people are destroyed for lack of knowledge. . ."* Hosea 4:6 We are really seeing this play out in our world. Most everyone wants to live by their own truth, whatever feels right. They follow their heart (and the heart is deceitful and desperately wicked) and are devastated when life begins to fall apart. The serpent has lied to the human race and convinced them, since the Garden of Eden, that we are capable of thinking like God and deciding what is good and what is evil. Left to our own rudder, which is really *his* rudder, we live shipwrecked lives.

Marriages are hanging on by a thread as each partner tries to figure out how to make things work. Without the Word, there is no real insight. Without the healing love of the Physician, there is no cure for the pain of intimate relationships out of sync with God.

The relationship between children and parents has deteriorated. Lawlessness and disrespect are in our face. So many kids live like orphans and are doing the best they can to care for themselves. Without the Word, they have no rudder. Without the transforming power of the cross, they have no access to victory over the lure of sin.

We need the law to show us what's wrong. We need Christ to forgive us and empower us to live God's way. If I languish today in a wilderness of confusion and torment, I know that my only cure is much time in the Word and in prayer. Clarity will not be found any other way. The mirror of the Scriptures waits to show me where my face is dirty and how to be cleansed and focused in a new direction.

Without the law, I won't know where I've sinned. Without the law, I won't know how to make decisions about things that leave people stumped. Make me wise and discerning, Lord. Amen

RESTING ON THE CUSHION OF GRACE

That is why it depends on faith, in order that the promise may rest on grace and be guaranteed to all his offspring – not only to the adherent of the law but also to the one who shares the faith of Abraham, who is the father of us all.
Romans 4:16

I can be so terribly inconsistent. I know that when I came to Christ through faith in Christ, that I contributed nothing to the equation, but from then on I am tempted everyday to live my life trying to please God. The Christian life becomes all about my efforts and going back to the law. Grace is shut out.

What will please God today? I can make a list and try to live up to it. I can vow to be honest today and do fairly well. I'll only slip up twice. Does this double failure impress God? It's better than failing ten times, right? Or does God only accept a one-time slip up? The line of what's acceptable is vague, even tormenting, as I try to figure out what will make God happy with me. He is transformed into a judge, condemning or accepting according to my works, and I am kept off balance in a perpetual state of insecurity.

God is my Father, not my judge. I have been made perfect in Christ. God has promised covenant love to me and I can rest in that promise on a soft cushion of grace. This is not some poetic expression to inspire me to feel better. It is the greatest reality of the kingdom. My Father is a lavish grace-giver. I need grace because none of my efforts are perfect enough to be stamped 'holy and acceptable.' But, because of grace, I know that God sees me through the veil of the cross. Christ's atonement continues to work on my behalf today. As I sin, I repent, and I am washed clean yet again. There is no quota for how many times I can ask for forgiveness. I can come for cleansing, resting on grace, as often as I need it.

I love God. I love His Word. I obey with joy and good intentions. But failure to achieve perfection is a certainty. Instead of being hard on myself (which is so intrinsic to my nature), I take joy in the fact that God's grace is poured out upon my sin. The cushion, ornate and intricately made, is the perfect place to repose.

I rest on promises I don't deserve. I focus on You and Your great love. I celebrate Your grace. Amen

SOMETHING OUT OF NOTHING

God. . . gives life to the dead and calls into existence the things that do not exist. Romans 4:17b

Our God is so powerful. Though our hands are often empty and we're driven to despair, He can create something out of nothing.

When a woman has a knack for putting together a beautiful meal with just a few leftovers in the refrigerator, we say that she 'whipped up a meal out of nothing.' But she <u>did</u> have ingredients to work with. Everything in her meal was in her refrigerator or cupboards.

A magician or illusionist gains fame by appearing to make something vanish, or make something appear right out of thin air. But we all know it was an illusion. He is not God. He's just gifted with trickery and sleight of hand.

God is described in scripture as one who makes roadways in the wilderness and streams in the desert. He speaks, and things that did not exist at all, exist. That's my Father. That's my King.

Every child of God wants to know that a powerful God is aware of him. He is! Every person wants to be loved by someone they worship. They are! Every human being who has his or her back against the wall, and who is in serious trouble, wants to know that God can deliver. God can! With just a word, the earth shakes and things change.

Today, perhaps you're out of hope. You've tried everything you know to fix things and have finally exhausted all your options. Giving up, you've declared the whole situation hopeless. God can create options that are outside of your problem solving skills. He can create hope where there is none.

What needs to exist today that doesn't? Perhaps the need is external. Pray the Word of God and stand, in prayer, on His promises. Maybe the need is internal. Find scriptures; ones that speak of your need and stand, in prayer, on God's promises. Be tenacious. Man is into microwaving. God is into marinating. God wants to grow our faith as we come to the end of ourselves and finally learn how to trust His answers and His timing. For many of you who you have waited, in faith, with His Word on your tongue, perhaps today is the day of deliverance.

I review how You have worked in my life and give You glory.
Some of your answers were quick, others were so very slow,
and through all of my waiting, you were faithful to help me
rest on the cushions of grace. Amen

BECAUSE GOD SAID SO. PERIOD!

In hope he believed against hope, that he should become the father of many nations, as he had been told, "So shall your offspring be." Romans 4:18

If anyone could have floundered in his faith, it was Abraham. All he had were the words God spoke to him. He had no church to fan the flame of his faith. No bible. No bible studies. No fellow Christians. He was all alone and the only one in his world to hear God speak. He clung to God's words in a vacuum.

God calls us to Himself and, through His Word and the voice of His Spirit, calls us to live against the grain of our world too. Because the world hated Jesus, we were warned that they would hate us as well. Every great man of God in scripture stood against the tide of society. The eleven disciples of Jesus were all martyrs, except John. They had experienced the love of their Savior firsthand, heard His words, and the memory of it constrained them. Jesus commanded them to go preach to the ends of the earth and so they did. End of story.

Today, we stand in faithfulness in the vacuum of the workplace. We're the only ones who won't manipulate, won't engage in dishonesty, and won't use the company for advancement. What should cause others' respect can quickly turn to scorn.

We stand in faithfulness in the vacuum of our families. We are aware, because of the Word and the fulfillment of our times that Jesus could come at any moment. Because of that, we live focused and stay ready. Someone recently said, ***"You really believe that Jesus is coming out of the sky and to snatch all His followers off of the earth? You are all nuts."*** Yes, I believe because Jesus said so. Period.

Across the world, others are also serving God in a vacuum. The love of God, expressed in Christ, constrains them to live out their faith despite the prospect of great suffering. Entire families and towns have banished them from their homes. Others are in jail. Others are being tortured.

Do you know about Andrew White, the vicar of Baghdad? An Englishman, a husband and father of two small boys, was called by God to go to the Middle East. He has Multiple Sclerosis yet the love of Christ constrains him. He serves as pastor of an Anglican church, once 3,000 strong, in one of the better neighborhoods of Baghdad. He will not leave even though his life is threatened. He has seen six assistant pastors killed with car bombs. Out of 3,000 in his church, all the men except a dozen or so are left. Now, he serves a congregation of widows and orphans. He goes about town with a security detail of twenty-four armed guards provided by the Iraqi government. He has seen them all killed.

What gives me the courage today to obey, and ultimately it could be by threats of persecution? Daily infusions of the Word and a life characterized by prayer. As a trusting child of my Heavenly Father, my life should be summed up one way. *God said it. I obeyed. End of story.*

Give me strength for today and prepare me for tomorrow.
Amen

HOW FAITH IS KILLED

He did not weaken in faith when he considered his own body, which was as good as dead (since he was about a hundred years old), or when he considered the barrenness of Sarah's womb. Romans 4:19

When I consider God's promises to me, they are always outside the veil of feasibility. Because of that, it is dangerous to depend on other people to reinforce my faith. They are weak vessels and also view the impossible. Because they didn't experience the '*call*', their ability to sustain faith is weak. Noah, as he built the ark, was circumstantially cognizant of the fact that no one in his world had ever seen rain. An ark that would float on water was absurd. The ridicule he suffered could have been debilitating. Yet, for nearly 120 years, he believed God.

If I look to my circumstances to foster faith, that is not a sound decision. They will constantly shift. If Abraham had obsessed about his age and the barrenness of his wife, his faith would have been killed. As long as he directed his faith toward God, the one with whom all things are possible, his faith lived.

The only one who can sustain faith is God. As I read the Word and ask His Spirit, simultaneously, to breathe His Word into my spirit, faith flourishes.

Each of us must identify the reason our faith weakens. God promises us something, yet faith is a fragile thing unless nurtured by the Word and prayer. I am susceptible to some *'thing'* that will erode belief in God. For each person, that *'thing'* varies but it is imperative to know your Achilles heel.

- I may be someone who relies on other's respect. To obey God means to go against popular opinion and risk being misunderstood. Other's criticism can be a faith killer.
- I may be bent toward scientific thinking. Seeing is believing. If I weigh the odds of God of performing His miracle, rationality is a faith killer.
- Weariness and the number of years it has taken to see the promise fulfilled can cause me to give up. Tenacity has not been my strong suit. Admitting defeat and quitting the race are faith killers.

Lack of self-awareness has caused many to shipwreck. I must know myself and know what it is that has the potential to throw me into state of unbelief. Only then can I use the Word to fight against it. Whatever God has promised, He will provide the grace to believe that He will bring it to pass.

I do my part, Lord, to nurture faith and kill unbelief. I make my heart a place that is faith-friendly. I await the fulfillment of Your promises. Amen

WHEN BELIEVING HURTS

He did not weaken in faith when he considered his own body, which was as good as dead (since he was about a hundred years old), or when he considered the barrenness of Sarah's womb. Romans 4:19

Faith doesn't exist if I can possibly manufacture an answer to my problem. Faith begins when a situation is absolutely hopeless. There appears to be no solution. God says He can heal it, fix it, and reform it – yet I cannot see how. At that point, I choose to believe. But believing hurts because I must invest my heart when it feels like suicide.

Abraham was probably felt exhilarated when he received the promise of a child. High on spiritual adrenalin, he was full of faith. When faith meets the real world and the thrill of hearing from God is dulled by life, it begins to be tested. The miracle of Abraham's story and why God blessed him so, was that his faith did not weaken when he considered the odds against he and Sarah. They had always been barren. They were old. They had never known anyone their age that had conceived. It seemed preposterous to believe they could be the first.

Faith hurts ~ because it requires me to believe God though I have sunk comfortably into disbelief. I grew complacent when I threw my hands up and finally gave up. It was a relief not to trust anymore, to let my hope die. Faith challenges me to repent of that, to open my heart to God and the promise of change.

"Open my heart again?" you ask. *"No way! I'm doing that again."* But what if our faith could be the catalyst to the greatest breakthrough in our lives? Our faith is being tested and this is the moment to pass, not fail. God promised. God is mighty. God can deliver. When things are the bleakest, faith has a starting place.

When there is no proof that faith is rational, that's when I cling all the more to it. Let Abraham's faith be mine today in all the impossible places. Amen

PAIN AS A PLOTLINE

It [righteousness] will be counted to us who believe in him who raised from the dead Jesus our Lord, who was delivered up for our trespasses and raised for our justification.
Romans 4:24-25

Who delivered up Jesus to be crucified? Was it the Jews? Was it Pilate? The shocking answer is that God did! God delivered up His Son and then raised Him from the dead as a sign that He accepted Jesus' sacrifice as payment for man's sin. *He who did not spare his own son but gave him up for us all. . .Romans 8:32*

Pain is a powerful plotline in my story. It was never meant to be meaningless or wasted. While in the grip of painful times, I can feel like it's all for nothing. Doesn't pain just crush its victims and that's the end of the story? No! God always meant for my suffering to be redemptive. It has great purpose and meaning for me if I'm God's child but only when I cooperate with God to see redemptive things happen.

How can suffering be a good thing, something God can redeem? If I am willing to be shaped by God into the likeness of Jesus, it can:

- Bring me to the end of myself and turn my heart toward God.
- Cause me to see that Satan is one who seeks to kill and destroy. Like Jesus, through prayer, I take up my role as soldier to destroy the works of the devil.
- Teach me to learn 'praying without ceasing' so that I can depend on God moment by moment.
- Train me to know, trust, and cling to God's promises so that God can bring beauty out of ashes.
- Direct me to the point of suffering ~ to bring glory to God no matter my circumstances.

Jesus never got lost in pain's storyline. He never saw it as an end unto itself. He knew that all his suffering was leading to the cross, that place of ultimate redemption. Because He died, sin and suffering need never win in my life. They are temporary.

95

Because He rose from the dead, victory awaits me. In the meantime, as I take joy in the hope of eternity, God is glorified even in my tears.

Don't let pain shut me down. Remind me that I can do a lot while I suffer. I actively seek you, Your Word, and lifestyle of prayer. Amen

CHAPTER 5

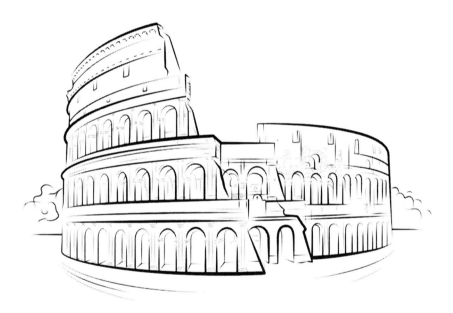

FINALLY AT PEACE

Therefore, since we have been justified by faith, we have peace with God through our Lord Jesus Christ.
Romans 5:1

*W*hen I function, daily, in a world of frantic activity, I dream of peace. When I work in an atmosphere where there is conflict and negativity, I dream of peace. When there is tension between me and those close to me, I dream of peace. When I'm plagued by all my foolish choices, I dream of peace. When I feel others' judgment, I dream of peace. When I worry about those I love, I dream of peace.

When I was younger, I would dream of sitting by a lake to listen to the water lap up on the shore. But, ironically, when I finally got there and though the atmosphere was peaceful, I found myself rehearsing all the things that made me feel stressful. There was not really any way to drown out the inner turmoil.

Paul nails the greatest need of my heart. It is to know peace with God. Since Christ's sacrifice on my behalf has made me right with God, I can immediately eradicate some of the most important reasons I fail to have peace.

My failures have been washed away by the blood of my Savior and He has put them behind His back, never to take them out again and say to me, viciously, *"Remember what you did?"* I am forgiven and that brings peace.

Condemning comments from others, even though spoken long ago, can ring in my ears. I can be plagued by a sense of being flawed and inadequate. But, I am accepted by God and feel the warmth of His favor on my shoulders. That brings peace and silences my accusers.

Fears that I rehearse, even in peaceful surroundings, can still threaten to undo me. Perfect love, given to me by God, casts out fear as I rehearse His love letters full of promises. The power of prayer is mine and that brings peace.

If you find yourself wound up tight, stop, take a minute and exhale. Be at rest. Be at peace. Breathe this prayer. Strength will be yours for this day.

Oh Father, I am loved by You and that love is never threatened! I am forgiven for everything I've ever done and I'm free of Your condemnation! I can cast away fear because You are in control of my life. You turn all things for my good and I rest completely in Your sovereignty. My circumstances can often be tumultuous but deep in my spirit, my heart abides in You. The current of Your peace carries me through the storm. How can I ever thank you! Amen

HOW HOPE AFFECTS ME

..and we rejoice in the hope of the glory of God. Romans 5:2

The word Paul used when he said we 'rejoice' is 'boast'. The word 'hope' is the same as 'certainty'. We boast in the certainty of the glory of God. John put it this way, *". . .but we know that when he appears, we shall be like him, for we shall see him as he is. And everyone who thus hopes in him purifies himself as he is pure."* I John 3:2 and 3

Hope is not just something relegated to a future time. It has present significance for how I live today. John's message reminds me that when I die, I will be glorified and be like Jesus. If I live in the certainty of that, *that* being my ultimate dream, wouldn't I want to start now by being like Jesus? If I live for that day, then why would I want to live in sin? I will start, even now, to prepare myself for that future glorification.

Our society has some sayings regarding hope. *"I hope against hope." "I hope for the best."* Neither has the feel of certainty. Biblical hope is defined as living in the certainty that what God promises, He will deliver. *"We have this as a sure and steadfast anchor of the soul, a hope that enters into the inner place behind the curtain. . ." Heb.6:19*

Though my body is aging, though it knows disease and decay, I live in certainty that on the day I expel my last bit of breath through my lungs, I will immediately take in my first breath of celestial air. My body will instantly be in its prime. I will have energy I've never known, even on my best day. My mind will not be bogged down with limitations and distractions. I will be free of all sinful bents and addictions. Because Christ rose from the dead and was glorified, He gave this same hope to every child of His Father's.

If I am waiting for that day, and if my heart is fully vested in its reality, I will start today to be like Jesus, think like Jesus, and feel like Jesus. Though I am limited in what I can do with decaying flesh, I <u>*can*</u> do something about my soul. I make it my goal to know the immeasurable greatness of His power toward everyone who believes. There is no ceiling for internal change for every one of God's children.

Everyday, my likeness to you, Jesus, should be greater than the day before. Keep me, by your grace, on this upward climb. I take deep joy in the promise of being like you.
Amen

THERE IS A 'BECAUSE'

More than that, we rejoice in our sufferings, knowing that suffering produces endurance, and endurance produces character, and character produces hope. . . Romans 5:3-4

One of my frustrations with the church, in the past, has been the misuse of scripture. It's as if snippets of the Bible were memorized, categorized internally on a 3x5 card, then spit out again in what was considered an appropriate situation. I can't count how many sermons I've heard over the course of my lifetime on 'rejoicing in suffering.' It was a command by rote, completely void of the scriptural context of intimate relationship with God. Add to that the fact that the command to rejoice was followed up with an important 'because'.

I don't rejoice in suffering because I enjoy hurting. I know this is ludicrous and if I'm told that God expects that of me, that He enjoys hurting me, this creates such a crack in our relationship that only truth can fix it. How many of God's children have shut God out of their lives because they are angry He didn't stop the pain in their lives! Satan loves errors in theology because of their potential to damage our trust in God.

I rejoice in my suffering today and rejoicing has two components; grief and joy. The groaning of pain <u>can</u> coexist with a deep abiding joy because of the knowledge that God always uses our pain, as He did with Jesus' suffering, to bring redemption. God is hoping that we will trust Him through our trials so that He is given the opportunity to bring full redemption and meaning to what we have endured.

How many have come to Christ because pain drove them to God's arms? How many have discovered that, in coming to the end of themselves, they found the power of Scripture? That is my witness. A life of ease numbed out my need of God.

Suffering does produce endurance, character, and hope. When going through something excruciating, I lean on my previous experiences in the desert. Where I once would have panted and fainted, I now have spiritual muscles to endure, to stand on scripture, to find a strength in prayer that was not available to me ten years ago.

If anyone has ever told you to be joyful in suffering, ended their sermon there and walked away, perhaps you became wary of God. Let these truths repair the breech in your relationship. Whenever things are really hard, I dig into the Word, abide in Christ deeply in my spirit, and I say out loud, *"I'll tell you one thing. The redemption of this pain must be more beautiful than I can imagine."* The greater the pain, the more stunning its outcome. May we live to see it.

You are Redeemer! Your death on Calvary was redeemed. You bore the sins of the world. Then, You rose again to give us resurrection power. I can't wait to see all of what you do with the suffering of Your church. Amen.

HOPE AND SHAME

. . .and hope does not put us to shame, because God's love
has been poured into our hearts through the Holy Spirit
who has been given to us. Romans 5:5

Hope does not put me to shame. What does that really mean?

David said, *"Indeed, none who wait for you shall be put to shame." Psalm 25:3* At the time David was writing, enemies surrounded him. They had him in a snare. Though he had an opportunity to kill his most formidable enemy, King Saul, he chose to walk away with sword in hand and wait for God to deliver him. He also spoke in the same chapter about the sins of his youth being enemies.

I am surrounded by enemies as well. There are three. 1.) The world is an enemy because it is unfriendly to Christ and to my proclaimed faith. 2.) My flesh is my enemy as I am so prone to sin. Because I know myself much better in my fifties than I did in my twenties, I remember the sins of my youth. I was blind to their destruction and consequences. Sometimes I sinned by intention, other times because I had no insight. My sins and the bent of my flesh are definitely enemies. 3.) Satan is also my greatest enemy. Because He hates God, then he also hates anyone who belongs to God. That means me.

There can be shame in being despised. Have you experienced that? Your authentic self retreats behind some protective wall and a calculated plastic person takes charge. Jesus Christ is the only one who can heal shame. I must be tutored by His Spirit as I meditate on the Word for shame to be replaced with confidence.

How do I meditate? Here are some powerful ways I've found to interact with Scripture.

- Before reading a word, I ask God to open my heart and give me spiritual understanding.
- I focus on a short portion of scripture. Meditation is not about quantity, but quality. I meditate best when it involves just a few verses.

- I read a passage over and over, knowing that scripture is multi-layered. Each time I read it, the Spirit of God takes me to deeper understanding.
- I ask God to help me feel what He feels about the passage I'm reading.
- I investigate the stories of the people who wrote the words. What were their circumstances? Knowing that gives me insight into the passage.

My healing from shame takes intentional work on my part. Jesus doesn't just show up and heal shame without my participation. My education in the scriptures is key and must be love-driven. He loves me and therefore, I learn. And as I do let the power of His Word wash over my shame-sick soul, Jesus slowly lifts my head.

Your healing is not quick but slow and intentional. You want me to understand where shame exists and why it's there. Your Word is my light, leading me to dark places that need Your grace. I continue to take You by the hand for such a journey as this. Amen

GOD'S LOVE AND MY SINFULNESS

For while we were still weak, at the right time Christ died for the ungodly. For one will scarcely die for a righteous person-though perhaps for a good person one would dare even to die- but God shows his love for us in that while we were still sinners, Christ died for us. Romans 5:6-8

So many pastors today have abandoned the subject of sin. I have heard a few say, *"People already struggle with poor self-esteem. They live hating themselves. Talk of sin will only make it worse."* By avoiding teaching on sin, they cannot give an accurate picture of the love of God. Joyce Carol Oates, a contemporary author says, *"We human beings are the species that clamors to be lied to."* We want someone to tell us that we're not that bad ~ that God should love us because we're basically good people. Here's the dilemma. If God only loves good people, how magnificent is His love? It's more human-like than God-like and not very impressive at all.

As long as I run from the truth that I am sinful to the core of me, I won't find peace with God. God's love is only stunning when it is set against a backdrop of my sinfulness.

When I realize that I could walk to the ends of the earth but not find God, I will appreciate the cross. When I realize that I could spend every last ounce of energy giving to others selflessly but end up in hell, I will appreciate the cross. God's love came in the face of Christ at a time when all hope for me was lost. I was limp, in a weakened state, trying to earn His favor but failing miserably. My sin separated me from His heart. I was completely powerless.

Then Jesus came! He saw my sin but came anyway. When I didn't want Him, He wanted me. When I wanted to try everything and everyone else first, He still loved me and came. See what kind of love He offered?

If the subject of the love of God bores me, or someone I know, perhaps we have lost sight of what kind of love it took for Jesus to come and save us. His love cost Him everything. . .and He gave it all up willingly so He could say to each of us, *"Not guilty anymore!"*

With all my sins forgiven, You invite me to come close –
forever – nothing threatening our relationship. There is no
peace but this, Lord. Amen

PARANOIA

Since, therefore, we have now been justified by his blood,
much more shall we be saved by him from the wrath of
God. Romans 5:9

If you grew up in a family that didn't express themselves well, you probably experienced other's disapproval without words. A tone, even a look, communicated that you had done something wrong but you didn't know what. If you dared ask, you might have heard, *"Well, you should know. I shouldn't have to tell you."* That was the end of the matter.

Entering adulthood doesn't automatically erase the nagging sense of insecurity you feel about those closest to you. If they have a bad day, you automatically assume you are the problem. If they are quiet, it can undo you.

All of us were born with the keen sense that God was angry with us, that we were alienated from Him. And we were ~ until we made peace with God through Christ. When I made Jesus my personal Savior, all my sin was forgiven and God's wrath was satisfied by Jesus' sacrificial death on my behalf. I need to let that sink in on a bad day.

Too many of God's children, and I know from personal experience, live with nagging doubts that God is disappointed in them. We mistake His quiet working in our lives as displeasure and punishment. What can be done about our uneasiness? A review of doctrine and honest praying.

> *Father, Jesus paid for my sins. I am in right relationship with you. You see me as justified, perfect in Christ. You are for me, not against me. You draw near to me even when I can't feel it. I can always draw near to You without fearing rejection. If I've sinned, You will always show me so peace can be mine. Heal my experiences with imperfect people. You are God, and not like them. Amen*

FEAR OF GOD'S ABANDONMENT

> *For if while we were enemies we were reconciled to God by the death of his Son, much more, now that we are reconciled, shall we be saved by his life. Romans 5:10*

Since God pulled out all the stops to make a way for us to become His children, no longer His enemies, and since that 'way' was the death of His Son, won't He now fully invest Himself in us? If He sent Jesus to the cross for an enemy, how magnificently would

He treat His friends? I can't even fathom the goodness in His heart toward me.

Whenever I have had to fully invest in a relationship here, I value it all the more. Becoming a mother and pouring out my life for my children, strengthens the bond we share. With each passing year, my feelings for them only intensify. My desire to bless them grows, not diminishes. So it is with God.

May this not be just theoretical. When life gets really hard, why would I even entertain the thought that God has stepped out of my life? Could He forget me? Could He fail to provide what I need? Could He act in a way that would give me valid grounds for distrusting Him? Impossible. He already gave His Son's life for me. He's secured a relationship with me at great cost. He's making a home for me in heaven so that we will have a relationship forever. It is not threatened by anything or anyone.

Paul reminds me of this later in Romans that nothing can separate me from the love of God. Famine, hardship, persecution, even death cannot divide us. If God loved me enough to send Jesus to bear the cost of my sin, won't He do the easy stuff now that I'm His?

A well-placed confidence in His proven love erases the fear of abandonment.

Your love and Your character can <u>never</u> be in question after what You've sacrificed for me. If my heart fails to 'feel' the truth, it is based on a mirage, one that is enhanced by the lies of your enemy, Satan. I fight against them by speaking Your Word out loud. Bring Your Word to my mind so that my heart will not fail. Amen

I HAVE NO JOY BECAUSE. . .

. . .we also rejoice in God through our Lord Jesus Christ, through whom we have now received reconciliation. Romans 5:11

Jesus came to show me what God was like. That He came is a miracle. That He would leave heaven so I would know His Father is a miracle. That He would die in order to show me the vastness of His Father's love is a miracle. That He would be so radical as to forgive all my sins and never bring them up again is a miracle. That I would have nothing to feel guilty about is a miracle. That I could dare go behind the veil and approach God intimately is a miracle. There are enough grounds here to rejoice all day, every day, no matter how well or poorly my day is going.

Yet, I've lived much of my life without joy. What was the problem? I have found, for me, that no joy means one of two things, and how I wish someone had told me this twenty years ago.

1.) *I have not allowed the truth of God to impact my heart.* Symptoms? I know a lot but feel little. I can pick apart doctrinal stands on issues but never let the truth of them affect me. I can preach humility but be arrogant. This is the fruit of study without meditation; about knowledge void of experience. The cure? I come to God everyday with the Word in my hand and ask Him to awaken my heart to the message. *"Search my heart, do surgery on my heart if necessary and let me feel what You feel, Lord, about this passage."* This begins a transformation that, over time, produces joy!

2.) *I believe things about God that aren't true that block joy.* I can be full of contradictions. I say that I believe Jesus came to save sinners but then I have trouble admitting that I _am_ one. I can easily give testimony that God is love but privately believe that He is punishing me when things go wrong. I must ask God to make me self-aware, in touch with my emotions. When I feel helpless, what do I believe that is causing me to feel helpless? Therein lies the lie. When misjudged and feeling outrage, what lie do I believe about God's justice and His sovereign rule? I must name it before I can know freedom. I must hold up my emotions, the beliefs behind them, to the truth of God's Word. My beliefs, and the feelings which mask them, must be subject to Truth, always.

Joy begins when I *know* the truth. Joy begins when I *feel* the truth. Joy begins when I am delivered from misjudgments about God. Joy begins when my heart of stone is touched by King Jesus and begins to beat hard with passionate responses to His glory. I was made to feel joyful about God, not a shortsighted joy that is dependent upon in my circumstances.

Those who have been martyred walked to their death singing. Help me know what they knew. Amen

SPIRITUAL UNIONS

Therefore, just as sin came into the world through one man, and death through sin, and so death spread to all men because all sinned. . . Romans 5:12

A spiritual union, as in who I am united to in spirit, determines what I will believe and even what choices I will make. To be bound to Christ, to enjoy the flow of His abundant life, is to be like Jesus in how I handle my life, both on the outside and on the inside.

Paul is about to tackle some of the heaviest parts of his teaching and perhaps, because it is difficult, it is often skipped over. Can we afford to do that? May God give us each understanding.

On the one hand, I understand the nature of a spiritual union. My parents wanted me to make friends with good kids because they knew that a bad spiritual union could take me down a destructive path. A good parent also wants their children to marry well; to become united with someone who loves Christ more than anyone else. Parents know that two Christians, bound to Jesus, will enjoy the kind of relationship God had in mind when he created the institution of marriage.

Unfortunately, each of us still experiences the fallout from getting involved with the wrong person. Something allured us and sucked us in. It might have even looked godly. Oh, we can feel the stinging consequences for a long time.

Paul is emphasizing the fact that every person alive was born bound to Adam. That spiritual union was not something we chose at birth. It just was – because Adam's sin infected every descendant with a sin nature. What are the evidences that I was bound to Adam completely, and that I still fight the lingering effects of that union in my flesh?

- I am drawn to things God doesn't love.
- I value people and things more than I value God.
- I have a hard time breaking bad habits.
- Destructive relational patterns are often my defaults.
- Instead of praying, I try to figure things out on my own first.
- I want to make others pay instead of forgive.

Becoming a child of God means entering into a spiritual union with His Son, Jesus, so that I am delivered from the curse of that fateful union with Adam. Eternal life, not death, begins to define me.

I will become like the One I worship, like the One with whom I spend the most time.

Adam brought spiritual death to me, even as an infant. Thank you for calling me to Your heart so that I could experience the beauty of this spiritual union. I cling to You without apology. Amen

STUCK IN UNFAIRNESS

Yet death reigned from Adam to Moses, even over those whose sinning was not like the transgression of Adam, who was a type of the one who was to come. Romans 5:14

Paul doesn't let up! For ten verses he hammers this point about me being related to Adam. I was one with Adam. I suffered because of Adam's sins. I was judged 'in Adam'. That doesn't seem fair. You mean that I was born under God's condemnation because an ancient relative sinned? The answer is yes and it's easy to get stuck there. Most do.

I think of my ancestors, the ones that I did know. Their sins infected our family, even three generations down the line. This principle is true whether we're talking about Adam or our great grandparents. We suffer the consequences of those who lived before us. Is our predicament without hope? Is God that unfair? Without an understanding of why Jesus came, God can seem like a tyrant.

The moment Adam and Eve sinned, God put a plan in motion for a Savior, a plan He conceived before the earth was ever created. Jesus was called "the Lamb" before there was time so God's extravagant love pre-dates the creation of man. Wouldn't I be moved to discover that my earthly father cherished me enough before I was born to make provision for my every need for as long as I would live? I would be endeared forever to him. God has taken care of me, prior to my birth, for my life here on this earth and for all eternity.

The moment I chose Christ, the consequences of Adam's sin in my life died and I was unified with Jesus. Because He is sinless and has always *been* sinless, there are no ancestral sins to dread, only an anticipation of the abundant life and the fruit of His righteousness.

From Adam ~ to Christ. Such a short phrase but one that speaks volumes about the power and love of God.

I know, Lord, how painful it is to suffer because of a family's sin. But you made a way out. I live in You, the righteous Savior in whom I have nothing to dread. Thank you! Amen

A PICTURE OF ABUNDANCE

For if, because of one man's trespass, death reigned through that one man, much more will those who receive the abundance of grace and the free gift of righteousness reign in life through the one man Jesus Christ.
Romans 5:17

I don't know anyone who doesn't love getting a great deal. *"If you buy one of these, we'll give you five of that."* It seems too good to be true and we wonder where the catch is but we seem to do it anyway. God's provision of the Lamb was truly the picture of abundance. His offer left mankind staggering. There were no tricks. His offer was a picture of gracious abundance.

Here's who God is and how generous His heart is ~ Through Adam's *one* sin, we all died and were eternally condemned. Through Christ, our *many* sins are forgiven and we are eternally blessed. The icing on the cake is this ~ through His death we are not just restored to Adam's position before the fall. That would be enough over which to dance. But no, we are restored *and* we will reign with Christ.

I went from a state of complete depravity to a position of reigning in righteousness. How is that possible except for God's abundant heart! It's called 'my justification through faith.'

Satan would have me believe that God is a withholding God. He is quick to tell me that God is passive, watching me suffer and withholding deliverance and healing. Romans 5:17, committed to memory, is my response when Satan appears to me in my own wilderness of testing. Like Jesus, the Word is on my tongue. I don't cave to Satan's offer to get me out of pain earlier than God would. I wait for God. His timing is perfect, His grace sustains me until then, and however deliverance looks, it will be the picture of abundance.

I can't believe your heart. Who has ever loved me like you?! Amen

MUST KNOW THE BAD NEWS TO APPRECIATE THE GOOD

Now the law came in to increase the trespass, but where sin increased, grace abounded all the more, so that, as sin reigned in death, grace also might reign through righteousness leading to eternal life through Jesus Christ our Lord. Romans 5:20-21

Who feels ecstatic over being forgiven? The one who knows how deeply he has sinned and offended God. Who embraces salvation with his whole heart? The one who despairs of being condemned with no way out. The person who doesn't feel any 'need' makes a lukewarm Christian.

Paul really wants me to understand this! Everyone born after Adam was born in sin. But, when the law was given and came alongside to offer a parallel look in the mirror, the awareness of sin increased. The light came on and the bad news of our sinful condition ushered in feelings of hopelessness.

Utter hopelessness was God's plan because unless I see how sinful I am, I won't search for grace. God has as much forgiveness, as much grace, as I need. But if I don't see how badly I need it, I won't ask for much nor appreciate it when I get it.

Can I write a song today about God's abounding grace? Does the mere subject of it begin to stir my heart and bring me to tears? It should. My perceived need of it determines how much, or how little, I value Christ.

Jesus called the Pharisees 'vipers' not only because they were spiritually blind but also because they thought they had 'no need'. They took issue with everything He said. *"That's not true!" "You are of the devil." "We're not sinners. We don't need You."* As long as outrage and defensiveness reigned in their heart, Christ had no value to them.

I am to live with the cross ever at my side. It is not for salvation only but for the daily transformation of my sinful nature. One of the most important prayers I can pray daily is this ~ *"Show me who I am today and how much I need You."* My need of Him will ever be in my peripheral view.

Lord, I think I get it. I can afford to need You because You have <u>more</u> than I need in response. Your radical grace is always near. Thank you. Amen

CHAPTER 6

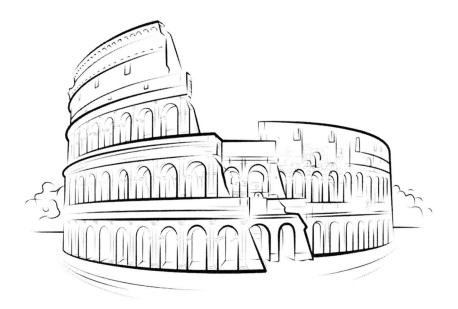

ABUSING A GRACIOUS GOD

What shall we say then? Are we to continue in sin that grace may abound? By no means! How can we who died to sin still live in it? Romans 6:1-2

*T*hink of the most gracious person you know. How easily was it to accept what they offered? Perhaps you're the kind of person that squirmed, trying to put a limit on what they wanted to give. Or, perhaps in the folly of immaturity, you took their gifts for granted and felt entitled to more of the same.

No matter what a man or woman gives, it is nothingness compared with the gracious gifts God gives. Whose offering can exceed the forgiveness of sin, the removal of condemnation, and the start of a new life that begins now but lasts forever?

Paul asks a redundant question. Should we continue to sin and offend such a gracious God? May it not be!

The stumbling block for any of us is that Satan has disfigured the face of a gracious God. When suffering doesn't cease, when we don't get the answers we want to the prayers we whisper, we assume God isn't really on our side. Gracious? Hardly. And yet Isaiah said that *'God longs to be gracious to us and He waits to have compassion on us.' Is.30:18*

The Old Testament saints and the New Testament apostles all made the grace of God a recurring theme. They did this despite their hardships. On what did they base their experience of grace? On God's longsuffering nature, on His willingness to forgive without regard for whether or not they would continue to make the same mistake again, on His many provisions of strength, on His ability to change the lives of people. They knew that heaven was 'not now'. They were ambassadors to a dark world. Ah, but on the inside? God was gracious to transform the inner landscape of their soul so that they were full of evidences of His grace and glory. I, too, have tasted and I want so much more.

No matter how big my appetite is for You, You are gracious to exceed what I ask for. I vow to hate sin more because of who You are. Amen

THE IMPLICATIONS OF GOOD NEWS

We were buried therefore with him by baptism into death, in order that, just as Christ was raised from the dead by the glory of the Father, we too might walk in newness of life.
Romans 6:4

I was baptized at 14 in a little country Baptist church in upstate New York. The familiar scriptures of Romans 6 were recited as I waited to be lowered into the water and then raised with Christ. I must confess that I had no clue about the implications of what was happening to me. I could have spouted bare truth, i.e. *"buried with Christ and raised to new life in Christ."* What would this all mean for me later as I lived my thirties, forties, and fifties? It would define the battle of my life and, most likely, yours as well.

I am no longer defined by sin and lies and that is worthy of great celebration. I feel deep joy when I understand that I am not destined for death, but resurrection life. What's behind it though is daunting to apply.

Everything thought, every past lie spoken to me, every nickname I was called and I absorbed, and every untruth about God when I'm in pain, these are what I am called to examine. Since I have been raised with Christ to new life, I am to shun and renounce any vestige of what Jesus died for.

Years of deception can send me plummeting without an understanding that there is spiritual disease that needs the cross. I can easily dress in grave clothes and live in the darkness of an internal tomb. Jesus is always standing just outside. He is calling me out of darkness into the Light. This is a daily battle. Anything that is not of God's kingdom must be recognized and dealt with. Living in the Light can be intimidating, even frightening, and initially, always feels like I can barely grasp it. With practice, walking in the Light becomes instinctive. It is my new default.

Show me what's in the dark. Hold me by the hand as You do. Amen

INSTRUCTION BEFORE EXPECTATION

So you must also consider yourselves dead to sin and alive to God in Christ Jesus. Romans 6:11

I can't believe it. This is the first time in the entire book of Romans that Paul told the Roman Christians to _do_ something. There were five whole chapters of instruction before there was an expectation for obedience. What a foundation Paul laid for us to understand our sin, our relationship to Adam, God's provision of a Lamb, and what Jesus _really_ gave to us freely when He died. Now, in light of all this, Paul says, **"Consider yourselves dead to sin and alive to God, in Christ Jesus!"**

Part of what has been wrong with the raising of my generation is that we grew up in authoritarian environments; both within our homes and within the church. Questions of 'why' weren't tolerated. If asked, the answer was always, **"Because I said so. Period."** While there is certainly a time when a command must be given and obedience must instantly follow, this should be the exception.

Authoritarian figures in the church gave commands in similar fashion. **"Forgive!" "Rejoice always." "Trust God!" "Let go and let God." "Be a good soldier."** These are all biblical principles but each one is given scripturally after much instruction. However, from the pulpit, the loving instruction part was usually absent. Because of that, so much of my generation (and the children _we_ raised) are biblically illiterate. They hear the commands ring in their ear without knowing how to sit under the counseling of the Spirit as they search the Scriptures.

Martin Luther wrestled with the tone of the scriptures as he worked to translate the New Testament from Greek to German. He remarked to a friend, *"The Scriptures should be read as a mother talking to her children."* What is contained between Genesis and Revelation is instruction, in the context of a father/child relationship, followed by commands to do something. It's as if God says, *"Now that you understand these things, go and do the following."* Instruction, then obedience. If I live my life trying to obey a series of axioms, God seems cruel. He appears to be a stern parent expecting me to 'do' without regard for relationship, confusion, questions, and frailty. Oh, God is not like that. His plan is that I will read, I will listen in prayer for personalized application, then I will obey.

You are such a kind Father, the best of teachers. And when I don't think I have the strength to obey, Your Spirit helps me. What more can I ask! Amen

BACKWARD

For the death he died he died to sin, once for all, but the life he lives he lives to God. So you must also consider yourselves dead to sin and alive to God in Christ Jesus. Romans 6:10-11

I realized this morning in an even deeper way that *my* generation, the one that has raised children and had prominent positions in the church, has had it backwards. We have seen the fallout. Have I discipled others like Jesus? Have I mentored like Paul?

His message to the Roman Christians is not one long list of *'Do this and don't do that!'* In fact, the first five chapters of Romans do not contain *one* command. It is all teaching. *This is who Christ is. This is what sin is. This is our spiritual condition. This is what Christ did for us. This is how much He loves us.* On the broad foundation of that, we are finally told what to do and what not to do. Loving instruction has a context.

Jesus built a foundation with his disciples. He loved them, He ate with them, He lived with them, and upon such friendship He began to teach them. Why is it that Christians have a reputation for being moral policemen without any joy? When my children were small, I'm afraid I spent more time quoting verses than I did telling them how much Jesus loved them.

To put it simply, I have heard it said that if God's children really understood, on a deep personal level, how much God loved them, their obedience would sky rocket. If they really believed the reality of their mystical union with Christ, they would live by faith.

Scripture is only treasured when internalized within the context of knowledge and revelation by the Spirit of God. I am asking God to prepare me to hear all the commands that are to follow in Romans. Whether or not I want to engage with them reveals whether or not I've really internalized the meaning of everything Paul has taught me so far.

I commit the rest of my life to prepare the foundation of listener's hearts. Help me, by the power of Your Spirit, to share that the joy of being loved by You is what captures other's attention. Amen

WHAT REIGNS?

Let not sin therefore reign in your mortal body, to make you obey its passions. Romans 6:12

To reign is to prevail. To reign is to rule. To reign is to have ultimate power.

Sin can reign but only with my permission. Even though Christ died for it, and I have the choice, and the power granted to me by the Holy Spirit to walk in resurrection life, I can still choose sin and allow it to gain the throne of my life. I think of the many things I have said about my life, or my environment, over the years.

Confusion reigns here.

Depression reigns here.

Anger reigns here.

Passivity reigns here.

I knew these things to be true; each at different times and I admitted it in utter frustration. The air reeked of the fruits of unrighteousness and what I was really saying was that God was not in charge on that day. Sin reigned. Sin prevailed but only because it was allowed to.

Paul spells the truth about sin plainly. It has its passion because of the energy of the prince of the power of the air behind it. He promotes it, sugar coats it, breathes it, stirs up our emotions to want it, and the lure is irresistible without Living Water and Living Bread. Only by consuming the Word will sin become easily recognizable and truly distasteful.

Reign in my heart, King Jesus. If you wouldn't say it, think it, feel it, or do it, I ask for your grace to live like You. Amen

IMAGINE

Do not present your members to sin as instruments for unrighteousness, but present yourselves to God as those who have been brought from death to life, and your members to God as instruments for righteousness. Romans 6:13

I know that heaven awaits but Jesus came to announce that the kingdom is here now. I am to spend my life asking the question, "What would heaven's response look like in this situation?" That answer, determined by scripture, is my guideline for how to pray. Specifically, this is what it looks like for me.

- If Jesus were my husband, what would He say about this?
- If Jesus could come in person today and talk to me about my child, what might He say?
- If Jesus were to come and pastor our church, what might His first steps be?

These answers give me a glimpse into the prayer life of Jesus when He taught us to pray, *"Thy Kingdom come, Thy will be done on earth as it is in heaven."*

To take this even further, which is what Paul is getting at in today's scripture; I consider all the things a human can do with his body. What will my hands be doing when I get to heaven? What kinds of things will my mouth say? How will I reign with Christ and what does that leadership look like?

In a glorified body, I will be using all my members for righteousness. As I imagine that, and I can because of all the pictures scriptures paint, I begin to see how I am to live now.

The kingdom is here now and I can begin to live in it as I <u>will</u> live in it – through the power of the Spirit.

Direct my imagination toward holy dreams. I am yours.
Amen

WHEN I DON'T WANT TO

For sin will have no dominion over you, since you are not under law but under grace. Romans 6:14

For years, I numbed out to Christian realities like sin and grace. I knew how they were both defined and I believed I understood them. However, I had no knowledge of the limitless expanse of sin within myself and the unfathomable expanse of grace within Christ.

I was like a patient who feels mildly ill, goes to the doctor, and just wants a pill for whatever is wrong; not wanting to know how sick they are nor what disease they have. I treated sin like that. I had a vague sense that I was a sinner but didn't understand how serious it was. I was completely unacquainted with myself through the mirror of the Word.

I found out the hard way that if I didn't take sin seriously then I didn't need to explore grace. A simple definition from the dictionary sufficed. Only as God showed me my great sin and the consequences of it without a Savior, did I begin to take hold of Jesus' feet and pour out thanksgiving for my pardon from a condemned life. If salvation from hell had been all He'd given me, that would be enough. But daily, there is still grace; as much as I think I need, and even more that I don't know I need.

Paul is beginning a section of *"Do this, do that!"* The commands are strong. *"Kill sin. Hate sin. Train to be a soldier. Fight the fight. Engage in the kingdom clash."* The person who knows he is sinful and holds on to grace like he would a life preserver will take on each command. When we don't want any part of it, we need to pray two prayers:

Show me my sin, Lord. And give me the heart to know Your grace. Amen

IF ONLY I COULD GO BACK

But what fruit were you getting at that time from the things of which you are now ashamed? For the end of those things is death. Romans 6:21

What are the things you regret? Regret is a powerful emotion and if I choose to live in it without having placed all my hopes in a God who redeems, I will become depressed and withdrawn. There were words spoken that I can't take back. There were a series of selfish acts that seemed so small at the time but yielded great pain for those around me. That is the cruelty of sin; what looked like no big deal led me to do it a second time, then a third, and it wasn't long before guilt became my ever-constant companion. I have thought many times, *"If only I could go back and do it right!"*

Wisdom runs deep in the heart of a repentant sinner. I am passionate about the lessons I've learned from my mistakes. Give me a soapbox (and God has) and I'll proclaim loudly, *"Don't do it! You can't afford the ultimate payoff of shame and regret."*

The real tragedy is the child of God who has come to Christ but has never tapped into *'abiding in Christ'* to experience the power of His Word to redeem each place of shame. Many, including myself for a few decades, lived in the bitter place of regret. I numbed my pain with service to God, hoping to lessen my guilt. This proved futile and led to an emotional crash in my forties.

Where is joy on the other side of regret? That's tomorrow's devotional. To fully indulge in God's gracious offer of sanctification, I have to stop everything and look honestly at how my sin has shaped me. Is there something I've done that still causes me to shrink and become depressed? As a fly feeds on rotting flesh, Satan feeds on guilt and shame. The sweet fruit of repentance is mine if I'm willing to do live by faith. Every memory where my body still slumps as it remembers can be impacted by the message of God's redemption.

You never intended for your children to live in the tears of regret. The tears of repentance are meant to lead to the joy of forgiveness and redemption. Give us the oil of healing for every place that still makes us wince as we remember.
Amen

THE OTHER SIDE OF REGRET

But now that you have been set free from sin and have become slaves of God, the fruit you get leads to sanctification and its end, eternal life. Romans 6:22

Regret is always a powerful topic and many of you express why you struggle with it. You are not having trouble moving on for your own sake, but for the sake of those you hurt. The consequences of past choices are ever in front of you in the lives of family and friends who are still paying for your bad choices.

I know. This is the result of growing in Christ. We spend much of our adult life discovering the things we could, and should, have done differently. We apologize to those we love over many things, asking them to forgive us.

The question is this: How can I walk in the joy of resurrection life when the pain of my choices is crippling to others?

If those we love see that we have a deep abiding joy in Christ, that we believe in God's ability to heal and redeem, does this seem out of place to those we hurt? I believe that the key is joy in the midst of humble sorrow; faith in the midst of unhealed pain.

Have you ever known someone who faced tragedy yet trusted God? They wept, they were broken, yet they trusted God in the midst of it. That is joy – in sorrow. This is the way we express regret; brokenness amidst a joyful confidence that God will move and heal those we love. Humbly, tearfully, we ask for their forgiveness. Expectantly, we show them our faith for the day when God will heal anger and alienation.

If I wallow in guilt, never able to hold my head up to those who hurt, I communicate: 1.) That I don't really understand God's forgiveness. 2.) That I don't really believe that God has enough power to use my mistakes for their good.

God knew our history before we lived it. He gave us our children, our parents, our siblings. He knew we would make mistakes and cause others harm. Yet, he still predestined us to be in those families, to be parents of those children. Just as He used <u>our</u> past hurts as catalysts to find Him, He will use <u>their</u> hurts (suffered at our hands) to bring them to the end of themselves. Their pain is their opportunity to discover the power of His love and the abundant life He offers. My faith inspires their faith.

I pray with tears. I pray with joy. Faith and tears <u>can</u> be married. Help me so that we can be whole. Amen

STRIVING

For the wages of sin is death, but the free gift of God is eternal life in Christ Jesus our Lord. Romans 6:23

I learned this verse as a small child. Did you? I was taught that this was the Gospel in a nutshell, the foundation of salvation by faith. But like many things I memorized, the beauty and meaning was absent until I lived a lot more life.

This verse alone is the reason many people ignore the scriptures and the revelation of God in nature. Their personal theology is this.

My sin earns me death.
My righteousness (good deeds) earns me life in heaven.

If they believe in God, they spend their life trying to tip the balance of the scales on the righteousness side. All their striving has to earn them <u>something</u> in the eyes of a loving God, right? But God's theology is this:

Your sin earns you death.
Your righteousness earns you death.

What kind of God is that? All my attempts to love, be charitable, serve in the church, perform heroic acts for my family, these earn me death? Yes, because the problem of my sin nature has not been addressed. I can't undo the penalty of death no matter how hard I try.

God is neither unreasonable nor uncaring. Because my righteousness cannot earn me anything but death, Jesus stepped in the picture to offer Himself as a sacrifice on my behalf. On the other side of Calvary, he offered me the gift of eternal life. There was a stipulation ~ I had to own the truth of my lost condition. I had to agree with God that my sin and my righteousness weren't good enough. Only then could I embrace Jesus as my Savior and accept His death, on my behalf, as a free gift. This alone gave me eternal security.

My future is based on this, Lord. You – plus nothing else. Today, you owe me nothing but everything you give, which is everything you have, you freely give because you love me. This fixes any arrogant bent of my heart. I stand in a humble place. Amen

CHAPTER 7

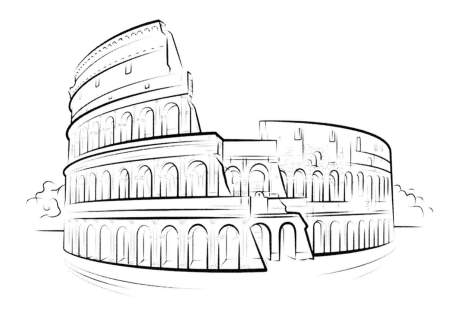

DEATH TO THE LAW

Or do you not know, brothers ~ for I am speaking to those who know the law ~ that the law is binding on a person only as long as he lives? Likewise, my brothers, you also have died to the law through the body of Christ, so that you may belong to another, to him who has been raised from the dead, in order that we may bear fruit for God.
Romans 7:1, 4

*E*ach person has been born under the burden of moral law. I have a conscience. I know when I've sinned. Embarrassed, I hide my sins and failures. I know that I'm deeply flawed, evidenced by my early discomfort around God. This moral code is binding. The bar is set so high that there is no way I can possibly live up to it. Nevertheless, I tried. I hid my sins and flaunted self-righteous attempts to look good to others and God. It didn't work.

What does it mean for me to 'die to the law through the body of Christ'? It is to throw up my hands and abandon striving. It is to admit that there is NO way I can be a law-keeper in order to make God happy. I wrap my arms around the reality of a Savior who died so that He could pay my debt to the law and take my death sentence. I die, with Christ. The law is behind me. I arise from the dead, with Christ, to another way of life.

On the other side of the tomb is a whole new existence. I am no longer under the condemnation of moral failure. Once, my good deeds were simply good behavior to make God happy. Now, my good deeds are the result of the Spirit of God birthing righteousness in my heart. Christianity is not behavior modification. It is Spirit-enabled righteousness that begins in my spiritual womb.

I am pregnant today with much fruit. The Spirit lives in me and is generating works of righteousness that will glorify God. What I do now, through the power of the Spirit, I could never have done under the law. I used to be an angry performer of works. Today, I am to be a spring of Living Water from whom righteousness flows like gushing fountain.

Is all my striving a thing of the past? If not, then I have not fully applied the freedom that Your death and resurrection offers. Take this home to every place in my heart. Amen

WHAT HAPPENED TO PASSION?

For while we were living in the flesh, our sinful passions, aroused by the law, were at work in our members to bear fruit for death. Romans 7:5

Passion can be evil. It can also be good. It is a neutral thing. When I became aware of the law (the moral code of what is good and bad), my passion was ignited to break the rules. Tell a child *not* to do something and rebellion is ignited. Passionately, I wanted to do what was not good for me. Satan knew how to prepare sin's party so that it looked inviting; looked like it was tailor-made for me.

Once I embraced Jesus, learned to understand and love God, what happened to my passion? It was supposed to ignite in a different direction. What I used to love, I was to hate with a passion. What I used to hate, I was to love passionately!

The nature of being lukewarm, a condition that God hates, means being void of passion. Does this describe my church, my Christian friends, or me? There is nothing more dangerous to my soul than to hang around children of God with no passion.

Think of the last time you were set free through hearing a sermon, or from your time in the Word and in prayer. You were stirred to the point of tears and joy. You just had to tell somebody. Passionately, you took your news to a few Christians and shared your 'pearls.' They were polite, they listened, but their response lacked God's emotional response.

If I make lukewarm Christians the hub of my fellowship, I am in a position to share the most beautiful and personal things of the Spirit with those who will not confirm them. When I am undone, they will remain unmoved. Chances are, the next time I go to them, I will reign in my emotions. It won't take long for me to become emotionally flat in order to fit in.

My church home needs to be a place that passionately hates what God hates and passionately love what God loves. God has a heart that beats with deep emotion. If his children fail to feel what He feels, and express it, there is grave spiritual illness. Perhaps it's time for many to change their spiritual company.

Thank you for the spiritual partners you have brought into my life. Oh, how they love you. Not just in word but in passion. Never let me leave company of those who are on the move for the kingdom. Amen

AFTER ALL IS SAID AND DONE – IT'S BEAUTIFUL!

Likewise, my brothers, you also have died to the law through the body of Christ, so that you may belong to another, to him who has been raised from the dead, in order that we may bear fruit for God. Romans 7:4

Let's not miss the forest for the trees! After all the delicate study of law, works, grace, abundant life, sanctification and justification, it boils down to this ~ I belong to someone else now and the effect of that is changing my life everyday, forever.

Ever feel like an orphan? You wonder where you belong. Who will fully embrace you? Even in families where there were mother and father figureheads, kids can feel like orphans. For the rest of their lives, they're looking for someone to invite them into a place of belonging. Driven, having stretched out their arms indiscriminately, others 'owned' them and hurt them. There are no safe masters except Jesus.

The decision to marry Him, to give myself completely to Him, is something I will never regret. He is the perfect bridegroom and never disappoints. In that marriage of complete contentment, I am changed by His love and the influence born of proximity.

What is marriage? Love. Chemistry. Commitment. Intimacy. Partnership. Respect. Encouragement. Often knowing each other's thoughts. I can't really enter into marriage if I marry an author, live in another state, and simply read his books. Yet, that's the experience of most Christians. Isn't that sad?

Let the marriage begin. The Christian life starts with a decision to enter into the kingdom through the door of Christ. But most get just inside the door and freeze. Afraid to trust. Afraid to commit. Afraid of intimacy. Afraid of change. How shall we be free to worship, glorify God, know ourselves, and bear fruit if we never enjoy marriage! Jesus is the ever patient bridegroom who waits for us timid ones with arms outstretched. Let's go home all the way.

I am not technically married to you. I'm fully married. I'm deeply in love and will never look back at another master.
Amen

LIVING AT ARMS LENGTH

But now we are released from the law, having died to that which held us captive, so that we serve in the new way of the Spirit and not in the old way of the written code.
Romans 7:6

"Your mother died." When I heard those words spoken by my father, my whole world rocked. The life drained out of me at the implication. My next questions were, *"How?"* and *"When?"* And yet the words, *"Jesus died!"* can have so little meaning. Jesus, the One I say I love more than anyone else.

Two days ago, here in Athens, Georgia where I live, a group of men stole a car and put the driver of the car in the trunk, who was able to escape out of it while the car stopped at a red light. When the police caught up with them, one of them shot the police officer in the face. A back up unit arrived and this same man walked up to squad car, aimed his gun through the driver's window and pulled the trigger, instantly killing the other police officer (who was a Christian leader in a local church). It has made national news. People are appalled. They feel the horror of the story and are asking, *'why'* and *'how'*. It was unfair. And, it was a tragedy.

So now, let me hear the story of Jesus again. He died. My whole body sinks. *"Why?"* For you. *"What do you mean?"* He died because you were held captive and couldn't be with Him. The only say to free you was to give His own life as a ransom!

As with any death that is personal to me, I feel sick. I grieve. Then I begin to understand that I don't need to be separated from Him anymore. The chasm that used to keep us apart has been bridged. Slowly, I begin to take first tentative steps onto the bridge. Then my pace picks up. Finally, I run full speed toward the person on the other end. It's Jesus. He's not dead, but alive. He's waiting for me, kneeling, arms open wide to welcome me into that place where we are never apart. We're together, in my spirit. He's closer than the air I breathe.

Am I really living conscious of Him? Or am I still acting like I'm on the other side of the bridge, mechanically obeying the scriptures as though my life depended on it. Jesus died – tore the veil in two – and invites me to abandon my obsession with rule keeping. Instead, I get to enjoy living with Him. Obedience takes care of itself because perfect Love has that effect on me.

The prison of keeping the law is behind me. I belong with You and Your love can energize everything I do. I'm living in that reality, Jesus. Amen

GUILT THAT LEADS TO FREEDOM

What then shall we say? That the law is sin? By no means! Yet if it had not been for the law, I would not have known sin. Roman 7:7a

The law is really my friend. It's true. Without an awareness of God's moral plumb line, I wouldn't know what sin is. Without sin, there wouldn't be guilt. Without guilt, there wouldn't be a need. Without need, I wouldn't seek a Savior.

Sometimes putting it another way drives the point home. With an awareness of God's righteous judgments, I understand that I have sinned. Because I have sinned, I feel guilty. Because I feel guilty, I have a need to be reconciled to God. Because I seek peace between us, I pursue a Savior who can not only forgive my sins, but wash them away and give me His righteousness.

Guilt is a good thing if this is the result. Guilt can turn into a bad thing if I believe Satan that my sins are too severe for God's forgiveness. What started out as productive guilt can become a tormenting guilt as the 'accuser' holds my failure up to my face day after day. Convinced that God can't possibly forgive 'that thing', I hate myself and never know the freedom and joy that Jesus offers.

If I was the family scapegoat, if everything was made to be my fault, then I have an over-reactive guilt trigger. I can feel guilty over things that aren't my fault. How do I know if God is speaking to me about sin or Satan is speaking to me in order to lead me down a bad trail? Here is what I've discovered because I was/am one who feels guilty easily. God's forgiveness is swift; joy is on the other side. God leads me to an awareness of my sin in order for me to feel remorse. Once I repent, He extends forgiveness and the issue is over.

Satan induced guilt however is one that has no resolution or closure. It's that nagging sense of 'being bad' that never allows the truth to change my mind. I believe I don't just _do_ bad things, I _am_ bad.

Guilt can be productive if it leads me to the cross. But guilt can also be destructive if I live in the bondage of self-condemnation.

The law was good. It led me to You. You danced on the day I trusted You to wash my sins away. Let Your joy infect me so that I will cast the sins of my past into the depths of the sea. Amen

FALLS LIKE A SWORD, THEN SAVES

It was sin, producing death in me through what is good, in order that sin might be shown to be sin, and through

the commandment might become sinful beyond measure.
Roman 7:13b

Scriptures, without application, do nothing for me. It was the Word, falling like a sword, that opened my heart to the awareness that I was a sinner. The Word exposed my heart, made me take a look in God's mirror, and showed me the way home to His heart.

"People perish for lack of knowledge," Hosea said. My journey into the Word, who is Christ, had only just begun when I became a Christian. Scripture only started to unveil what I needed to address. James said, *"Receive the Word implanted which is able to save your soul."* On the day of salvation, I was saved from eternal condemnation, but each day, my soul is in the process of being saved from the bondage of sin. How does it happen? The Word falls. It exposes sin. I repent. Then, the Spirit of God brings change. This transformation takes a lifetime.

A process like this just doesn't sound like much fun. Who would want to do it? Why would I hunger for the chance to go to a book that was going to expose sin in my life? If it's for the wrong reason – my stamina for this journey will grow weaker by the day. But if it is for the right reason, I will not be able to stay out of the book. Joy, on the other side of remorse, will be my companion.

I grew up in a legalistic environment. The command was, *"Read the Word. Just do it!"* There seemed to be no joy attached to it. But now, thank God it's all-different. Why do I run to the Word? Because sin separates me from the One I love so much. If I repent, I get more of Jesus in my life. Sin and daily repentance brings high dividends.

I had no idea that I would be on this journey with you, the adventure of a lifetime. I love how You are changing me.
Amen

WHY SIN WINS

For I do not understand my own actions. For I do not do what I want, but I do the very thing I hate. Romans 7:15

If someone asked me the question, "Would you like to be like Jesus today?" I would say yes. That is the deepest desire of my heart. So what happens when my desire is overridden by my next sin? Was my intent just not strong enough? Was I just trying to do this on my own without the Holy Spirit's help? Ok, so what does it really mean to tap into the Spirit's power? Once again, we are often handed clichés without explanations. *"Change is only possible through the help of the Holy Spirit."*

Most of my sin is not pre-meditated. I love Jesus and would never set out to offend Him and create a distance in our relationship. Yet, today I will sin. Why is that? I've been praying about that through the night and asking God to help me understand this better.

Sin happens for several reasons.

1. I don't know myself well and so I don't know where I habitually cave. Only as I understand my weaknesses (through time in the Word and the instruction of the Holy Spirit) can I be strategic to plan ahead for what I'll do when tempted.
2. I have learned to sin, by default, and it's an entrenched pattern from childhood. Perhaps my family did it and it naturally became part of me. Anything deeply entrenched, ignored for a period of time, becomes a stronghold.
3. At the point of temptation, there is an immediate payoff that wins over the larger desire to be like Jesus. If I'm angry, I get a rush from telling someone off. If I'm depressed, I get a payoff from other's attention and pity. Satan's way is to offer counterfeit ways to get out of pain by sinning.

What is the answer for me, for you? It is to design a plan. I don't just wait for the next temptation and try to handle it when it happens. I take time with Jesus to look at my biggest area of failure. Then:

1. I ask God to show me why I do it.
2. I confess my sin of caving in and enjoying the payoff.
3. I find 3-5 scriptures that address my temptation and have them ever before me.
4. I ask the Holy Spirit to write them on my heart, keep them on the forefront of my mind, so that when I'm tempted, I can recite them out loud.
5. I commit this plan to God and ask the Holy Spirit to enable me to follow it – no matter the cost.

I am a child of the kingdom. I have a new father and no longer belong to this world. I am hard on my sin, serious about the power of the Word, and am destined to walk in the light. If those around me who yet live in the dark are not wincing because there is Light in their eyes, I haven't yet discovered what it means to live like Jesus.

I want to be radical about this, Lord. I want my life to affect other people as yours did. Continue to unveil the pathway to victory. Amen

WHAT IS CHRISTIAN MATURITY?

For I know that nothing good dwells in me, that is, in my flesh. For I have the desire to do what is right, but not the ability to carry it out. Romans 7:18

When a parent raises their child from infancy to adulthood, the goal is to set him free at age 21 to soar on his own. Along the way, a family looks on and notes the child's progress. The dependency of a toddler morphs into growing self-sufficiency as he learns to do things on his own. Handholding lessens with age.

As a human, I am prone to take earthly contexts and impose them on scriptural principles. When I think about being mature in Christ, I believe I should no longer be dependent and needy. I should be mature and learn to manage myself. I should practice restraint when needed and boldness when called for. Others should say of me, *"She's so mature in Christ."*

But this is all backwards! As an adult who engages God as my Father, I find that He starts undoing self-sufficiency and turning me back into a child. I discover that what I *think* I should be able to do, I can't. When I think I should be good, I find that I'm not. In fact, the closer I get to my Father, the more sinful I discover I am.

Christian maturity is to be utterly convinced of my own sinfulness and fully confident that I am helpless in His world. I revert to toddlerhood; unsure of my next steps, not able to climb the steeps of the mountain of faith without taking Him by the hand. If I venture out on my own, I fail. If I stray from His voice, I get lost. And, to make matters more severe, I have an enemy I can't see that is constantly waging war against me. My Father is the only one who knows him, knows his war plans, and can equip me with the necessary battle gear that will give me victory. God is teaching me how to fight but I can't learn war strategy when out of ear shot.

In short, Christian maturity is to be a small child. Dependent. Needy. Words the world despises but concepts God loves and fosters. The more I need Him, the better He likes it.

I have often felt shame that I can't do anything without you, but help me to see that this is progress, not regression. I am your child, always. Amen

REACHING BUT NEVER GRASPING

For I do not do the good I want, but the evil I do not want is what I keep on doing. Romans 7:19

Body, soul, and spirit are so connected. My spirit is often willing, even eager, to walk as Jesus walked but that is difficult when issues of body and soul enter the picture. I remember walking around a lake near my house one morning with our dog, Freska. It was a beautiful Spring day, the kind I love. No humidity. Seventy degrees. A faint breeze. I was rested and relaxed. I remember saying to the Lord, out loud, *"I feel like I could take on anything for the kingdom today."* Immediately I heard in my spirit, *"Be careful, Christine! Your sense of balance is precarious."*

What He meant by that is this ~ What I want to do in my spirit becomes a challenge when my body is ill, or fatigued. If I had the flu, I probably wouldn't have said it. It is also a challenge when my soul is hurting. If I were grieving, in the midst of personal disappointment, I would have been consumed with that and probably not even noticed the beautiful day.

So much goes into committing, or refraining from, evil. As long as I live in a mortal body, on foreign soil, with sinful people, I will be imperfect. Glorified bodies with glorified appetites are things I long for but not yet experienced.

How can I hope to cope with all the dynamics of personal challenges to holiness? Grace. God's extravagant grace. It is poured out moment by moment as I express need. Need comes from self-awareness and a willingness to live in the grief, _and_ the anticipation, of the 'not yet'.

I get so frustrated with myself sometimes. That's what Your grace is for. Thank you for living in the trenches with me.
Amen

WHAT COMES BEFORE GOOD NEWS

Wretched man that I am! Who will deliver me from this body of death? Thanks be to God through Jesus Christ our Lord! So then, I myself serve the law of God with my mind, but with my flesh I serve the law of sin. Romans 7:24-25

My spirit is committed to Christ. So is my mind and heart but they are also bent toward sin. My flesh is ever breathing down my throat. I get weary of it, don't you? On the best of days, I sin. On the worst of days, I sin more. Often, I echo the words of C.J. Mahaney when he lamented, *"I am the worst sinner I know!"*

I can't believe we're exactly half way through Romans. Are you being challenged? Have you found the spiritual meals we've been consuming to be strengthening, enlightening, and even transforming? I have. But, I'm also aware that oftentimes the teacher gets the greatest reward from preparing the material.

I am so excited to start Chapter 8. Before I finish Romans later this year, I hope to have tucked away Chapter 8 to memory, following one of my mentors. That chapter alone would be enough spiritual food for a lifetime. Paul ends Chapter 7 with the cry of a broken man. He begins Chapter 8 with the news that, in Christ, he is not condemned for his sin and brokenness.

If I really want to grasp the good news that is about to come, I must also embrace the totality of my sinfulness. The hopelessness of one condition will increase the joy of salvation.

Lost and found. Condemned and forgiven. Object of wrath and object of grace. Could your love be more wonderful? Could your Gospel bring better news to a lost woman? How much you love me even though You know my sinfulness, I give you glory. Amen

CHAPTER 8

THREE PHRASES

There is therefore now no condemnation for those who are in Christ Jesus. Romans 8:1

*A*n old German commentator named Spener said that if the Bible was a ring and the Book of Romans its precious stone, chapter eight would be *"the sparkling point of the jewel."* I agree. I have waited for the day I would reach the eighth chapter and to be honest, this chapter is the one God used to show me that I should spend this year in Romans.

It begins with *'no condemnation'*. It continues with many verses that reveal there is *'no defeat'*. And the last verse proclaims the incredible news that there is *'no separation'*.

There are some reality TV programs about prison life. You watch for an hour and get to know what it might feel like to spend a day on death row, in solitary confinement, or as one of the prisoners on a regular cellblock. Terror overtakes most first-time prisoners as they come to grips with the danger of this new world where freedom and fairness, and having rights, are non-existent. Gangs rule and the guards turn their heads.

Have you ever seen footage of a prisoner who was sentenced for life but gets pardoned? The look on his face as he leaves the barbed wire gates and steps into the world outside is something to see. There are shrieks of joy as loved ones run to embrace him. The celebration of his new life continues for the rest of his life.

This is the message of this chapter. Sitting on death row with my crimes ever before me, with no possibility of a pardon, I look up to see a judge and some officials arrive at my cell. They unlock the door and tell me that I'm free to go. Someone has paid my ransom; someone I had cursed and treated like an enemy. This person became my Savior.

One day, I realized that because of what Jesus did, I no longer had to live on death row. If I embraced my Savior and accepted His ransom, I could leave my cell and walk out of my prison. Now, I live in the reality of His sacrifice for me. I've come to understand that my worst sins cannot defeat me. His sacrifice continues to impact my life and give me freedom from any kind of bondage. Even though I may offend Him over and over again with my sinful behaviors, I can never be sent back to death row. And, no matter what I do, I can never be separated from His love.

To be condemned by humans is often to be cast out of their presence. Only God gives us a real taste of forgiveness where love can never be threatened. Not by sin, not by fire, not by death. I am always in the embrace of the One who paid with his life for *my* life sentence.

Help me really understand how hopeless my situation was so that I can understand what Your sacrifice really means. I want to celebrate my freedom and Your love. In Jesus' name, Amen.

FULLY ALIVE TO GRACE

For the law of the Spirit of life has set you free in Christ Jesus from the law of sin and death. Romans 8:2

A well-known author of many Christian books tells the story of getting a ticket while driving through his neighborhood one evening. The speed limit was 25 mph and he was clocked at 29 mph. While he watched the police officer write up his ticket, he admitted to being more than irked. Who gets a ticket for going less than five mph over the speed limit! He told the officer just *that* but the policeman calmly replied, *"But what was the speed limit?"* *"Twenty-five,"* he muttered.

With the ticket in his hand, he drove home. And he was angry. He said to himself, with disgust, *"What's the big deal! I was just going 29 mph."* Then God spoke to him. This is often how Christians feel about their sin. We make horizontal comparisons with other people instead of the only comparison that matters; that vertical one with a holy God. We feel pretty good about ourselves and say, *"But I didn't do what he did!"* as we point to a real sinner outside our circle of friends.

The only way I will come to appreciate being declared free of God's condemnation is to understand that I was as guilty before God as any other person on Earth. The corruption of my heart was as much of an offense to God as one who commits murder or molests children. Every human being stands on death row and each one is the subject of God's wrath unless they look to Jesus for pardon. As His blood was poured out on Calvary, the same amount of blood was required for each person's justification; enough blood to eventually take the life of the Savior. Only the death of the Lamb could set any of us free.

If today's scripture fails to move me, I need to ask God to show me, yet again, what it took for Him to say, *"You are no longer condemned, Christine. You are free."* Only then will I be like the woman who washed Jesus feet with enough precious oils to equal her year's salary. Jesus explained her radical act of worship this way. *"The one who has been forgiven much. . ..loves much, but he who has been forgiven little. . ..loves little."* Grace is cheap – only to the ungrateful.

Forgive me for ever having been casual about my sin. I am the worst of sinners and each time I tell you I'm sorry, the cross is needed for you to forgive me. Wake me up to beauty of grace. In Jesus' name, Amen

DEFEATED OR HOPEFUL?

For God has done what the law, weakened by the flesh, could not do. By sending His own Son in the likeness of sinful flesh and for sin, He condemned sin in the flesh, in order that the righteous requirement of the law might be fulfilled in us, who walk not according to the flesh but according to the Spirit. Romans 8:3-4

Ever feel like you can't do anything right? If you live with this nagging sense of defeat, most likely you've lived in an environment where there were too many unreasonable rules.

I grew up in a home where there were many expectations. Children weren't really children but were expected to be little adults. While the rules weren't written and posted, they were communicated clearly even though unspoken. *No running in the house. No loud playing – like yelling, laughing. No water spots on shower walls. No leaving a faucet dripping or overusing water when washing the dishes. No bringing in mud or stones on your feet. No rolling suitcases over floor surfaces. No asking to use a restroom while visiting someone's house.* I'm a bit OCD even today; liking perfect order in drawers and cupboards. I've had to temper this bent as I raised my children.

As a parent, not only is it confining and unreasonable to impose such rules on children, it's defeating. A little kid never feels like he measures up. If he keeps nine rules perfectly but slips up on the tenth, he'll hang his head.

The Law was given by God, not to force me to be perfect, but to show me that I was *not* perfect; that there was *no* way I could be holy. The Law showed me my need for a Savior who could forgive my sinfulness.

As a child of God, I never need to look again at the Law, try hard to keep it, fail, and then hang my head in defeat. Jesus came, took my sin upon Himself, died for it, and fulfilled the Law on my behalf. It's as though I have stamped across my heart, "Perfect!" What a gift! The Law is no longer hanging over my head. My debt to it has been paid in full.

As God's child, striving is over. Spirit-enabled obedience is mine. Feeling like a failure should never mark the face of God's child. He took the Law, posted on the walls of heaven, and stamped them PAID IN FULL for every person who trusts Jesus as his Savior.

Oh Father, You are not a cruel Father. There are NO unspoken expectations. You were up front. You gave the Law. I could not keep it. I needed Your Son to be my Savior. He bore my punishment for breaking the rules. Now, You see me as perfect because of Jesus. I can hold my head up high and look into Your eyes with confidence. Amen

CARNAL CHRISTIAN OR UNBELIEVER?

For those who live according to the flesh set their minds on the things of the flesh, but those who live according to the Spirit set their minds on the things of the Spirit.
Romans 8:5

Bear with me. There is no way to interact with Romans and not engage with the deeper things of the faith. Today's scripture is a prime example. Many days, I track the number of people who open these devotionals and read them. The days the numbers are high tend to be connected to catchy emotional titles; ones that deal with fear, anger, abandonment, etc. The days the numbers are low are usually ones where a title is more intellectual than heart-oriented. I contend that we need both. Material that causes us to think *<u>will lead</u>* to an emotional response if we ask God to let it penetrate our heart.

This section of Romans 8 is controversial. Many believe that there are three categories of people; the unsaved, the carnal Christian, and the committed follower of Christ. I have always believed that but I am searching the scriptures and asking God to show me whether or not there are only two kinds of people; believers and unbelievers. Are those who live according to the flesh unbelievers? And, are those who live according to the Spirit believers? I'm beginning to wonder if that is the case.

Would you ask the question with me and would you prayerfully consider that the issue might be quite simple. We either follow Christ or we don't. The notion of a church half full of 'carnal Christians' might mean that we will all be surprised one day to see 'too whom' Jesus says, *"Depart from me. I never knew you."* Perhaps we are either ardent followers of Jesus (and have our minds set on the things of the Spirit) or we are hostile to Christ (and have our minds set on the things of the flesh.) In a few more verses, Paul will say that those who have their minds set on the flesh are *<u>hostile</u>* to God.

I am not saying that if I sin today, I am not God's child. I will sin – and I have *already* sinned even though it's 8:30 in the morning. The questions I must ask myself are, *"Where is my mind set? Did*

I sin with no regard whatsoever to the heart of God? Did I sin without a conscience? Will a line of sins follow today for which I will feel no tinge of remorse?" If the answers to these are 'yes', I am probably not a true disciple.

If I **am** a disciple, I am consistently conscious of the "One" whom I'm following. If He never crosses my mind, then how, by definition, can I consider myself a follower? Perhaps the church makes the issue too difficult. Children may understand these things better than we do. So, I continue to ask God to make things clear; clear enough to change me, challenge me, and equip me to teach the women God brings to my sphere of influence.

> *Lord, is it possible for a person to be backslidden and still have their minds set on you? I know many who thought of you constantly, but sinned, and were miserable. Oh, perhaps the test is this ~ Is the one sinning thinking of you at all? Bring me understanding as I continue in Romans, Lord. Amen*

THE LIVING DEAD

For to set the mind on the flesh is death, but to set the mind on the Spirit is life and peace. Romans 8:6

I've got my feet set in this new direction. Those who live according to the flesh are unbelievers. Those who live according to the Spirit are God's children. The reason I believe God led me to this conclusion is through the phrase "setting your mind".

To set my mind on the flesh is to be habitually consumed with things that offend God. How can I focus all my attention, as a consistent way of life, on the very things enemies of God think about and do? Doesn't that make me God's enemy? I believe Paul is saying 'yes'. *". . .but she who is self-indulgent is dead even while she lives." I Timothy 5:6* She is the *'living dead!'*

The unbeliever lives for himself. He is consumed with getting his needs met his way. He has no thought of God except for the occasional nagging at his soul that something is wrong.

The believer has been born again into a completely new reality. God has become his father. He is being re-parented by a perfect Parent. Everything he used to love and want has been transformed. His mind and heart are set in a new direction. His heart – made new – is aware of a deep peace that he is finally right with God. He is not perfect, but he is on the path of righteousness and his mind is habitually set on the new reality of the kingdom.

Lead me into all truth. In Jesus' name, Amen

PROFILE OF AN ENEMY

For the mind that is set on the flesh is hostile to God, for it does not submit to God's law; indeed, it cannot. Those who are in the flesh cannot please God. Romans 8:7-8

Sometimes it's helpful for me to take a spiritual truth and flesh it out inside an earthly illustration. Then, I can see it. Through the night, I've been asking God for a good analogy regarding these verses.

Suppose that there is a righteous man in my community. Many are employed by him, respect him, and he is rich in friends. Wanting to be associated with someone upstanding, I brag to my family and friends that I am also his friend.

However, another reality exists. He does not know me at all. Privately, I am jealous of the admiration he receives. I conduct my life in opposite ways from the way he lives his life. When I hear him quoted, I take issue with most everything he says. Truth be known, we agree on almost nothing. I avoid being around him like the plague and I don't have any desire to be around his friends. Am I _his_ friend? Hardly. If I _were_ to know me intimately, we would quickly be at odds.

Those who live by the flesh cannot please God, cannot call Him their friend. The way God thinks and feels and the way an unbeliever thinks and feels are irreconcilable. It is like oil and water. An unregenerate man or woman cannot understand God at all. His ways confuse them, his presence of holiness grates on their nerves. Unbelieving people do not want to be around the people God calls His friends. Their peculiarity makes them the subject of ridicule.

Enemies of God may spend much of their lives trying to please Him and placate Him. Satan allows them to believe that they have made progress with all their charitable acts of compassion and kindness. But when all is said and done, God will ask them what they did with Jesus.

Am I God's friend today? If I love His ways, if I have my mind habitually set on Him, if I resonate with His passions and my feet are walking in the direction of His righteousness, this is proof that He is mine and I am His.

Once I became Your friend, nothing could ever nullify our relationship. I am Your friend for life and I will never lose the wonder of that. Thank you. Amen

ALIVE TO YOU

But if Christ is in you, although the body is dead because of sin, the Spirit is life because of righteousness.
Romans 8:10

How does a child of God explain the spiritual phenomenon of what it's like to be God's child? To an unbeliever it doesn't compute because human language is inadequate to really capture it. I can begin to understand John's dilemma when his spirit was taken to the third heaven. How would you describe that experience with words that are so confining!

One of the realities for the child of God is that he is alive to God. I understand this, don't you? Everything God says and does impacts my heart.

There are many situations that can cause us to feel estranged from others. Even though we may be near them in proximity, what we do doesn't interest them. Where we came from and what has shaped us is never probed. Our tears are not noticed. Our words are dismissed and forgotten. It is as good as being dead to them.

When someone is alive to us, how differently it feels. The contrast is so stark that it can feel frightening at first, but then exhilarating.

Paul is making this point. If Christ is in me, the Spirit is alive to me. I am alive to Him and He is alive to me. See the pinks of an ocean sunset and my first thought is that the God who lives in me made that.

Every word He says is alive to me. Scripture flies like a sweet arrow deep into my heart and I care deeply about thought. I also have the assurance that my words fly to His heart. He waits for my company, longs for my stories, and is stirred by my words of affection.

Nothing He says or does is insignificant to me. And nothing I say or do is insignificant to Him. We are fully alive and engaged by one another. This automatically translates to progressive sanctification. I am changed, second by second, by every thought of Him.

I've been dead to others. Oh, I know the contrast. I'm wonderfully alive to You and no one can steal it or change it. This joy starts my day. Amen

MY FUEL OF CHOICE

But if Christ is in you, although the body is dead because of sin, the Spirit is life because of righteousness.
Romans 8: 10

I've been up a while praying. Convicted. Aware that something is out of sync and asking God to counsel me and show me. After feeling that I heard Him speak to my spirit, He urged me to get up and go to the next verse in my Romans journey. He assured me that my 'bread' would be there. I couldn't imagine how, knowing the subject matter of my prayer and the perceived subject matter of Romans 8. But here I am; humbled and in awe before my Father that, once again, He has gone ahead of me and prepared the spiritual meal. He knew that the instruction He gave in prayer would be confirmed by His Word.

I was up praying about the incredible pressures I am facing all around me, both wonderful and awful. I have before me a new incredible opportunity for ministry but that venture alone could completely dominate my time. Added to that are the pressures that come with walking on the front lines of battle. In prayer, I cried out for clear vision about how to walk these days. God's message was clear and may only have been for me. But in case it was also for you, I share it.

"Christine, your pressures are great. The demands are too much for any human. The fuel needed, physically, spiritually, and emotionally, is substantial. Because you need so much of it, you fill up your reserves with me – plus other things that give you the impression that your tank is full. It's tainted gasoline. Me – plus other fuel – does not make you run the race well. Don't run to other sources of fuel. Fill yourself up with me and I will give you the stamina and longevity that will be required of you."

Getting up off my knees and opening up Romans, the very next verse, I am confronted with the same thing being said another way. The body is dead and, ironically, looks to <u>dead</u> sources of fuel to keep it running. The Spirit gives life; life to the spirit and life to the body. Jesus said to His disciples (after sending them into town to buy food so that He could talk to a Samaritan woman), **"I have food to eat that you know nothing about."** Fuel. This, He said to them, as they returned with a meal for Him and found Him wonderfully distracted. He was doing His Father's will and had just seen a woman dip into the well of His own Spirit.

I'm taking stock of my fuel sources and giving God permission to say, **"Keep it! Or, pitch it."** I'll be freeing up my tank for more of Him.

At 4:30 in the morning, this sounds 'cutesy'; perhaps even corny. If this was only for me and touches no one else today, bear with me.

Sometimes it's hard for me to tell whether pieces of my journey are just for me or are to be shared. Tomorrow will be another day and I'm glad you're with me as God teaches me a day at a time. Romans sure has wide applications.

I dip my cup into the deep well of You. Amen

HAS MY PAST BEEN ALTERED?

If the Spirit of him who raised Jesus from the dead dwells in you, he who raised Christ Jesus from the dead will also give life to your mortal bodies through his Spirit who dwells in you. Romans 8:11

Harry Ironside, one of the first pastors of Moody Memorial Church in Chicago, said. . ."*Christians are people whose past has been altered.*" The resurrection power of Jesus has forgiven their sins and forever stripped Satan of his right to damn them. What power! Without Christ's death, my sins would have been enumerated and posted on my *own* cross. I would have died the death of one condemned. Hell would have been my end.

If my past has been altered, forgiven, then why does my past still affect me so much? Is it possible that the same resurrection power that raised Jesus from the dead can *also* make me new, in *every* way, on the inside?

If an angry mother raised me and I still tremble in the presence of anger, Christ's resurrection power can deliver me from fear and make me bold. I can be calm and prayerful though others rage.

If I was raised to be someone's puppet and never had a thought or dream of my own, Christ's resurrection power can deliver me from the control of others. I can be free to follow Christ and follow His plans for me.

If I was criticized relentlessly for most everything I did and still feel a crippling fear of doing something wrong, Christ's resurrection power can deliver me from playing it safe. I can become a Joshua who goes forward in the God's confidence to conquer spiritual mountains.

How does this happen? Not by a simple prayer and one-time event. While Jesus washed away my sins through one event, His own death, the process of being made new on the inside is progressive. It's something God does, but with my full cooperation and involvement.

Wouldn't it be tragic to get to heaven and see a picture of who I *could* have been if I had trusted Jesus, and His Word, to really change? If I am a radical disciple, a woman who has great faith in the transforming power of Christ and every Word He speaks, I will cease to resemble the person I was in my past. Jesus calls each of His children out of the grave, offers to slowly unwrap the grave clothes, so that we can be free to live in resurrection power. To what extent am I allowing that?

I just realized, Lord. It's called sanctification. Peeling away the grave clothes. May it be! Amen

A GIFT YOU CAN TRUST

So then, brothers, we are debtors, not to the flesh, to live according to the flesh. Romans 8:12

Gifts are funny things. The giving of them can be altruistic; the giver loves me and I feel loved by receiving the gift. But another kind of person can give a gift that is self-serving. By accepting it, I feel the pressure to repay. Feeling indebted to someone I do not trust is a *heavy* burden.

Early in my twenties, I responded to overtures of friendship with a person who turned out to be extremely manipulative. She lived fifteen hours away from me so our visits were sparse. However, every time I arrived at her home, or she arrived at mine, she kept bringing out gift after gift. I was so uncomfortable with the number of them *and* the obvious expense of them. She couldn't really afford them.

I will tell you that they didn't feel good to me. One day, I tried to explain my discomfort to her yet again. I told her that I was struggling; that I felt such a burden of indebtedness that her gifts were no longer bringing me joy. She listened and her face showed no emotion. I finally asked, *"Do you understand that I feel so indebted that it's really bothering me a lot? I mean, how long would it ever take me to pay you back?"* Before she had time to think about her answer, this is what came out of her mouth like a shot. *"Forever!"* she said, with a casual shrug of her shoulders.

That day was a turning point in our relationship. I came to understand that her gift-giving was to make sure that my sense of indebtedness kept me in her life.

Can being a debtor be a good thing? I have found that the answer to that question is yes. It depends on the giver!

Justification and sanctification are related to each other. Jesus has given me a staggering gift, one that I can never repay. He has erased my sin that condemned me and declared me righteous by His death. He justified me!

My response? I am a debtor. It's safe to feel that way because His love is pure. There are no hidden agendas. He wants me to be His and wants to share His home with me forever. Because of my gratitude, I say 'thank you' by presenting myself to him for a sanctifying process. It will require daily sacrifice as I give up what I 'think' I want with what He tells me is best for me. But my sacrifice is nothing compared to what it took for Him to offer me my salvation.

Jesus, I give myself to you today with no reservations or restrictions.

ARE WE ALL CHILDREN OF GOD?

For all who are led by the Spirit of God are sons of God.
Roman 8:14

Isn't everyone who lives on planet earth God's child? Many think so and refer to the human race as children of God. It is a warm, fuzzy concept that usually expands to include the belief that angels are all around and are sent to protect us. The biblical truth is that everyone who lives on planet earth is God's _creation_ but not necessarily His child. The dividing line is what one does with Jesus.

In John 8, Jesus tells a few Jewish people, including leaders, that the only ones who were really disciples were the ones who followed His teachings. Those who didn't accept Him as the Messiah and follow His teaching were slaves of sin. The Jews were indignant, insisting that they were related to Abraham and were not slaves to anyone. Oh, how blindness snares us all. They had been slaves of many nations during their long history. Even while they were saying this to Jesus, they were under the domination and authority of the Roman Empire. Pride does blind us!

It is not possible to be led by the Spirit of God if I have not embraced Christ. The only way the Spirit of God comes to live in me is through belief in the death and resurrection of Jesus.

Just before Jesus was arrested, He told His disciples that He was going away but that it was better for them if He went because He would come to 'be with them' another way. So who is the Spirit of God? The resurrected Jesus – who is the Son of God – who is the Spirit of God – who is God. The three are one.

There will be moments today when I sin. I will do things, think things, and say things that will not be like Jesus. That does not nullify my position as God's child. What I really need to ask myself is this ~ What am I like the rest of the time? Do I have a heart that is bent toward following Jesus? Would others say of me, *"I can tell that she loves Jesus by her life!"* That does not mean that they never see me sin but that when I do, I care deeply because I have _not_ been like Jesus.

Another paraphrase of today's scripture is this, from Jesus' teaching: All who love Jesus and prove it by following His teaching as a way of life ~ are sons of God.

There are two families on this earth. There are two fathers. Only those who love and serve God, in Jesus, belong to the family of the Living God.

Never let me forget the great privilege of knowing I am your child. I show how much it means to me when I follow You. Amen

ADOPTED! AND THAT'S FINAL

For you did not receive the spirit of slavery to fall back into fear, but you have received the Spirit of adoption as sons, by whom we cry, "Abba! Father!" Romans 8:15

It's really hard to say what might be the most important verse in Romans 8, but this one would be in the top five. If I'm an insecure person, never knowing if I belong somewhere, then this verse is at the very top.

I grew up in a family where I seemed so different from my parents, and certainly different from most of my extended family. I didn't know if I belonged or not. Complicating this was my parent's bent toward quietness. They did not reveal how they felt about you; your value, your gifts, your presence in their lives. I grew up looking at them, asking the unspoken question, *"Do you think I'm okay?"* I was the good girl trying to over perform in order to win their words but I rarely did. Except for a phrase or two on a greeting card, my heart lived wanting and fearful.

God does not withhold what we need as children. He is generous with words, and word pictures, to let us know where we stand with him. Once we have accepted Jesus as our Savior, we don't ever need to live in fear of not being good enough anymore or of being cast out of His presence. No more spirit of slavery where insecurity spreads like a cancer throughout our entire being. Instead, we can rest in our adoption.

'Adoption' is *huiothesia* in the Greek, which means, *"to have an installation or placement as a son."* Adoption means being taken from one family and placed in another. It means receiving a whole new status that cannot be nullified, even if we're disobedient children.

In God's sovereignty, Ron and I adopted two children from birth. We were privileged to experience, in the natural, what God has done for us in spiritual realms. Ryan and Jaime are as much our children as if I'd given birth to them. We are their parents for life and nothing they might do or say erases their identity. And if they ever needed proof of their adoption, they have it in writing. One day when they were both young, a judge stamped the papers that made their adoption final. Their status was confirmed and made legal.

Satan, the father of all children (unless adopted by Christ,) is the worst of fathers. He is not nurturing but cruel. Though we all belonged to him, there was never a warm sense of security. Everything Satan isn't, God is! Whatever we experienced as children that left us scared and feeling inadequate, can be erased in the arms of our new Father. It's never too late to ask for what we need. The healing we seek rests in the power of His words and the Spirit who breathes them into our needy hearts.

I never knew security until I found it in You. There's no peace like the peace I feel because I'm Yours. Thank you.
Amen

A HEART THAT LEAPS

The Spirit himself bears witness with our spirit that we are children of God. . . Romans 8:16

I've read this verse for years but never knew what it really meant until God showed me one morning what my heart does when I read His words, when I hear a kingdom story, when I sing certain worship songs, and when I see a beautiful natural sight and exclaim. My heart leaps and strains toward God. I can feel it bend in His direction, moved, open, stirred with adoration.

It has to be related to what Elizabeth felt in her womb when her unborn baby, John the Baptist, was in the presence of Jesus for the first time. Jesus was also in Mary's womb and the two women were greeting each other. Elizabeth felt John leap within her. Metaphorically, I believe this perfectly captures what happens when the Holy Spirit bears witness with our spirit.

Don't get me wrong. There have been periods of spiritual dryness in my life when I felt almost nothing. God seemed distant even though I knew He wasn't. I read scripture and it was dust in my mouth. But, this should be a temporary place on a Christian's journey. For the most part, our hearts should be leaping.

Each morning before studying Romans, I ask the Spirit to rise up within me to teach, bring understanding, make my heart alive to the passage, and then be in control of my pen. Each time He does that, my security in knowing that I am His child is further reinforced.

What I'm feeling led to write today is not meant to spread doubt and fear. I feel these words are intended to comfort those of you who **_do_** doubt. If you care deeply about the words of Jesus, feel moved by Him and what He says, you are experiencing what Paul is describing.

I am not a big fan of the 'What would Jesus do?' bracelet. Christianity is a heart-thing. I need to be asking, ***"Would you help me feel like you feel, think what you think?"*** When He does that, my body is not my own. I want to live – leaping.

Some saints of old are depicted as bent in their old age. Perhaps they're bent toward you, listening, leaning toward heaven. The older I get, Lord, make my spirit more limber in Your presence. Amen

SUFFERING – THE PROOF OF SONSHIP

. . .and if (we) children, then heirs – heirs of God and fellow heirs with Christ, provided we suffer with him in order that we may also be glorified with him. Romans 8:16

Why is suffering talked about so much in the Bible? Why does being broken, in come circles, seem to be a badge of honor? Some Christians wear it with pride and look down on anyone who has not suffered yet in this life.

Paul has already given me ways to double check whether or not I am God's child. Why go over the top and talk about suffering, yet again?

The theology of suffering is an expansive topic but sometimes, like the reference to suffering in this verse, I make it too complex.

When someone is a friend in good times, it is easy to invest in the relationship and stay true. The love is not tested yet. Let hard times come to my friend, let my loyalty cost me my own comfort, and the true nature of my love will be revealed.

The story of Jesus proves this. When Jesus was healing, making food out of nothing, and stunning the crowd with one provision after another, there were fickle proclamations of love. They wanted *this* Messiah and King. He contributed to their physical well-being. But, as soon as He became unpopular for His teaching and became a wanted man, the crowd fled. Under the greatest stress, his disciples went and hid as well.

Suffering proves my fidelity. Each of us *has* walked, *are* walking, or *will* walk through dark times. What happens to my relationship with Jesus when darkness comes? If I blame him and shut him out of my heart, permanently, I might be a fair weather follower; and really, not a follower at all. Jesus, when in agony, did not back up from His Father and blame Him. He drew closer. His faithfulness in suffering proved His Sonship. My faithfulness in suffering proves mine.

This does not mean that if I once turned my face away from God, that I am really an unbeliever. Peter did that. Jesus knew he would do that and told him to not worry about his upcoming sin. (John 14:1) If however, I leave Christ and never return, never miss him, never feel convicted for turning my face the other way, I better examine myself. Fair weather friends never enjoy longevity in relationships and miss out on the joy of intimacy.

***I make my default response in suffering – drawing closer
to You. Amen***

<u>HEIRS</u>

If (we are) children, then heirs – heirs of God and fellow heirs with Christ, provided we suffer with him in order that we may also be glorified with him. Romans 8:17

If I'm materialistic here, then I will think of heaven as one big indulgence of 'stuff'. Being an heir of God means that I inherit God Himself. Can that mean so little to me? *"I say to myself, 'the Lord is my portion; therefore I will hope in him.'"* Lamentations 3:24 God promised His chosen people in Exodus that they would enter the land of promise but that promise was eclipsed by other passages where God spoke of Himself as their inheritance.

There is no more moving moment in a romance than when one lover pledges their heart to another. Watching it on the screen, I sometimes hold my breath to hear the words spoken. What is unfathomable is that God would make Himself the Lover of my soul and give Himself to me without any reservation. I was His enemy, and through no merit of my own, He made me His friend because of Jesus. Today, I will do things that offend Him, yet His heart will still stay true. As if that's not enough, He will give me other things as His heir.

1.) A home. He's building one for me. It will be perfectly crafted to my liking. I won't ever have to fear losing it. Here on earth, homes are fleeting and fragile. I can fail to pay the mortgage and lose it. It can burn down or be destroyed in a tornado in a matter of a few seconds. It can be broken into and precious things stolen. Not so in heaven. I'll have a home I'll never have to worry about.

2.) A banquet. There is a promise of abundance. I'll have an invitation to a dinner the likes of which I've never seen. It is the stuff of fairy tales. It will not be rushed and the joy of the fellowship across the table will have no trace of human drama.

3.) An opportunity to rule. Every time I am frustrated here by something I can't change, I remember that God promises His children the right to rule one day. I will share in the privilege of bringing about perfect justice and heavenly order.

4.) A likeness to Christ. I cannot imagine the gift of being like Jesus. Frustration with myself will be a thing of the past. Every habit here I can't break, every fear that plagues me, every trigger that sends me down a path of bitter memories, these will all go away.

When I look at others today and envy, forgive me. Amen

<u>WHAT WE CAN'T DEFINE</u>

For I consider that the sufferings of this present time are not worth comparing with the glory that is to be revealed to us. Romans 8:18

I was so moved this morning by a C.S. Lewis quote from his book, Weight of Glory. He defines glory as 'a longing for something that can hardly be expressed.' I want something deep in my soul and I just know it's not available to me yet.

I am choosing to quote Lewis because it just may move you as well.

"We are to shine as the sun, we are to be given the Morning Star. I think I begin to see what it means. In one way, of course, God has given us the Morning Star already; you can go and enjoy the gift on many fine mornings, if you get up early enough. What more, you may ask, do we want? Ah, but we want so much more—something the books on aesthetics take little notice of. But the poets and mythologies know all about it. We do not want merely to see beauty, though, God knows, even that is bounty enough. We want something else which can hardly be put into words—to be united with the beauty we see, to pass into it, to receive it into ourselves, to bathe in it, to become part of it. . . .

That is why the poets tell us such lovely falsehoods. They talk as if the west wind could really sweep into a human soul; but it can't. They tell us that "beauty born of murmuring sound" will pass into a human face; but it won't. Or not yet. For if we take the imagery of Scripture seriously, if we believe that God will one day give us the Morning Star and cause us to put on the splendor of the sun, then we may surmise that both the ancient myths and modern poetry, so false as history, may be very near the truth as prophecy.

At present we are on the outside of the world, the wrong side of the door. We discern the freshness and purity of the morning, but they do not make us fresh and pure. We cannot mingle with the splendors we see. But the leaves of the New Testament are rustling with the rumor that it will not always be so. Some day, God willing, we shall get in."

For any who are crushed beneath the weight of pain and words are not adequate to paint the anguish you are experiencing, the same will one day be true – but of glory, not suffering. That is our hope and part of the miracle of sustaining grace.

I am often like a fussy child not knowing what I want but hating how I feel. You know what I want and I'm destined to have all that and more. Fill my heart with the hope of glory. Amen

<u>PERPETUAL WINTER</u>

For the creation was subjected to futility, not willingly, but because of him who subjected it, in hope that the creation itself will be set free from its bondage to corruption and obtain the freedom of the glory of the children of God.
Romans 8: 20-21

The earth was cursed because of the fall of Adam . It was broken in half and everything in it was subjected to a state of brokenness and decay. We just have to live through the four seasons to understand that a cycle of life arrives with spring but cannot be sustained without going through the death and decaying process of fall and winter.

In The Lion, Witch, and Wardrobe, Narnia was under the control of the wicked witch of the North and the land suffered from a state of perpetual winter. Spring never arrived until Aslan died and rose again. Finally, the ice of winter melted and eternal spring was brought into existence.

Plants, animals, and even the hidden life of our planet were subjected to futility at the Fall. We are not alone in longing for a freedom from corruption. As I write this, our dog, Freska, is in significant distress. She was bitten by something yesterday and is agitated and in respiratory distress. Medication is not alleviating this quickly enough and we have been up a lot of the night with her. We don't have to look far to see that the earth, in this present state, is cursed.

Each of us feels the 'winter of the soul' in different ways and in varying degrees. Some of God's choicest servants knew little external joy. Depression, persecution, serious illness – these have visited most of the heroes of the faith. Their lives seemed to be in perpetual 'winter' yet they were not deceived. Very few believed that their present state of futility was an expression of God's disfavor. They understood that this was just 'life' here on earth. God subjected the earth to this state of decay and one day He would make it right again.

The Spring of Eden is on the horizon. Our momentary afflictions, and yes – they can be crushing, are blinks in the context of eternity. Nonetheless, the experiences we have with cold, ice, and death are real and can, at times, be crippling. We cry out in great distress and learn to lament like the Psalmists. Winter has forever affected us and we will not forget what it has been like.

The memory of things here will increase our joy when Jesus comes with power and delivers us. The greater our sorrows, the greater will be the joy of our freedom.

The futility of earth reminds me again of Your power, Lord.
You subjected it and You will deliver it. You alone have are
mighty and You are my hope for the future. Amen

MAKING IT PUBLIC

But we ourselves, who have the firstfruits of the Spirit, groan inwardly as we wait eagerly for adoption as sons, the redemption of our bodies. Romans 8:23

I have been adopted, technically, into God's family and nothing can ever erase the fact that I am now His daughter. But there is coming a day when I will go home with Him and He will make it public.

It's as if I'm still in the orphanage (Earth) and a letter arrived (the Bible) that has announced that I have been chosen. I've been paid for, my every need supplied, and the promise of my deliverance has been verified with a signature and a seal. I'm just waiting for the day when I can see the face of my Father, when I can be dressed in white and take part in the ceremony where He makes it public.

When a Roman child was adopted, there was a party where the adoption was made public. All of the family's friends were invited. A great feast was given. The father would present his new son with tearful speeches and much celebration. The son would sit in a place of honor. He would see and hear his dream of his new status come true. This is the picture Paul paints.

Now, I know the party is coming. One day, it will be reality. Now, the Spirit of God whispers words of love. One day, the words will be audible and the face of my Savior will afford a tangible look and lasting memory. For now, I rest in the promise of that day and it brings me strength.

I am never lost. I am yours. When I need reassurance, I listen to Your whispers and read Your words. Build in me solid hope for what 'is'. Amen

HOPE, PATIENCE, AND PRO-ACTIVITY

For in this hope we were saved. Now hope that is seen is not hope. For who hopes for what he sees? But if we hope for what we do not see, we wait for it with patience. Romans 8:24-25

Those who live without Jesus hope for things they cannot see and have no assurance of ever getting. *"I hope I get picked for the team." "I hope things work out okay." "I hope I will be loved today."* These are uncertain. The intense ache of the human heart in daring to hope is usually short-lived. It has been said that a seven-year-old child has already learned whether or not to dream. To the degree he has been disappointed in life, his willingness to hope is compromised.

Children of God also hope for things they cannot see but what they hope for already exists. They have a Father who has promised it. They hope for heaven; knowing it will be there when they take their first gasp of celestial air. They hope for deliverance; knowing that there will be one whether on earth or in heaven. They hope for healing; knowing that the Healer is vested in them and will provide it. They hope for redemption; knowing that no pain is ever wasted. Why? God said so.

Waiting patiently is not passive but pro-active. In order to keep hope alive (and keep the lies of hopelessness at bay), I must be reviewing the promises of my Father. I read the stories of my spiritual ancestors and their similar dark times in order to be reminded how God was faithful. I find scriptural promises that relate to my struggle and live in the hope of them, knowing that promises are a sure thing because of "who" it is that made them. I hang those promises on my mirror, on my walls, and post them in a prominent place in my car. This is the fight for faith.

Loss, grief, betrayal. . .these all visit the lives of Christians and non-Christians alike. Though weeping visits us all, the nature of our tears differs greatly. The laments of God's children are temporary and though they cry, they cling to the robes of their Prophet King and recite the promises of His good will. Resolution of the heavenly kind is just around the corner.

If I harbor disappointment today in any area of my life, it is only because my deliverance has not yet come. I know it will and my hope is sure in You. Give me grace while I wait. Give me strength to fight for my faith by speaking Your Word to the lies of my own soul. Amen

RAYER AND WEAKNESS

Likewise the Spirit helps us in our weakness. For we do not know what to pray for as we ought, but the Spirit himself intercedes for us with groanings too deep for words.
Romans 8:26

It is not a sin to be weak. Weakness is a human condition. Frailty plagues the most righteous man or woman, especially when in the midst of suffering. Quickly, every one of us loses our spiritual perspective. Our prayers reflect this.

Job was righteous. God said so. Yet he couldn't understand why he was suffering and his prayers proved his confusion. His friends thought they knew the mind of God and probably prayed for him, but wrongly.

The disciples, as much as they loved Jesus, proved to be weak prayer partners. In the garden, when Jesus needed them most, they feel asleep during Jesus' hours of anguish.

Elijah, a prophet of courageous proportions, succumbed to a weakened state after a great spiritual victory. Exhausted and emotionally drained, he prayed that the Lord would take his life. The flesh and the spirit are so integrally connected. When the body fails, the spirit is confused.

If I don't know how to pray for myself, how can I be sure anyone else will be able to pray for me correctly? The answer lies in my 'best friend' in intercession. The Holy Spirit. He is aware and fully engaged with my story. He knows my limited ability to understand God's sovereign plan for my life. When I cry out to God and I am wordless, much like a baby in distress, He hears my weeping and interprets it to the Father. He perceives my faltering words, my frustrating silences, and interprets those too. He tells my story better than I can and He tells it with omniscience. He prays about everything with perfect perspective.

So many days, I pray. . .. *"Oh holy Spirit, rise up in me and teach me how to pray. Form my words. Pray when my language fails."* When I despair that no one might be praying for me, I have been led to remember that Jesus, Himself, is praying for me. The

Holy Spirit is praying for me. Could the friendship of God be more perfectly proven than in this?

I rest in Your words, Your groanings, and even Your tears for the places in my life which have left me speechless and wanting. Thank you for being such a friend. Amen

WHEN I'M NOT IN THE KNOW

And he who searches hearts knows what is the mind of the Spirit, because the Spirit intercedes for the saints according to the will of God. Romans 8:27

There are many times I don't know how to pray because I don't know what God's purposes are for a certain situation. If I know I'm going to lose my job, do I bear down in prayer to keep it, or do I just assume God is using that loss to lead me somewhere else? If I'm experiencing a tragedy, do I ask God to take it away or do I assume that, like Job, God has ordained this chain of events to further His glory in some way?

This is where a prayer life gets stuck. I don't know what to pray for because I don't know the will of God. Because I don't know, I can abandon prayer altogether. That would be, and has been for me, a mistake.

That is the very time I need to rest with the Spirit of God in prayer and know that He is praying for my situation within the context of the will of God. He knows what it is. He knows how my present circumstances fit. There is comfort when I remember that though I am wordless, He is not. Prayer to the Father never stops. It is perfect prayer, and perfectly worded prayer.

For anyone today who might be tempted to think that lamenting over something God has ordained for His glory is wrong, let me assure you that lamenting is scriptural. The Psalms are laments – well ordered. If I take my very sick child to the hospital for a needed procedure, and that procedure is painful but necessary for my child's good, would I expect my child not to cry when he is hurt? Never.

There is such a thing as a lament in the midst of trust. While life hurts, I trust my Father's plan and reach out for His hand to get me through it. All the while, He is right there 'in and around me,' praying for me.

Never has 'resting in You' been more meaningful than this morning. Amen

THE ROMANS 8:28 CONFUSION

And we know that for those who love God all things work together for good, for those who are call according to his purpose. For those whom he foreknew he also pre-destined to be conformed to the image of his Son. . .
Romans 8:28-29a

I am like you. I hate the misrepresentation of this verse. I don't like being on the receiving end of it when others use this verse as a glib cliché. We often hand it out like a grandparent hands out penny candy to over-tired, whiny grandchildren.

This promise is a gem and so incredibly meaningful. Because of its mis-use though, as soon as I hear the reference, I feel a negative impact. I don't need to even hear the verse to feel the dread. I declare that it's time to lift the message of today's scripture high and truly understand it.

The 'good' Paul describes does not mean rich, healthy, or admired. The 'good' is what comes in the next verse. God's promise is that He will work all things, evil, sickness, failure. . ... to conform us to the image of His Son.

Isn't that really bad news? It is if I've been holding God responsible to fix my life and replace all my sinful choices with better ones. Golden ones. This is how the church often dispenses this verse as spiritual medicine.

Your child die? God will make it up to you and give you something good. Really?

You lose your job unfairly? God will give you a better one with higher pay and more influence. Really?

It is my experience that oftentimes God does advance His children through the path of adversity. Look at Joseph. But that spiritual reality has nothing to do with Romans 8:28.

When I quote this verse to someone who is hurting, I am really saying this. *"If you love God, God will use this 'crushing thing' to make you more like Jesus."* Do I really want to say this to someone who is in pain? This is almost an insult. My inference can appear to mean that they are not like Jesus so He sent them this adversity to help them shape up.

I believe this is a beautiful promise, but a personal one. Few are the friends who can quote this to me when I'm down. It may be just one or two people who have such credibility. But aside from that, I want to be sure that I treasure the promise today.

The bottom line to the whole issue is this ~ I do want to be like Jesus, the One I treasure, and I am more motivated to see my suffering as something that will help me think like Jesus, feel like Him, shine like Him, and act like Him. This deep desire changes the face of all my adversity even in the midst of weeping.

I can say that all the pain in my story has been good. It has been a gift because it has led me to worship and treasure You. Amen

WHEN GOD COMES CALLING

And those whom he predestined he also called. . .
Romans 8:30a

I do believe in predestination but not in limited atonement. Christ's death on the cross was for everyone. The call is universal and it is sounded out to all men and women. Jesus showed us the way to heaven, revealed that He is the door, and announced that He was the light of the world. But men have always loved darkness rather than light. Instead of the light being attractive, we are repelled by it. Christ is just not desirable to us. His light is too bright and we shield our eyes from it and turn away.

So, who will believe if all people love darkness? The ones God specifically calls; the ones whose eyes are opened to see His glory. Ah, this call is personal. This call came to us by name.

Whenever God speaks a word, it is effective. God spoke a Word and this dead planet began to pulsate with life. What once looked like Mars began to grow green.

God spoke a Word to a dead man, a decaying man, wrapped up like a mummy, and this man came to life. His body regenerated. *"Lazarus, come forth!"* was the call. God's Word produced life out of death.

God spoke a Word, called my name, and I was awakened out of spiritual death. The call prompted me to turn and look into the face of Christ. I understood His message of salvation and believed. If He hadn't spoken to me and opened my eyes, I would have continued on my death march.

Nobody knows whom God will call. Because of that, my heart reaches out to God in prayer for those who haven't yet heard their name spoken by God. Now, Christ is still unattractive to them, even repulsive. Once God calls their name, they will never be the same.

The call is powerful like dynamite. It transformed a brutal murderer into a zealot. The Damascus road was the place it happened. Paul was the man. I know this transformation, too. Don't you? The longer I live near Jesus and soak in His Words, the more I cease to know the old me. You'll never know how many times I read old journals and respond out loud, *"What was your problem, Christine?"*

The call is to a new life. Run, don't walk, to Calvary if you are hearing your name whispered in your soul.

Oh, still speak. I love how You speak to me. Amen

TAKING ON GOD AS AN OPPONENT

What then shall we say to these things? If God is for us, who can be against us?" Romans 8:31

Who is against me? The enemies of Christ – which are the world, the flesh, and the devil. All three are formidable.

I am valued by God. He has given me gifts to use. Yet real enemies in the form of the world, flesh, and devil undermine me on a daily basis. I am caused to question my value and my gifts are ridiculed, minimized, or ignored. Can they defeat God's purposes for my life? Sometimes it appears that they do and if I doubt God's power, I fear that they are winning.

The world (who rejects Christ) is also against me because I love the One they stand against. Those who are really offended by Him are also afraid or offended by me. I have extended family members, still unbelievers, who bristle at any mention of Christ. When with them, there are no questions asked about Daughters of Promise, my work, my heart, and what I may be reading or learning. I can be loving and attentive to them and their needs but Christ stands between us no matter how gracious I may be.

The flesh is also my enemy; the flesh in me and the flesh in God's other children. When I love what God hates and want my own way, my own flesh becomes the enemy to God's best plans for my life. When others love what God hates and want their own way, their flesh becomes the enemy to God's best plans too. Many churches have attempted to destroy a righteous man because their flesh took over.

The devil is also my enemy. He is a scheme-weaver; ever busy trying to undo the potential of God's children at work for the kingdom.

If I take the world, flesh, and devil and put them all together, and weigh them against the person and power of God, there is no contest. If I ever feel that people have destroyed my life or have ultimately kept me from God's purposes, I can rise up to hear good news today. Nothing and no one can win against God's sovereign purposes for my life. If I am following Christ, am prayerful and trusting, even the greatest setback is not going to ruin my future. Though it appears like I have been defeated, God is working behind the scenes to accomplish what I was born to do.

When Satan wages his best, thinks he's succeeded and dusts his hands off and declares, *"That's that!"*, I can know that God is preparing a word, an intervention, and a series of events that will bring a stunning new reality into view. I remember that the cross appeared to be Satan's greatest moment of victory. In reality, the cross was God's idea and Satan was a pawn in the greater plot of redemption.

I rest in the cradle of your power. Amen

GENEROSITY

He who did not spare his own Son but gave him up for us all, how will be not also with him graciously give us all things? Romans 8:32

Do I believe that God is gracious? Do I believe that his generosity has no limits whatsoever? While I know that God gave me what was most precious to Him, His only Son, I can believe that God withholds other things. When I perceive there's something I really need, and God appears to withhold it, I can question His generosity. Reinforcing my unbelief is the limited graces of people.

If I invited you to spend the weekend in my home and I worked hard to make your stay as perfect as possible, but then you announced on the last day that you'd like to stay for a month, or a year, my generous heart would be challenged.

Yes, God gave His Son but perhaps that's all He ever wanted to give to me. Am I presumptuous to ask for something in addition to my salvation?

Complicating this is the fact that I often ask for what is not good for me. I don't know that at the time I ask for it but God does. He says 'no' and withholds it for my good. But to me, it can feel cruel. In my 50+ years of living with Jesus, there are things I have begged God for. He took nearly 30 years to grant one of them. He finally did grant it and His glorious light broke through brilliantly. Only in hindsight can I see that He was gracious and He withheld. This review strengthens me for the next battle of faith.

Each of us has unanswered prayers. God's generosity is perhaps in question. As one who has survived some dark nights and enjoyed some brilliant spiritual mornings, let me put my arm around you and encourage you.

God has your answer. God is passionate about you and what you need. Whatever God gives, or withholds, is the result of His generosity. He longs to be gracious to you and is, in fact, doing so at this very moment. Be careful that an enemy who preys on the vulnerable does not extinguish your faith. Decisions made in pain are often bad ones. Satan knows that and will suggest mutiny when it might appear you have solid proof that God is not loving and gracious.

Nothing is too much to ask of God. Ask. And while you wait, know that extravagant grace is crafting your answer and your provision.

In a world that gives its sons and daughters away carelessly, you gave your Son, the One most precious to you. I pray this assurance goes deep into my heart. Amen

ACCUSATIONS

Who shall bring any charge against God's elect? It is God who justifies. Romans 8:33

I guess there is no way Paul is going to finish a powerful chapter like Romans 8 without bringing in the subject of justification. Perhaps he is aware that this is one reality that Christians down through the ages will fail to really grasp. Without an experiential understanding of justification, one that goes beyond the fine print in some doctrinal handbook, God's children will cave under the pressure of accusers. They will shrink and lose their confidence as soon as anyone points a finger.

I have sinned. People have had reasons to point a finger. I wore deep shame. Satan also accused me and he is someone who gets his facts right every time. But my hopeless story had a turning point. There was a rescue. Someone (Jesus) came forward and offered to take my life sentence of death. The judge declared me 'free to go'. The man who took my punishment wore my prison uniform and he offered me his garments. After I leave the courtroom, I know I will probably hear, *"There's Christine who committed _____."* But I will quickly answer, *"Didn't you hear? A man came forward and paid for my crime. He set me free. My debt to society has been paid in full."* At that point there is nothing for them to say. The key to my joy and celebration is knowing, and remembering, the power of the love of my Savior.

This verse has its roots in a story from Zechariah. Israel has sinned badly. Joshua, a high priest, stands before an angel of the Lord. This priest is there to represent his people so he is dressed in filthy rags to signify their sin. Satan is also there. Isn't he always? He makes one accusation after another against God's chosen people.

God speaks. *"I, the Lord, reject your accusations, Satan. Yes, the Lord, who has chosen Jerusalem, rebukes you. This man is like a burning stick that has been snatched from the fire."* The angel said to the others standing there, *"Take off his filthy clothes."* Turning to Joshua he said, *"See, I have taken away your sins, and now I am giving you these fine new clothes." Zechariah 3*

In a prophetic act, God justified Israel. Because of what Jesus did at Calvary, the court proceedings in heaven were forever re-written. Daily, Satan comes to God to accuse us. But as we stand there in our filthy robes, Satan is reminded that Jesus justified us. He took our punishment, took on our shame and guilt, and gave us His beautiful robes of righteousness. Daily, Satan is told that we are God's chosen people. Not guilty anymore.

Why would I ever wallow in guilt, Lord? Make this story live in my heart. It is the stuff of fairy tales, but true, only because of You, Jesus. Amen

HE SAT DOWN TO REST

Who is to condemn? Christ Jesus is the one who died – more than that, who was raised – who is at the right hand of God, who indeed in interceding for us. Romans 8:34

These are Paul's words for any child of God who doubts that they are really God's children. Is that you? Maybe the severity of your sins makes you doubt. Or, maybe you are in a spiritual desert and your experience of Christ is absent.

If you once came to Calvary, acknowledged your sin, asked God to save you ~ and then embraced Jesus to the point that you became His disciple for life ~ you are His child. No sin can ever condemn you. No spiritual desert can erase your place in God's heart and His future kingdom. Why?

Jesus died for your sin. Jesus rose again and proved that He was the Christ and His atonement was valid. Jesus is now seated at the right hand of God and His 'sitting' position means He finished what He came to earth to do. His work of atonement is completed and nothing can undo that.

The priests in the Old Testament never finished their work. Day after day, and year after year, they labored to perform their religious duties, even performing the same sacrifices over and over again because the Lamb of God had not yet come. There were no chairs in the Jewish temple, no sitting. Only working.

Many scriptures reveal that once Jesus ascended to His Father, God gave Him the seat of honor and glorified Him. Jesus finally sat down and rested. His seated position proves his statement from the cross when He said, *"It is finished."* He is resting just as God rested after the seven days of creation. His work was also finished.

I can know that I belong to Jesus, now and forever, because He is seated at God's right hand. His work on my behalf was completed on a cross, was proven by an empty grave, and is now reinforced by his seated position. I do not miss the power of this subtlety. If my sin were not forgiven, if I was not justified and perfect in His sight, Jesus would still be working.

Everything that you did for me is completed. The legal judgment of 'not guilty anymore' was rendered at the cross. Nothing, not even my greatest failure, can undo that. You are resting so I can rest in my salvation. Amen

A LOVE THAT IS FAITHFUL

Who shall separate us from the love of Christ? Shall tribu-
lation, or distress, or persecution, or famine, or nakedness,
or danger, or sword? Romans 8:35

My love for Christ has often been corrupted by tribulation, distress, persecution, danger, and sword. In my spiritual immaturity, love waned because of my wrongful judgments against Him. When painful times rolled over me, my distrust of Him spread like a cancer.

But my love for Christ is not the 'love' Paul is talking about. It is His love for me. Even though I pull back in fear, His love is ever present and engaging. Even though I pull back in distrust, His love continues to woo and build trust.

When I have allowed tribulation to erode my love for Jesus, it was only because I did not understand God's sovereignty. I could not see His panoramic view of my life and how stunning it is for His glory. With limited vision, I threw stones at His perceived plans for my life and told Him that He was doing a pretty lousy job of loving me.

Christ's love for me, the kind that does not ever diminish when the world falls apart, is a love I have to take by faith. When I see no evidence of it, faith must live. When I stand in glory and meet Jesus face to face, and I get to review my life with glorified spiritual understanding, I will fall to my knees for ever doubting His love.

Jesus Loves Me This I Know – is the most important song we have ever learned. It needs to play like a broken record in the rooms of our heart when anger and doubt are first present. How do we know Christ loves us? Because the Bible said so. If ever there were a promise to stand upon, this is at the top of the list.

I have been so childish, Lord. I'm still embarrassed by that.
When life was good, I said. . . "He loves me." When life
was bad, I said. . . "He must not love me." I vow to never
let tribulation rock this assurance again. Amen

THE BATTLE FOR FAITH

No, in all these things (tribulation, distress, famine, naked-ness, danger & sword) we are more than conquerors through Him that loved us. Romans 8:37

I've noticed over the years that Romans 8:37 is the life verse for many Christians. I've always been baffled by that because I've never been sure what the verse means. To claim to be a conqueror of suffering would lead me to believe that by doing *'something'*, I can get rid of the suffering. Is there some magic prayer, or the reciting of a series of verses, that will eradicate tribulation, danger, and distress?

Only time with God and getting older has revealed the meaning of this promise. I've finally learned that what God is enabling me to conquer are the temptations that come along with suffering; i.e. despair, hopelessness, the feeling that God has forsaken me, and every other sort of bad theology that is usually embraced when trials come.

What are the weapons God makes available to me to ensure that I will come out of suffering with my faith in tact? The Word of God. It is a rudder that keeps my head on straight when my heart is on the roller coaster of life. Good theology is a necessity. Solid beliefs about God and His sovereignty are my anchors in the storm. While my emotions are tossed around like twigs in a tornado, God's promises hold my beliefs in check.

Ultimately, this is a battle for faith. If my theology remains sound while the storm around me roars, my trust in God does not waver. All those who abandon God in hard times do so because their trust erodes into distrust. Their feet were not firmly planted on the solid rock of the Word, who is Christ.

I will never survive a trial, with my relationship with God in tact, if I am not meditating on the Word and asking God to write it deeply on my heart. The forces of pain and the voice of the accuser are just too strong a force when they come against me in a weakened condition. God is a strong tower that prevents my defeat. When I cling to every Word He speaks, His arms hold me fast. I can conquer every mental and emotional frailty.

The three men in the fire were not singed. You were there standing in their midst. No matter what I suffer, Lord, keep the flames from touching the borders of my faith. Amen

HIS LOVE AND HIS PRESENCE

For I am sure that neither death nor life, nor angels nor rulers, nor things present nor things to come, nor powers, nor height nor depth, nor anything else in all creation, will be able to separate us from the love of God in Christ Jesus our Lord. Romans 8:39

The love of a husband or wife, the love of a child or dearest friend are powerful forces. When we're in trouble, they'll come. When we're sick, they'll sit with us. When we're in danger, they go with us if they can. But because they're human, there are limits to where they can go.

When I'm going in for life-threatening surgery, they must leave me at the door and wait in the waiting room. When my soul is hurting, there comes a point of separation. They must sleep, go to work, attend to their own lives, and if it's a friend, they must go home. While their love is powerful and appreciated, their presence is limited.

There is no place on earth or in heaven I could go that God is not with me. He loves me, He's with me, and He's more powerful than the forces of evil and of nature. He made it all.

When Jonah was swallowed up by a great fish and spent three days in the belly of a big fish, God was right there with him. No friend could have done that. When Neil Armstrong walked on the moon, God was right there with him. When he faced the dangers of re-entry back into our atmosphere, and could have easily bounced off and headed forever into space, God would have gone with him there too.

The people nearest to my heart promise me their prayers and their love no matter what. I am deeply moved by that and rely on it. But how much more am I moved by God's promise of love, the assurance of His prayers, and the comfort of His presence? No surgery room keeps Him out. No maximum-security prison locks Him out. If I travel to the remotest part of our planet, He is there too. Feeling alone is always an illusion.

The greatest way to combat loneliness is to nurture my relationship with You in prayer and meditation and ask daily, "Show me your glory and make me more sensitive to Your presence." Amen

CHAPTER 9

ANGUISH

I am speaking the truth in Christ – I am not lying; my conscience bears me witness in the Holy Spirit – that I have great sorrow and unceasing anguish in my heart.
Romans 9:1-2

*A*nguish is not a word to throw around carelessly. Used too much by someone who loves drama, this person finds himself in a position like the boy who cried 'wolf' too many times. When he really did encounter the wolf, no one believed him so help never came. Words like anguish should be used sparingly.

Anguish is to be severely broken. A cry of anguish is a wailing cry. The posture of anguish is to be bent over, cut in half by forces of pain. Paul is experiencing anguish over the spiritual condition of his nation, the Jewish people. They have been given it all; God's favor, God's glory on Mt. Sinai, God's covenant, God's law, the right of adoption to be God's people, but when Jesus came, they threw Him away.

The strong anguish he feels comes from his own heart that has been steeped in the spirit of Jesus. Jesus once stood on the hill outside Jerusalem and wept over the spiritual condition of the same group of people, His people. To be like Jesus is to feel as He did over the lost.

"Conscience bears me witness," means that his heart has been quickened, illuminated, and under the direction influence of the Holy Spirit. I am challenged by the reality that Paul gave the Holy Spirit permission to take over his mind and heart and cause him to feel how Jesus feels about the Jews. His feelings were captive to the feelings of Christ.

There are occasions when I will pray a similar prayer. *"Rise up in me, Holy Spirit, to make me feel what you feel about this, and then to speak what you would speak."* Boy, does He answer. The effects are such that my feelings are intensified many times over. My words are not what I could ever come up with and they come out with force and persuasion or I just don't have words to explain the depth of my heart.

So the question for me is this: Why am I not praying this prayer about everything? Why pray this every now and then? What would happen if I prayed often for the Holy Spirit to rise up in me and cause me to feel how HE feels about the church I attend, the Sunday School class I'm going to teach, and even my neighbors? Am I willing to invest my energy to feel the anguish that will come over me?

Paul knew the anguish of unbelief; both his own and that of the Jews. He remembered how long he murdered God's chosen people because of spiritual blindness. As he recalls his history, anguish would be his companion as he recalls the torture he inflicted and the lives he took. As he looks into the faces of unbelieving Jews, perhaps he sees his own face. Humility is a sweet companion.

I'm so serious. Take over my heart today. Amen

WHEN MAN TRIES TO BE A SAVIOR

For I wish that I myself were accursed and cut off from Christ for the sake of my brothers, my kinsmen according to the flesh. Romans 9:3

This is a hypothetical cry but one made out of great momentary distress. They were *'words for the wind'* as Job put it. Paul knew that it was theologically impossible for Him to make Paul a savior of the Jews.

It wasn't the first time someone had made a request like that. Moses did the same thing. God was angry against His people because, even though He had just delivered them miraculously out of Egypt, they had collected gold throughout the camp and had made a golden calf to worship. God was going to judge and wipe them out and start a new Jewish nation from Moses' seed. He would become a new 'Abraham.' What a promise. A self-absorbed man might have jumped at the chance. Moses didn't. He pleaded for the lives of his people even if it meant being blotted out of God's book.

God turned down Moses just as He turned down Paul. And He will turn me down when I am in such anguish over a loved one that I step in to rescue them. There is only one Savior, one Deliverer.

Our prayers of corporate repentance move the heart of God and bring revival and grace to those who don't deserve it. When a family bands together to pray for a lost father, or son, God hears and is moved. But when those same family members rush in to rescue that loved one from the consequences of his choices, this just interrupts God's plan.

Because of my gift of mercy, I have attempted (in my immaturity) to get people out of pain. If I loved them, I would do anything to see them spared. I have learned the hard way that I only stood in the way of them coming to the end of themselves. Pain was their friend, driving them to God and repentance.

God wouldn't let Moses give his own life for the people. Jesus did that. But God did hear Moses' cry and saved a remnant of the Jews. He judged the rest; the remnant saw and believed.

God wouldn't let Paul give his own life for the Jews either. Jesus did that. God heard Paul's prayers and a remnant of Jews came to Christ because of his ministry.

God won't let me be the savior of my people either. Jesus is that! He hears my prayers and moves in the hearts of His chosen ones. I can be assured that the pain they suffer because of their lifetime of choices will be a saving pain. God's arms are ready to embrace them if the heat of His love and correction melts their stubborn rebellion.

Put a check on my gift of mercy, Lord. Give me the grace
of restraint. Amen

IS "IT" THE PROBLEM?

But it is not as though the word of God has failed.
Romans 9:6a

When those we love have heard the words of Jesus read to them and still exhibit unbelief, what is the problem? Is it the Word of God that is ineffective or is it the depth of their unbelief? I can jump to the right answer, as though it were on a test, and say that the Word of God is never ineffective but the inconsistency is not lost on me here.

It wasn't until 2009 that the light of truth about this very issue broke through to my heart. Until then, I wrestled and self-condemned. When I taught a group of people and it appeared to fall flat, my heart began to sink before the session was even over. I never considered that the reason people's faces registered 'nothing' was because of unbelief. I concluded that the Word must have been ineffective *and* I had been an ineffective communicator. I reasoned that if Jesus had stood in my place and preached the same message, there would have been a great sweeping of His Spirit.

This was a mental stronghold, one that led to an emotional stronghold. My beliefs often led me to this place of such despair, believing I had failed God. God helped me realize that the problem lay in my definition of 'effectiveness.' Was Jesus not effective when He preached to the Pharisees and they took up stones to stone Him? Was Jesus not effective when, after all His teaching and miracles, the crowd walked away? He turned to His disciples and asked, *"Do you want to leave, too?"*

The Holy Spirit showed me that if Jesus had taught in my place, perhaps people would have been even more repelled and become even more resolute in their unbelief. The Gospel draws and it repels. No middle ground.

The Word of God is always sharp, always powerful, always effective. When there fails to be a harvest, the problem is not that the Scriptures are old, outdated, and no longer useful. The problem is unbelief. Since Eve believed the lie of the serpent and wandered into unbelief, nothing as changed.

So, I wrap my arms around my Bible today and hold it close to my heart. I vow to use it more. I will read it more in prayer. I will speak it over those I love when they are sleeping, when they are hurting, when they face a crossroads. Though some might feel little when the words are spoken, the Word is never ineffectual. It blazes a trail of trail of light wherever it goes – and sometimes that path is right into the unbelieving heart.

Teach me to speak the Word as You spoke it, Lord. It will cause some to hate You and some to love You more. Thank you for teaching me to rest in either outcome. Amen

THE TRUE TEST

But it is not as though the word of God has failed. For not all who are descended from Israel belong to Israel, and not all are children of Abraham because they are his offspring.
Romans 9:6-7a

Supposedly, 85% of all Americans call themselves Christians. Sadly, many are not according to the definition of a Christian in biblical terms.

The Jewish people, as a whole, call themselves Jews and sons of Abraham. Sadly, most are not according to the definition of a 'true Jew' in biblical terms.

The distinction between a Jew and a 'true Jew' goes back to the patriarchs themselves. As Abraham looked forward 'by faith' to the coming Lamb of God, all of his true descendants did the same. They were the remnant of Israel, not the whole. When the northern and southern kingdoms were taken into captivity and lived as apostates, there was a remnant that remained faithful. When Jesus was about to be born, though the whole of Israel was engaging in lifeless religious ritual, there was again a remnant that were true children of Abraham. Joseph and Mary, Elizabeth and Zechariah, Simeon and Anna; these were some of the ones *"who were waiting forward to the redemption of Jerusalem." Luke 2:38*

The Pharisees were insulted, and indignant, when Jesus told them that they didn't know God and were not children of Abraham. It was prophetic of the day when God will say to so many, *"Depart from me, I never knew you."* Jesus could easily stand in one church after another today and deliver the same message. *"You do not know me, or my Father."*

The majority of those who call themselves Christians believe that Jesus was the Son of God and that He died for their sins and was resurrected. Upon that confession, they declare themselves to be a believer. But even Satan believes that.

The true tests are these. As a Christian, I am a Christ follower in all of my life. I hunger after righteousness because Christ is righteous. I am repulsed by sin because my heart has been changed. I am willing to count the cost and pick up the cross that goes with identifying myself with Christ. I have exchanged everything I used to worship with the glory of Christ. He is my one and only treasure. The way I live my life proves it. I live to make much of Jesus, not myself.

Christians did not coin the word 'Christian'. It originated in the wicked city of Antioch. It was what unbelievers called those who followed Christ. *"They are of Christ,"* the people remarked. Believer's devotion to Christ was evident in everything they did. Would my world today say the same of me?

True tests are good for the soul. Lord, break through the deception so that I see myself as you see me. Amen

ELECTION

"Through Isaac shall your offspring be named." This means that it is not the children of the flesh who are the children of God, but the children of the promise are counted as offspring. Romans 9:7a-8

I've known this major section of Romans was coming. Of all passages in scripture, Romans 9-11 are the most difficult to understand. Election, God's choosing some to be His children and passing over others, is a huge stumbling block to many believers. This is the very teaching that causes a breach in their relationship with God. They rise up in judgment rather than seek understanding.

The Holy Spirit will help each of us understand His Word. I don't know how He will do it except I'm counting on His faithfulness. Just as we've taken the first section of Romans verse by verse, we will jump into this section one verse at a time as well. I need your prayers and want to assure you that you have *my* prayers as you learn along with me.

If you have kept God at arm's length because the doctrine of election appears to be unloving, I pray that these next weeks will vindicate the justice of God in how He chooses to act. God rules righteously. This ~ we must take by faith as we begin to look at something we don't understand.

James Boice, a present day theologian, argues that all of life is about election. When I feel moved to witness to one family member, I am doing so with an unconscious decision to pass others over. When Jesus sent out the disciples to Samaria, Asia, and Antioch, these cities were chosen over other possibilities. When Jesus chose the twelve disciples, it was to the exclusion of thousands of others who would have benefitted from three years with Jesus. And yet, by choosing twelve, few would argue that Jesus was cruel to the masses.

I am convinced that any struggle I have with 'election' is because of my limited perception. I'll never know until eternity why Jesus chose twelve disciples and why he chose you, and me, to be His present day disciples. Quite frankly, this makes evangelism easier, not harder. When I sow the seed of the Gospel, those who are supposed to respond – will. Their ears will be opened by the wind of the Spirit and spiritual understanding will hit them with a wave of such force that they will fall to their knees.

Holy Father, I worship You no matter what You do. Though human perception screams to prove Your guilt, I will not bite the apple of unbelief. Amen

THE BEGINNING OF ELECTION

Not all are children of Abraham because they are his offspring, but "Through Isaac shall your offspring be named." Romans 9:7

Jewish history began with election. Abraham did not go looking for God. God came looking for him. There was no possible way for Abraham to find God without God's intervention. He lived in Ur, a place where everyone worshipped idols. No one there had ever heard of the true God. Abraham's entire generational ancestry practiced paganism. Who could witness to him?

God came looking for him and called him out from his family and his land. He was to leave his family's idols, go with God, and never look back. Sounds like salvation, doesn't it?

Then came Isaac. God chose, from Abraham's two sons, whom He was going to bless and call to Himself. Abraham had a son through natural efforts with Hagar. Ishmael was passed over. The one God would choose to bless would be the product of His own miraculous intervention. When physical bodies were too old to conceive, and Sarah's womb was too old to carry a child, God's hand touched them somehow and made the impossible possible. <u>The one who would be chosen would be Isaac – the child of a supernatural birth.</u>

The miraculous work of God in bringing about the life of Isaac out of a dead womb is what happens to every child of God in spiritual realms. I cannot manufacture spiritual life in myself. I am spiritually dead. (Eph.2:1) I am Sarah – with no hope of bringing new life about. God must come and supernaturally touch my spiritual womb, my spirit, and bring life to it. With that touch comes a call to leave the idols of my past and follow Him.

At that point, I become as peculiar to the world as Abraham was. As a Christian, I am never homogenous with my environment. Choosing the way of righteousness (the new appetite of my resurrected spirit) sets me apart. When family members keep clutching their idols, my choices to worship only God with my life will separate me from their mainstream. When this separation happens within society, it's tolerable. When the sword cuts into the family fabric, there is the sound of tearing and that is excruciating.

To be the elect of God brings humility and joy but it also brings a high cost. Daily sanctification.

I am not a natural child of Abraham. But You, miracu-lously, have made me his spiritual child. This makes me so happy. Thank you! Amen

THE ELECTION OF A CHILD

Through Isaac shall your offspring be named.
Romans 9:7b

Whom God elects, He draws to Himself. He makes them His own and ownership means the full authority to do whatever He wants with His children.

Abraham was called. Isaac was called. And once Isaac was named as the next in line for the promise, Abraham was account-able to God for the life of his son. When God spoke to Abraham and told him to take Isaac up the mountain and offer him up as a sacrifice, Abraham obeyed. He obeyed because God is God, but I suspect he also obeyed because Isaac belonged to God, not him. God had elected him before his conception. Nowhere was there a recorded conversation between Abraham and God where Abraham raged, *"How dare you do this to my son!"*

As a mother, there is nothing, absolutely nothing, more painful than seeing your child suffer. And how they do. They are often hurt at the hands of bullies, betrayed by best friends, overlooked by someone who appeared to have the keys to their dreams, and even violated sexually by someone everyone in the family trusted. When that happens, a parent can back up from God and cry out, *"How dare you let this happen!"*

Just as Abraham trusted God, by faith, that the tragic plotline He seemed to be weaving for his son would have a redemptive end, we must do the same. It doesn't mean there won't be tears, but tears will be mixed with faith and trust.

God provided a lamb and Isaac lived to marry and produce the next in line for God's election. Jacob. If your child is in an impos-sible place with no seeming way out, know that your child is in good hands. God has a firm grip, and a sovereign one. He will provide a lamb but not without our prayers, our fasting, and our tears. Through it all – He understands when we have our hands on the hem of His garment, when we cry out with tears of joyful expectancy. You know we can because they do not belong to me.

Oh, how many children appear to be stuck in some tragic plot; one that never seems to progress toward the light. Pour grace over the shoulders of each of us who are parents. Grace to believe. Grace to pray with expectancy for the Lamb to arrive. Amen

THE LOGIC OF GOOD BOYS AND GIRLS

When Rebekah had conceived children by one man, our forefather Isaac, though they were not born and had done nothing either good or bad—in order that God's purpose of election might continue, not because of works but because of him who calls—she was told, "The older will serve the younger." Romans 9:10-12

As a human being short on divine perception, I try to find loopholes around the truth that God elects who will be His child without any one of us earning our way into His good graces.

Paul re-tells the story of Jacob and Esau. He reveals that both are full-blooded Jewish children of Isaac. Yet, before they were ever born and had done anything good or bad, God had <u>already</u> chosen Isaac. This is a struggle, isn't it? I want to believe that Jacob's heart was bent toward God and Esau's wasn't. That's why He chose Jacob. But that just isn't the case. Their spiritual destiny was decided for them before conception.

So whom does God elect today? Can I tell ahead of time who will be God's child? If I have two children and one has always been a good boy and the other has been trouble from the start, does that give me a hint as to the one God will choose? No. The Gospel is just as much needed for both. I remember that the 'good boy' in the prodigal son story turned out to be the one who had <u>no</u> heart for His

Father. His performance had been self-serving. The rebel, in the end, embraced his father after radical mercy was extended to him.

The subject of election can be a stumbling block to my faith because I'm like the older brother. I believe that I'm good, am impressed by the good things I do, and I in no way resemble the rebel who spurns the love of God. Surely God is more pleased with me. When a prostitute, drunkard, or murderer comes to the altar, it can make me squirm. The passion in their testimony is in stark contrast to my own lifeless praise to a God who has been equally merciful to me.

God is not impressed with my 'good girl' behavior. The question I must ask myself is this, *"Am I aware that I have received radical mercy?"* I was once completely lost, even though outwardly good, and was condemned to a Christ-less eternity. My good girl behavior was self-serving. If I don't own my lost-ness, praise will be stuck in my throat.

Crush any vestige of self-righteousness. Show me how lost I was so that your love and mercy are alive to me. Grant me the full joy of my election. Amen

DOES GOD ELECT AND CONDEMN?

What shall we say then? Is there injustice on God's part? By no means! For he says to Moses, "I will have mercy on whom I have mercy, and I will have compassion on whom I have compassion." So then it depends not on human will or exertion, but on God, who has mercy. Romans 9:14-16

I'm writing prayerfully, and with trembling, about these passages of scripture. These are, admittedly by teachers, scholars, and theologians, the most difficult to understand in all of Scripture.

It is impossible to have God choosing some without the counterpart also being true; that He passes over others. There is a blessing and a condemnation happening simultaneously. But does God really pick out people to condemn? To understand the answer, I have to look again at election.

To see the glory of Jesus and believe, my eyes had to be opened. God's grace and the wind of His Spirit came to me, and enabled belief. Although I, of my free will, chose God, He gave me the grace to understand the Gospel.

It is not so with those who are _not_ elected. God does not open their eyes to see the truth. However, God does not _cause_ them to disbelieve. He is not the author of their condemnation. Those who are condemned choose to reject God on their own. Their condemnation is the result of their sin of disbelief.

So, all of us are tempted to rise up and say, *"That's not fair. God is like that?"* In order for my faith in God to stay in tact and not be eroded by my many questions, I must take this doctrine and put it in the context of the whole of Scripture. God loves. God rules righteously. It is not His will that any perish. We do have the free will to choose or reject Christ. God is trustworthy.

In the stable foundation of God's love and mercy, there is the doctrine of election and reprobation (passing over of some). To rise up and put God on trial is to put myself in a position to never understand these concepts. God teaches the humble. When I don't understand, I don't question God. I dig in deeper and cry out, *"Have mercy on me. Teach me."*

I trust Your character, even in this. Amen

THE DEATH ANGEL AND MERCY

For he says to Moses, "I will have mercy on whom I have mercy, and I will have compassion on whom I have compassion." Romans 9:15

When a Jewish household put blood on the doorposts of their homes, the death angel passed over. Their first-born sons were saved. Why were they saved? Many Jews believed it was for the wrong reasons. Some concluded that they were saved because they were Jews and therefore deserving. Others believed that God was rewarding them for the suffering they had endured. I'm sure there were still others who thought they were better, more moral, than heathen Egyptians.

None of these were true. They weren't true for the Jews in Egypt. They aren't true where we are concerned. God simply has mercy on people who are undeserving. Why He chooses some and not others is a spiritual mystery.

Where I can get trapped is when I begin the argument, *"If God were just, he would choose everyone, right?"* What I need to understand is that this is not a justice issue. If God had acted justly, we would all be condemned to hell. This is a mercy issue.

For reasons we may never know, He reached out in mercy to one group of people, the elect, when they deserved condemnation. Their lineage and their belief that they were morally superior to others played no part in their salvation.

The whole human race deserves Hell. God chose to elect some of us and grace us with the spiritual understanding necessary to believe. He did not grant this mercy to others. Do I have enough faith in holy character of God to believe this and not stumble?

When my belief is dependent on adequate spiritual understanding, I have nullified the need for faith. Really, I shouldn't be tripped up by why God doesn't elect everyone. I should be focused on why He elected me; one who deserved to die. Trust, gratitude, and faith toward a God who acts in ways that defy human explanation should be my heartfelt responses to concepts like election. I'm working on it.

Lord, this concept is as vast as Your mind. How can I grasp but one grain of sand in the ocean of truth? I search for understanding because I love You – not because I distrust Your wisdom. Amen

EVIL AND THE GLORY OF GOD

*For the Scripture says to Pharaoh, "For this very purpose
I have raised you up, that I might show my power in you,
and that my name might be proclaimed in all the earth." So
then he has mercy on whomever he wills, and he hardens
whomever he wills. Romans 9:17-18*

The Egyptians oppressed the people of God for 400 years. Great
evil was perpetrated upon them. The Hebrew people were beaten,
suffered injustice, and everything else that makes up the stuff of
slavery. Rage and hopelessness simmered beneath the surface of
every soul. They took on the mindset of a slave and just accepted
whatever came their way.

Can God be glorified when suffering exists? Are those who per-
petrate such evil subject to the sovereign hand of God? The comforting answer to both questions is "Yes!"

God told Moses to tell Pharaoh that He, Yahweh, was the one
who put Pharaoh in power and kept him there. God did this so that
His own glory could be revealed. It was to be showcased incrementally. Every time Pharaoh refused to let God's people go, the stakes
went up and another level of God's power was unleashed. Each
plague was worse than the one before. People's eyes were growing
wider and wider at the power of this *"I Am"* – God.

God did not cause Pharaoh to sin through unbelief. Pharaoh
made his own choices. But, on that parallel course of history, God
also hardened Pharaoh's heart so that His glory would be revealed
by the miracle of His people's release from oppression.

I am asking the question now, just as you are. If God hardened
Pharaoh's heart – AND Pharaoh freely chose to sin through unbelief,
how are both simultaneously possible? Logically, isn't it an either/
or? Once again, this is the mystery of election and free will.

How does this play into our modern day oppressors? Who is it
that confines you? Who causes you to feel that you are their slave? If
the abuse comes through a family member, God would have you be
pro-active to get to a place of safety. But if you work in an oppres-
sive environment or are being persecuted under an ungodly regime,

God is biding the time. His glory is released when we love and forgive our enemies, and when we lose our lives for the sake of Christ. And, He is also glorified upon our release from Egypt. It may be today. It may be when we step over the threshold into eternity. God's glory is always showcased and its brilliance coincides with His perfect plan for our lives.

Can I trust You while in Egypt? If I cling to You and stand on sound doctrine, I can. I've seen Egypt and I've seen your powerful hand of deliverance. Oh, I pray for each one reading these words today, Lord. Strengthen their spiritual fiber so that they can stand in the fire. Amen

DEMANDING ANSWERS

But who are you, O man, to answer back to God? Will what is molded say to its molder, "Why have you made me like this?" Has the potter no right over the clay, to make out of the same lump one vessel for honorable use and another for dishonorable use? Romans 9:20-21

I was created for the glory of God. My body, soul, and spirit – and how they work together – display His brilliance. Before the creation of the first human being, He decided what would make man thrive; what would make him happy and productive. The divine strategy? To live a life that glorifies God.

To glorify God is to give Him a place of honor. To de-glorify God is to put Him on trial and dishonor Him. Never will I do anything that destroys me more from the inside out than when I arraign my Creator in the courtroom of my heart. In pride, I rise up to believe that I am qualified to be His judge. I drag Him to the witness stand, demand answers, and wonder why He is silent. He is an uncooperative defendant and as a prosecutor, I am out of line and stand in contempt of court.

To think God guilty because He chooses some and not others is to insinuate that all people are innocent and deserve His salvation. The fact is ~ all are guilty. Every one of us is on death row and perfect justice has already been served. But Jesus marched into hell on the other side of Calvary and earned the right to snatch some sinners from the fire. That God would choose to save anyone is cause enough to walk humbly. That He passes over others is not for me to judge nor understand.

I just have to know this, and I do. He is merciful. And He is just. And in both, He is glorified.

When I try to understand the mystery of Your ways, I do so with trust and reverence. Forgive me for ever putting you on trial for anything. Amen

PAUL QUOTES HOSEA

As indeed he says in Hosea, "Those who were not my people I will call 'my people,' and her who was not beloved I will call 'beloved.'" "And in the very place where it was said to them, 'You are not my people,' there they will be called 'sons of the living God.'" Romans 9:25-26

Paul has been clear. Not all Jews are the true seed of Abraham; only those who come by way of Christ, through faith. Not all Gentiles share in the promises of Abraham either; only those who come by way of Christ, through faith. Each resulting child of God was pre-destined to be the recipient of grace while also exercising free will to choose or reject Christ.

It is of grace that Paul speaks now; the same grace Hosea offered his unfaithful wife, Gomer, after she betrayed his love, walked out to a life of prostitution and ignored his pleas to come home. He even looked after her from afar and made sure her needs were met financially. Patiently, he waited with a broken, longing heart. The analogies to every repentant sinner are humbling.

When I was unfaithful and spurned the love of God, He called out to me. I was His enemy and yet He pleaded, *"Come, I'm offering to make you mine and give you a place in my family."*

When I carried on like an unrepentant prodigal, He continued to call me *'Beloved'* and loved me anyway. Instead of shaming me in public and washing His hands of me, He sacrificed the life of His Son so that I would understand my sin and His love. The hands that could have brought judgment were nailed to the cross instead, offering every sinner the promise of restoration. The story of Gomer (and Israel) is the stunning reminder that no one can mess things up so badly that God ceases to want them. Grace knocks incessantly at the door.

Gomer's three children bore the names of judgment but You changed their names. You condemn and You restore. You strike and You heal. Bring someone home to You today who has been far away for a long time. Amen

CHAPTER 10

HOW DEEPLY DO I LOVE UNBELIEVERS?

Brothers, my heart's desire and prayer to God for them is that they may be saved. Romans 10:1

*H*ow do I feel about unsaved people in general? While my heart may break for a close family member who has yet to embrace Christ, my heart is not that engaged when it's my city. Too often, I am someone who shakes her head and says, *"They're hard-hearted. There will be eternal consequences if they don't repent."* I may pray for them but nowhere with the urgency that Paul describes. Would I exchange my own salvation for theirs if God would allow me?

The unceasing anguish Paul feels is not a momentary kind of sadness. Anguish, which like Paul I *have* felt over some relationships in my lifetime, never really leaves. It's the thing that tears at your heart and makes your whole body ill. You can't sleep, can barely eat, and though you carry on with life, you are going through the motions while feeling sick to your stomach. Anyone who really knows you and loves you can see that something is very wrong.

Paul invested his heart in the lives of the Jewish people. He felt sick over their collective lost-ness. He wasn't in anguish over one particular rabbi or priest in the temple with whom he'd bonded. He had God's heart for humanity. Isn't this just like Jesus standing on the border of Jerusalem, seeing the city through God's eyes, and weeping over their spiritual condition? Yes, this must be holy anguish.

Two things before I close. 1.) Paul takes a lot of hits for being a confrontational type-A personality. This inference intimates that he lacks sensitivity and heartfelt emotion. I used to say that about him too. I have repented of it. The reference to *"unceasing anguish"* and the openings and closings to his letters to the church are usually dripping with emotion. 2.) I often stand in the back of a church full of women before speaking and feel their spiritual condition. I am often in tears. But before I become self-impressed, this is far removed from the anguish Paul describes over Israel.

God sure has a lot of work to do in me. I'm humbled. Embarrassed, as well. As I begin Romans again, the sword of Paul's writing already strikes my flesh. The Word has come, pierced my heart, and I am again on my knees.

I am ready for the rest of Your message through Paul, in Romans. Don't hold back, Lord. All for Your glory. Amen

ZEALOUS BUT LOST

For I bear them witness that they have a zeal for God, but not according to knowledge. Romans 10:2

To many, zeal counts for everything. Zeal means sincerity and in our present day society, it is believed that if one is sincere, then a person is entitled to whatever opinion they hold.

Paul would be the first one to tell us that zeal can be misguided. No one was more passionate to protect the Jewish traditions of his spiritual fathers than Paul. So much so, that he hunted down followers of Jesus. He believed them to be heretics. His zeal was commendable but it worked against the purposes of the God he believed he loved.

I have known a few pastors and Christian leaders who were so zealous to protect their people from the influence of what they considered liberal views on lifestyle preferences, that they considered a large sector of the body of Christ enemies. Nasty letters, disparaging remarks from the pulpit and in print; these may have convinced their followers that their zeal was commendable but it was really misguided.

My zeal, my passion, must be surrendered to Christ. I want to be passionate about truth but not so passionate about peripheral issues that I alienate the body of Christ. Zeal must cause me to pick my battles carefully, prayerfully, to make sure I feel strongly about the things that Jesus feels strongly about. Much of the things I'm zealous for may just arise out of personal baggage. This is the 'zeal – not according to knowledge.'

Passion is a stunning thing when it is pure. But when it is not, it can leave a wake of bodies in its path.

Am I passionate about the right things? Is my passion holy? Only You can tell me. Amen

WHAT HE IS, I AM NOT!

For being ignorant of the righteousness of God, and seeking to establish their own, they did not submit to God's righteousness. Romans 10:3

No one likes to be shown up. Ever have a family member who needs to 'one-up' everything anybody else says? It's about impossible to share anything exciting because before you finish your story, this person is already trying to top it. Their listening skills are poor at best. They do listen, but not to understand the person who is speaking. They listen only to preoccupy themselves with how they're going to answer and remain the center of attention.

Imagine being shown up by God? That was the prospect for the Pharisees when they stood in front of Jesus and his holiness burned like fire against the grain of their self-righteousness. If they could compare themselves with true sinners, their confidence in their own righteousness would remain steadfast. Held up against the righteousness of God however, in Christ, their goodness paled in comparison.

There is a story recorded in Luke where this contrast was most evident. The Pharisees accused Jesus of healing on the Sabbath but when He answered them, His holiness was on full display. What was their reaction? Luke 13:17 *"When he said this, all his opponents were humiliated."* The Pharisees were shown up. Unable to cover their sin, they were actually humiliated; something we don't read anywhere else in the Gospels.

I am not righteous; only God is. I can spend a lifetime running from this truth, trying always to justify myself in others' eyes and redeem their perception of me. Or, I can own the truth of my sinful condition. The real question is this: Is it safe to be exposed for what I am before a righteous God? The answer is yes. It's frees me in every way possible to accept the undeserved gifts of love, forgiveness, and redemption. It underscores the truth of the Gospel that what I have, in Christ, has not been earned. What I have, He has freely given because His nature is to love and lavish grace upon the undeserving. My part is to come humbly with empty hands.

Perhaps any who have not yet been overwhelmed with the love of God is due to the fact that they have not yet stopped striving to redeem themselves.

What you are, Jesus, I am not. If I have become more like You, it's only because Your Spirit has changed me. I owe everything to You. Amen

THE LAW WAS A POINTER

For Christ is the end of the law for righteousness to everyone who believes. Romans 10:4

The Law was never an end unto itself. It was designed by God to be fulfilled in Christ. The sacrifices that were made were just pointers to the once-and-for-all sacrifice of Christ. He gave His life as the perfect Lamb – doing away forever with the need to sacrifice anything else. He was morally perfect and because of that, He was the only One who could fulfill the law and forgive sin.

Yet everyday, people live as if the law still exists and as if, by keeping it, God is appeased.

Unbelievers live their lives by a self-made set of scales. They perceive bad deeds on the one side and good deeds on the other. By 'keeping the law' enough times, their good deeds outweigh the bad and earn them God's favor and an eternal home in heaven. The problem is, God never suggested this exercise in morality. He declared from the beginning that man was entirely sinful and needed a Savior. The law was given to frustrate man, not give him a goal he could achieve, and cause him to see that it was impossible to keep it.

In desperation, he would look for a Savior who could forgive his sin and give him a new heart that was bent to obey.

Here is what's troubling though. As a believer, I can live my life by a self-made set of scales too. I can know, intellectually, that God accepts me. I can know that He is my Father. But justification is blurry. Believing that God sees me as righteous as Jesus is out of reach if I look at myself instead of Christ. To keep God happy with me, I perform. I become a rule-keeper, a law-keeper. I try to do enough things on the 'good deeds' side of the scales to outweigh the bad so that at the end of the day, God weighs them and decides I can be in His good graces.

Romans 10:4 is to be taken by faith! Christ put an end to all law keeping. In Christ, I am complete and holy. When I sin, He forgives but He also continues to declare me justified and righteous. This is the radical good news of the Gospel. I don't need to perform to keep my Father happy. I just need to obey because I am happy over such a love as this.

No more tiptoeing. No more dancing on egg shells. Peace with You brings rest in my obedience. Amen

GIVING UP IS A GOOD THING SOMETIMES

But the righteousness based on faith says, "Do not say in your heart, 'Who will ascend into heaven?' " (that is, to bring Christ down) "or 'Who will descend into the abyss?' " (that is, to bring Christ up from the dead). Romans 10:6-7

Think of someone you know who is a bit deluded and out of touch with reality. Have that person in mind? Now, imagine asking them later this morning, *"What are your plans today?"* Their answer, *"Two things are on my list. First, I plan to make a trip to heaven to bring Jesus down to earth. If that doesn't work, I'll assume He's dead and go down into the belly of the earth and retrieve Him that way."* I think you'll be calling 911.

These examples are preposterous. Yet, these are the lengths Paul goes to ~ to make sure I understand that believing that God will just accept me outside of Christ is as ludicrous as believing that I can plan a trip to heaven or hell and make it happen. I don't have one ounce of power (or goodness) to be righteous. The only way God will be able to look at me and see His Son's pure character will be if He gives Christ's righteousness to me as a gift.

I am not mechanically inclined. I can't tell you how many times I'll try to put something together, or fix something broken, and come to a screeching halt. I get so frustrated. I end up looking at the clock and waiting for the hour when Ron will walk through the door. I may round the corner with the broken pieces of 'something' in my hands and exclaim, *"I tried, but I can't fix it!"* He takes a look at the pieces and usually within three minutes, he's got it together. He's so nice as he's never rubbed it in.

My eternal destiny doesn't depend on whether or not I can fix a juicer. Eternal life starts, or ends, on whether or not I'm willing to approach God and exclaim, *"I just can't do it! There's no way I can overcome my sin no matter how hard I try."* Though my Ron is gracious, God is even more so. He knew we couldn't do it even before we were born, even before we started trying to fix our broken condition. He sent the Lamb of God to 'fix it and finish it.' We have to humble ourselves, declare our hopeless condition, and embrace a Savior.

Who has to ascend into heaven? Not anyone – if Christ is his or her righteousness.

The lost. The frustrated. The hopeless. These are the ones
You came to save. I'm glad that plan included me! Amen

DANGER OF FAMILIARITY

But what does it say? "The word is near you, in your mouth
and in your heart" (that is, the word of faith that we pro-
claim); because, if you confess with your mouth that Jesus

is Lord and believe in your heart that God raised him from the dead, you will be saved. Romans 10:8-9

Gospel language is familiar in so many parts of our world. In our country alone, all one has to do is turn on a sitcom, or listen to a popular primetime interviewer, to hear them use terms like "Christian," "born-again," "saved," etc. Extended members of our family, hostile to Christ, have watched Billy Graham more than a few times and mock the terminology he uses during the invitation. The Word is surely 'near them' and unless they open their hearts to Christ, they are without excuse.

I am shocked by how many movies and television programs make Christianity an open target in their material. Pieces of scripture are quoted out of context and always with disrespect. Those who follow Christ are portrayed as horribly out of step with the times.

Never has the Gospel been more available with the Internet and fun gadgets like iPads, Smartphones, Kindles, and Bible apps. But not all who know and use the gadgets know the Savior. The word is near them, even very familiar to them, but knowing it and confessing Christ as Lord with sincerity of heart is a completely different matter.

Is there such a thing as a closet Christian? What about the one who won't associate with Christians and says that he privately believes? That makes me nervous, I have to tell you. Stating an allegiance without apology makes it real. Oh, the power of speaking what is in the heart. It has an effect on the one who speaks it and it definitely penetrates the conversation one has with others.

In this post-Christian era, I can't afford to hide. I shouldn't mince words either. Prayers for boldness, shared words with others that are heart driven; these have always been the hallmarks of God's servants who go out and change the world.

Where can I speak where I've been shy? Show me. Amen

IN FRONT OF FAMILY AND FRIENDS

If you confess with your mouth that Jesus is Lord and believe in your heart that God has raised him from the dead, you will be saved. Romans 10:9

Did you ever date someone you knew your family wouldn't like or approve of? Chances are, you dated in secret. There was a lot of shame involved. Fear kept you from bringing that person home to meet the family. You hid how often you saw this person, how strongly you felt about the relationship, and just prayed no one would ask any questions.

This is how many 'believers' feel about Jesus. They made a closet decision to embrace Him but then they keep it a secret. They are afraid of what others might say if they openly disclose their love for Him. He's like a shameful date where they must keep the object of their affection out of sight.

No wonder Paul, under the inspiration of the Spirit, makes this strong statement about open allegiance. We must take Jesus as Lord, publicly, just as we take a husband or wife, publicly. We invite family and friends to the wedding. We stand before all the people most important to us to declare our love and make our life-long vows. With a radiant face, we reveal our deep love and affection for all to see, sealing the ceremony with a kiss and the blessing of the clergy.

Is not taking the bridegroom, Jesus, worthy of such a declaration? With the radiant race of one who trusts in Christ, I openly declare my decision to take Jesus as my Bridegroom. I dare reveal, with the shining face of a bride on her wedding day, how deeply I feel about my Lord. *"Those who look to Him are radiant, and their faces shall never be ashamed. Psalm 34:5*

When my heart has been impacted by beauty, I have to talk about it. Standing at the rim of the Grand Canyon, by myself, may be a private experience but not for long. Hearing a beautiful piece of music late at night may be experienced privately but not for long. I find that I must share what is life changing.

If my life has forever been changed by the moment when God revealed Himself to me, in Christ, confessing Him will not be burdensome, but a necessity and relief. Before Moses even opened his mouth to share what had happened on Mt. Sinai, the people knew. How? A shining face.

Does mine? Make it even more, Jesus. Overwhelm my heart with the beauty of everything it meant when You called me to be yours. Amen

TEST OF ADMISSION

For with the heart one believes and is justified, and with the mouth one confesses and is saved. Romans 10:10

Confession for the early church (and ultimately for me) was important because the times were perilous for Christians. To admit that you were a disciple of Christ was to potentially sign a death warrant. A person didn't play at Christianity like it's easy to do today in a country where Christianity might even bring power, opportunity, and prestige.

Still, I don't want to underestimate the cost, even today, for so many. There are those who are hated in families, scorned and cast out, just because they love Christ and put His ways over the sacred family way of doing things. To proclaim an allegiance to Jesus over father and mother can carry heavy consequences.

God knew this and gave us scriptures about 'shame' for comfort. Isaiah 28:16 *Thus says the Lord GOD, "Behold, I am the one has laid as a foundation in Zion, a stone, a tested stone, a precious cornerstone, of a sure foundation: 'Whoever believes will not be in haste.'"* If I embrace Christ and give Him my life, He will give me the strength to show my face, speak of my love and devotion, without hiding and nullifying my faith in front of others who are antagonistic.

And this one. Romans 9:33 Look! *"I am laying in Zion a stone of stumbling, and a rock of offense; and whoever believes in him will not be put to shame."* The phrase 'put to shame' comes from a phrase that means 'to fly away and escape conscious danger'.

Confession is so important. It is a test of our sincerity. Jesus admitted that He was one that would be stumbled over. One does not make a decision to follow Him without counting the cost. Comfort now but eternal condemnation and separation from Him later. Or, eternal life and intimacy with Him now (embracing the dangers) and eternal security later.

So much about Jesus makes me stumble; both in coming to salvation and in the ways of discipleship. His truth, though liberating, is convicting and uncomfortable. But just as He gives me the grace to bear up against outward pressure, He also gives me the grace to stand under the power of His conviction. When I follow, no matter when and where, there is abundant life.

Run away? May it be never! But if I do, it will only be momentary until I come to my senses. You are worth any cost. Amen

CALLING OUT

For "everyone who calls on the name of the Lord will be saved." Romans 10:13

So how can there be any confusion about the way of salvation? Calling on the Lord, plus nothing, brings salvation. Paul doesn't tell me to do ten things and then come and call on the Lord. I bring nothing but my plea.

How can any person living on this broken earth not believe that there is a need for salvation? Evil is everywhere. It is so obvious that something is wrong, even as we look within ourselves and see our anger, entitlement, and self-righteousness. Self-help books abound and they abound because no self-help strategy has ever worked to eradicate evil and bring lasting righteousness. The Savior owns that. The Savior must transform.

It has, historically, been hard for me to ask for help, to call upon anyone for something I need. The reasons for that are way too numerous to talk about here but if there was only one 'cry' in me, one call for help, it must be this one. There is no way for me to be saved using my own ingenuity and pure grit. When all is said and done, my eternal destiny depends on whether risk believing Jesus, open my mouth and call on Christ.

There are some today who believe the invitation is not for them. How tragic to know that I am lost, that a Savior is the only answer, but then fear that I am exempt. The word 'everyone' must be announced from every preacher and platform. No one is too bad, or too good, or too lost, or over qualified. We all appear before Jesus the same way; empty handed, sinful, and helpless. It takes humility to cry out, *"Save me."* Perhaps that is the stumbling block. Powerlessness is perceived as our enemy when, instead, it's the pride that deceives us from accepting our powerlessness that will take us to a God-less eternity. *"Help me, Savior!"* changes everything.

I would have surely believed your invitation was not for me. Oh, thank you for opening it to everyone. Amen

IDOLIZING MY REPUTATION

How then will they call on him in whom they have not believed? And how are they to believe in him of whom they have never heard? And how are they to hear without someone preaching? And how are they to preach unless they are sent? As it is written, "How beautiful are the feet of those who preach the good news!" Romans 10:14-15

It seems that in almost every instance in the New Testament, the apostles are preaching the Gospel in a way that includes their story. They reveal when they met Jesus, what they believed at the time, how lost they were, how they came to understand that He was the Christ, and how that is changing their lives. Even when Paul stood before King Agrippa and his life was at stake, Paul told his story.

I am convinced that some are not in the kingdom yet because of the way the Gospel is communicated. People fail to include their story in the presentation. With a wagging finger, they talk of sin and its consequences. With persuasive speech, they speak of Christ's coming, His death and resurrection. But there is one important element missing ~ a personal testimony.

What do you and I have in our hands? Our story. If I am a Christian and I'm not on a continuous growth curve, if I'm not living 'in Christ' and in the Word, if I'm not in an experiential relationship, then my story is sterile. I can tell others of the day I made a 'decision' to accept Christ but I tell it like I might tell about the day I met a memorable person on a plane. It doesn't reveal connection and life-change.

For over ten years now, the Spirit of God keeps telling me the same thing. *"Christine, you are not sharing enough of your story."* To me, it seems that this is MOST of what I do. But to Him, there is so much that I'm not sharing. While I consider it too personal, or too risky to tell, He wants me to offer my life's story up as a sacrifice. I am being asked to share how Jesus has changed me at the point of desperate need. That's the stuff effective Gospel presentations are made of. Has my family heard it? Have all my friends? Have my neighbors? I'm realizing as I write this that there are some close to me who don't know my story at all. Ironically, *you* may know through this devotional – but my neighbor may not.

No one can argue with a personal storyteller. I am willing to lay down my reputation, yet again, to the more personal parts of my story. The only one who needs to look good is You, Lord! Amen

WHY IS THAT?

But they have not all obeyed the gospel. For Isaiah says, "Lord, who has believed what he has heard from us?"
Romans 10:15

When Isaiah laments about how few believe, he has spoken for God's servants past and present. Evidence for God is all around us.

Evidence for the life, death, and resurrection of Christ is irrefutable. Yet still, so few believe. Why is that?

Sin is so infectious and has done such a number on the spiritual condition of people that they cannot see the Light. Sin deceives and blinds. When a preacher delivers the Gospel under the most powerful anointing He has ever experienced, and then only a small percentage of his audience responds, he may cry out in his spirit as Isaiah did. *"Why, Lord? Why don't more get it?"*

I will spend a lifetime with Jesus and live in the life of the Scriptures and never fully understand the full nature of my own sin. I believe that I am fully alive to Christ and mostly free to see the power of the Word and yet my old nature still veils my ability to see the Light. Paul said it another way. *"Now I know in part; then I shall know fully, even as I have been fully known."* I Corinthians 13:12 This is why it's called a sin nature. My 'nature' is to be blinded. It's in my spiritual DNA from Adam.

I heard of a woman recently who was bitter over how her Christian father had failed her. She announced that she couldn't fully forgive until her father understood the full extent of his sin and showed proper remorse. Forgiveness was conditional upon his total absence of spiritual blindness. That will never happen. Though he could come to the place where he sees *'in part'*, he will never fully understand his own sin until eternity.

I'm glad that Jesus forgave me and made me His without me having to fully understand all matters pertaining to my sin. I have, still, no idea all the sin, in me, that Jesus died for. I just know that I am a sinner and needed forgiveness. Not until eternity when my eyes are open to behold His glory will the blackness of sin be on full display. One day, I'll realize how veiled Jesus was to me when I am free from this body of death.

The narrow way is marked by those who know they've sinned. But none on the narrow way know how badly they are infected. No wonder so few respond. Satan has blinded the minds of the human race. The entrance of the Word giveth light – a little at a time.

I can't afford to spend ONE day out of Your Word. Turn on the light more and more today in my spirit. The risk will be

seeing my own sin. 'Tis no risk though when I see the light
of Your glory and feel inexpressible joy. Amen

DEALING WITH PERSONAL FAILURE

But they have not all obeyed the Gospel. For Isaiah says,
"Lord, who has believed what they have heard from us?"
Romans 10:16

It's easy to assume that Paul writes his epistles theoretically. But I believe that in this, and in many other passages, he writes personally. Perhaps this verse reveals his greatest heartache. He has gone out, preached to the best of his ability, yet few have believed. He pulls out an Isaiah lament from the O.T. because he identifies with it. He probably finds comfort that another preacher validates what has been his own experience. *"Who has believed our message?"*

How much does this passage reveal about the personal responsibility Paul felt for other's rejection of Christ? You might wonder if I'm reading too much into it. I don't believe I am.

For any who open their mouth to share the Gospel with their heart engaged, there are minefields emotionally. Before speaking with a family member, or a class, or a congregation, you can prepare well. You can spend hours in prayer. You can ask others to pray for you. You can pray scripture over the group, asking God to make every Word effective. But then most of the time, only a few will listen. Even fewer will respond. To the one who preached, is that not internalized as personal failure? It would be the rare person who didn't struggle with it.

For any who have a temperament where they put way too much pressure on themselves, this will be a spiritual battle. I know. It was my Achilles heel for many years until a year or so ago. If I had worked hard to prepare, if I had engaged others to fast/pray for me and for the group I was speaking to, if I had trusted God to make my teaching powerful, if I had asked God for a special anointing to teach, then I had an expectation of a certain result. When few showed visible signs of life change, I took it personally. I concluded that something had to be wrong with what I had done. I cited the examples from the New Testament when the apostles went out in the power of the Spirit and thousands believed. I failed to take into account that this was the exception. More often than not, Paul (for one) felt like no one had believed, so few were the conversions.

The Spirit of God had to work on me and take apart this destructive stronghold in my thinking. He worked with me to define 'effective' teaching. He reminded me that Jesus was certainly effective, yet there was one in his intimate circle who grew disillusioned with him and ended up trading him in for silver. Did that mark Jesus an ineffective mentor/teacher?

When ten hear the Gospel and one responds, it probably has little to do with effectiveness. Jesus experienced the reality of these numbers, certainly. I am called to give my all and pour my heart out for those who listen. After that, the results are up to God. *"Men love darkness rather than light."* However, for those who have been predestined to find the narrow way, God will shine a light on the beauty of Jesus for them. He will open their eyes wide; they will see His glory and believe. For all who shrug their shoulders and walk away, I am not responsible.

To every other overly responsible person reading this, I say to you. . . We must stop our striving and live. God bears the burden and invites us to 'shake the dust off our feet' on the other side of preaching. Even with family. Bearing the burden for other's spiritual blindness is a plot Satan has conceived and feeds. Jesus is the lifter of our heads.

Break the chains of false guilt. Set perfectionists free and use my story of failure, Lord. Amen

PROOF OF TOTAL CONFIDENCE

So faith comes from hearing and hearing, through the Word of Christ. Romans 10:17

Life-saving advice means that what was shared with me was so valuable that I couldn't wait to go away and apply it. I have complete confidence in it.

One of the meanings for faith, in the Greek, is 'to have complete confidence in something.' The evidence of confidence is application.

Abraham had faith in God. How do we know that? He left his home village of Ur and took off for a new life. Saul had faith after experiencing Christ on the road to Damascus. How do we know that? He went from hunting down Christians to becoming 'the hunted.' Peter and Andrew had faith after hearing Jesus' call to them. How do we know that? They left their fishing business and their families to follow Jesus, even unto death.

Many today say that they believe in God; that he lived, died, and spoke the truth. They equate belief with faith. Yet, there has been no action that has proven their confidence. Words are cheap without evidence of life-change.

Ultimately, this is not a devotional about unbelievers vs. believers. It is more personal. I must ask myself the question, *"Do I have faith that Scripture is true?"* I answer *'yes'* without even blinking. But if that's true, am I acting upon what I read without hesitation? Am I one who looks for loopholes? Do I rationalize why I haven't obeyed yet?

Or, am I bold in my application? Will I stand up for truth in a meeting where it will cost me something? Will I take on a challenge God has led me to if I fear I'm not qualified? Will I risk offending family or even a good friend by charting a different course from them? Will I leave a group where I'm comfortable if God is telling me to join a different Bible study, Sunday school class, or even go to a different church?

Difficult obedience is the proof of faith. *"Faith comes by hearing"*. . ..yes, but faith is more than saying "I believe." The essence of faith is a confidence that bears proof through actions.

I believe You, Lord. In everything You speak, I believe You. Where do I need to act on it today? Show me where I've been lying to myself. Amen

"NOBODY ELSE SHOULD HAVE IT EITHER"

But I ask, did Israel not understand? First, Moses says, "I will make you jealous of those who are not a nation; with a foolish nation I will make you angry." Romans 10:19

I may not want something and even turn up my nose at it but at the same time, I don't want anyone else to have it either. Jealousy has many manifestations.

The Jews rejected Jesus and though He called them "His people", they did not call Him 'their Savior'. When the apostles were sent to the Gentiles, the ones the Jews believed to be spiritually inferior, their jealousy erupted. This is not the first time in scripture that one group rejected Christ but were then jealous of those who embraced what they had rejected.

In Acts 5, the Sadducees (a stricter group of religious people than the Pharisees) saw the popularity and power of the apostles and were so jealous of them that they began persecuting them severely. We might believe that if they didn't want Jesus, they simply wouldn't be interested in anything the apostles were saying or doing. But, that's not the way it worked nor the way it works today.

Jealousy is not rational. Even though the Sadducees didn't want the apostle's faith, they *did* want their charisma and influence, which was really the anointing of the Spirit (though they didn't understand that.) Their own teaching was probably lifeless, full of rules and regulations. They were proponents of the law and sticklers for keeping every "i" dotted and "t" crossed. Their listeners would have been bored. The only ones who enjoyed their company were like-minded legalists. They had few converts and I'm sure it was hard to watch the apostles' zeal and see thousands embrace a faith you believed was misguided.

Today, a similar jealousy can be among us. Those who have been the spiritual fathers of a certain church can come to see the church as 'their church.' But when the move of the Spirit is quenched by familiarity and tradition, God takes the fire and zeal to a new generation. Those who look, dress, and worship differently suddenly occupy their seats, once considered to be reserved for pillar families in the congregation who had claimed them as their own spot Sunday after Sunday. There can be an indignant and unrighteous response, believing that God has done wrongly in extending the Gospel to an untamed and undeserving crowd. God uses jealousy to stir up the pot and allow the impurities to come to the surface.

To personalize: Am I rejoicing over the ways the Gospel changes lives? Am I grateful for the favor God puts upon others if I am in a wilderness? Can I express my joy over the providence of God and trust His sovereignty? If any twinges of jealousy stir in me as I read or write this, I have an issue with God and He invites conversation in prayer.

Bless my enemies and help me mean it in all seasons of my life. Amen

THE PAIN OF BEING INVISIBLE

Then Isaiah is so bold as to say, "I have been found by those who did not seek me; I have shown myself to those who did not ask for me". Romans 10:20

God disciplines Israel for their rejection of His Son by taking the gift of salvation and relationship to someone else, the Gentiles. To the Jews, He was virtually invisible or, if perceived, unwanted.

There is pain in being invisible. I've been in many family rooms while traveling over the years. Sometimes there was a child in the family who acted out, and even cried out, *"Look at me. Look at me."* Initially, their antics were cute. When they turned desperate, it wasn't funny anymore. There was an undercurrent of rejection and the child pulled out all the stops to get noticed. As a guest, I came to realize that this was a way of life for this child.

It's almost unbelievable that God could be invisible. His handiwork is hung on the walls of nature. His grace is poured out in so many large and small ways that I can't count them. Yet, I turn my vision somewhere else. Does God feel pain when He is invisible? Yes. But not in the same way we do.

A child, one who wants to be the center of attention, wants something for himself. God, who also wants our attention, desires it because He has something to give. His hands offered Israel His very best, Jesus. He gave Him up to earth, put Him on full display, and He was rejected. In Jesus, there was the greatest gift of all for the Jews; the perfect sacrifice for their sins, the Messiah they had been seeking for thousands of years.

I'm stopping now to listen to the heart of God. *"I was ready to be sought by those who did not ask for me; I was ready to be found by those who did not seek me. I said, "Here I am, here I am," to a nation that was not called by my name." Is. 65:1* Sounds a lot like *"Look at me. Look at me."*

Are there people I've given up on in prayer? Then I've made God's gift of salvation invisible. Are there personal issues I believe are hopeless for change? Then I've made God's gift of transformation invisible. Jesus cries out, *"Here I am. Here I am."* He has always held out the gift of Himself and all that comes with Him. Do I make Him feel unwanted?

There's nothing more tragic than to embrace Him as Savior but push Him aside when He offers me the rest of the abundant life. The stubborn Jew who failed to see Jesus can be me. Before I condemn them for their blindness, I take the log out of my own eye.

Show me where I'm not believing You today. I want to see you. Amen

PUT YOUR ARMS DOWN?

But of Israel he says, "All day long I have held out my hands to a disobedient and contrary people. Romans 10:21

Consider what it's like to run into someone you haven't seen in a while. You're excited; you call out their name, and then move swiftly toward them. You're not aware there's a problem between you so you quickly extend your arms to invite a warm embrace. But to your shock, the other person freezes and stands there. There is an awkward moment when your arms are still extended but the hug is definitely being refused. How long will you hold your arms out in front of you? Five seconds max, most likely. The rebuff stings and we tend to remember these moments of rejection for a long, long time.

It's one thing to be rejected by someone shy and cautious. We're willing to give them time to warm up. But it's quite another to be turned down by one hostile to you. It can be embarrassing to wear your heart on your sleeve, to look anxious or even desperate for them to return your affection. Hostility brings and un-godlike response. We want to run the other way and do everything we can to avoid being around that person.

God does not feel that way. He loves. Period. His love never cools. No matter how long it takes, He woos those who want Him and those who don't. He keeps His arms out. Not even for a day, but throughout the ages, His arms stay extended. He is patient, gracious, vulnerable. . . .and chooses to proclaim His love even with the risk of it never being returned. He does not hide from His enemies but pursues them. He is not defensive, playing it safe until they warm up. No, His arms are extended.

Good news for any believer who is unjustly angry with God and has been away from Him for a while. Perhaps they're too afraid to come home. No, God's arms have been extended from the moment they left. This is also good news for the most hardened unbeliever. No matter how badly they've sinned, God's arms are extended. He does not raise and lower them according to our good deeds. Who loves like that? Only One!

You are a God like none other. Keep reminding me that no one loves me like You. When I'm tempted to love someone or something more than You, show me a picture of Your arms extended. Amen

CHAPTER 11

NEVER FORGOTTEN

I ask, then, has God rejected his people? By no means!
For I myself am an Israelite, a descendant of Abraham, a
member of the tribe of Benjamin. Romans 11:1

*E*ven though God took His love and grace to people outside of Israel, does that mean that His grace was closed to Jews? Not at all. Paul used himself as an example. Though he had once been antagonistic to Christ, killing so many who declared themselves to be disciples of Jesus, even he came to faith.

There is always a remnant. God is always looking for those who have a heart that is bent toward him, even in the slightest way. Even though there may be a history of antagonism, of spiritual blindness and failure, God's love prevails over all of it if I move toward him with my whole heart. Even though God may deal with men harshly, we are not utterly rejected.

Oh, how His love is unlike mine. He woos, keeps His arms extended, through years of slander. He keeps His invitation open though others vow never to respond to it. He sees what a person can be through the life-changing work of the cross even though they love to sin and offend Him. In this astounding age of grace, while His invitation remains open, He offers a long-suffering kind of love that is so un-human-like that it is hard to even write about it here. There are a few people I would describe as incredibly patient with others but patience is marked by months and years rather than decades, lifetimes, and generations.

In one stunning moment, Paul encountered Jesus and his spiritual blindness was cured. God had been waiting for Him. He embraced the One who extended the invitation into grace. While Paul could have had many human reasons for self-hatred throughout his Christian experience, reviewing how he had come against the church and those precious to God, he understood the work of the cross in his life. Though he was humbled by radical forgiveness, he chose to walk in joy rather than to churn in some kind of unproductive remorse about his past.

No unrepentant child, spouse, parent, or friend. . ..is outside the reach of God's call. Jew or Gentile, patiently waits for His remnant. He is actively waiting for a response, speaking to them with a voice of love.

Even Paul believed. Even I believed. Who will be next? Maybe it's the one I'm about ready to give up on? Help me remember the miraculous stories of grace. Amen

START WITH WHAT YOU HAVE

God has not rejected his people whom he foreknew. Do you not know what the Scripture says of Elijah, how he appeals to God against Israel? Romans 11:2

If there are two believers on my street but a hundred who hate Christ, I can paint with a broad brush and say, *"No one believes!"* But what about the two? If I pastor a church of a thousand and only twenty are serious disciples, do I lament *"My church is dead!"* What about the twenty?

This is Paul's argument. The number of Jews that embraced Christ were so few compared to the nation of Israel that it was easy to paint with a broad brush and say, *"The nation is lost."* But what about the remnant? Paul uses Elijah as an example to reassure us that God IS a promise-keeping God. He made a covenant to Israel and drew them close. Though the majority rejected His love and spurned His covenant, there was still a remnant who believed. God always has a remnant. In Elijah's day, there were 7,000.

I have to be willing to work with what I have. If I am the parent of five children and only one walks with God, I certainly pray for the four but I rejoice in the one! I invest everything I've got in that one child! If I teach a Sunday school class of thirty and only three really catch the heart of the message, I praise God for the potential they represent.

The cup 'half empty' cannot overwhelm me. That is how Satan discourages. He has me focus on the proportions and uses the scales tipped in his favor to convince me of ineffectiveness. But I must remember today ~ the way is narrow. Only a few find it. And of the few that find it, the way again is narrow because few are willing to pick up their cross against the lure of Babylon. The irony is, if I were a pastor in China, I'd find a higher percentage of converts and disciples. The Gospel explodes in persecution and grows weak in prosperity.

The point of today's devotional is this ~ Satan is a liar. God is <u>not</u> on the losing side. God always has a remnant. That remnant is a wondrous thing – worthy of my joy. I assess my 'remnant' today, thank God, and give them everything I have to see them 'burn and shine' like John. The world has been turned upside down by remnants!

I turn my ears away from the accuser who loves to look at numbers and discount Jesus. Jesus used twelve, not thousands. I choose to focus today on the potential of a few. Thank you for them. Amen

UNWORTHINESS AND GRACE

So too at the present time there is a remnant, chosen by grace. Romans 11:5

People can tell a lot about what's important to me by how much I talk about it. I have stories I repeat, I know that. Part of it might be aging but most of it is due to a desire to keep talking about what has impacted me the most. These are the defining moments of my life.

For Paul, it was the moment God snatched him from unbelief by an enormous act of grace. A moment before his conversion, he orchestrated the stoning of Stephen. He held the coats of those who needed a free arm to throw the stones but the next minute, he put his face in the dirt of the Damascus road. The one who had offended Jesus was offered outrageous forgiveness and grace.

From that moment on, Paul's theme was grace. Nearly every reference to the topic of grace in the New Testament is Paul's reference. A hundred and twenty eight times. He never forgot his sinfulness. But then, he also couldn't get over God's graciousness.

Grace and a sense of our unworthiness must go hand in hand. If I ignore either side of the equation, it distorts badly. Grace without unworthiness is entitlement. Unworthiness without grace brings self-condemnation and misery.

It seems to me one side of the equation describes most everyone in the church who experiences some kind of spiritual imbalance. A spiritually ill believer is either self-righteous or self-punishing. My father-in-law, a well- known evangelist now with Jesus, used to say that you can't get a person saved until you get them lost. Kind of another way of saying that they won't be attracted to grace until they know they feel unworthy.

As a Christian, I must continue to acknowledge my need of grace. If I'm afraid of my issues, running from any reminder of my own brokenness, I will live in the deception of self-sufficiency and turn my head the other way when God graciously offers me Himself. I will believe that the only thing I needed was salvation and nothing else.

The themes of my life need to be an awareness of my sin and God's incredible grace. My joy is God's goodness. My lament is my sin. And oh, how the first outweighs the latter.

You are so gracious to me that I cannot take it in. Exploring your goodness will take me an eternity. Amen

FAMILIARITY AND STUPOR. A BLESSING BECOMES A CURSE

Israel failed to obtain what it was seeking. The elect obtained it, but the rest were hardened, as it is written, "God gave them a spirit of stupor. . ." Romans 11:7-8a

Many who are familiar with the Bible, with the sacraments, with the history of the church, even with basic doctrine don't have a personal relationship with God. Their knowledge and familiarity is really their enemy. When their pastor preaches under the fire and anointing of the Holy Spirit, they are interested only for drama's sake and the opportunity to talk about it over Sunday dinner. The fire did not make their heart burn. The anointing did not bring tears. This is the stupor of which Paul refers.

The blessings (scripture, covenant, vast love of God, undeserved privilege of being a chosen child of God) actually become their stumbling block. What is so familiar deceives them into believing that they really possess it.

A story in scripture paints this vividly and tragically. Malachi, a prophet sent to bring a warning to the priests of Israel, faces an unreceptive and hostile audience. They were surprised and indignant at Malachi's words and could not see that their heretical teaching had led the nation of Israel astray. They were in a stupor.

They answered him, *"How have we defiled? How have we wearied God? How have we robbed him? What have we said against Him?"* They presumed to be chosen but lived in rebellion and unbelief. A strong judgment was pronounced against them. **"If you will not listen, if you will not take it to heart to give honor to my name, says the Lord of hosts, then I will send the curse upon you and I will curse your blessings. Indeed, I have already cursed them, because you do not lay it to heart."** *Malachi 2:2* Jesus said it another way. *"These people honor me with their lips but their hearts are far from me."*

I am not one who wants to cause a believer to doubt. Just the opposite. But I also want to encourage honest soul searching. Have I been baptized because it was the proper outward sign but since then, have had no inward commitment? Am I relying on communion for forgiveness of sins and an entrance into eternal life? If so, the blessing of remembering Christ through this sacrament actually becomes a cursed thing.

A spiritual stupor holds members of every church in its grip. There can be a tender move of the Spirit, even an electrifying move, but those who are not alive to Christ will not be moved. Nothing lights a fire under them because their spirit is, most likely, still dead.

David said, *"Let their table become a snare and a trap."* The extravagant love of God was presumed upon. Familiarity with the subject of religion is a dangerous thing.

> *Smash any trace of stupor about anything. Even your children can be lulled to sleep. Oh God, wake us up. Amen*

STUMBLING AND GOD'S GLORIOUS OUTCOME

So I ask, did they stumble so that they might fall? By no means. Now if their trespass means riches for the world, and if their failure means riches for the Gentiles, how much more will their full inclusion mean! Romans 11:11

When one I love stumbles over Christ, even vehemently rejects him, can that act mysteriously bear fruit in the kingdom? Yes! A rejection of Christ, temporary as in the unbelief of present day Israel, can be used in a sovereign way by God to advance the kingdom. The Gospel came to Gentiles like me because Israel stumbled. And it will be the Gentiles who become the catalysts to lead the nation of Israel *back* to God. Things come full circle in the mysteries of God. He weaves a path mankind could never think of. We get lost in the tragic story line. God's plotline transcends tragedy to culminate in redemption.

Example. Earth was once pristine. Perfect. Man's sin cursed it. Now, it is broken and will ultimately come to completely destruction. God will redeem it and make it new again. We will enjoy a new Earth and walk again in Eden. Full circle.

What does that mean for any loved one who can't yet see the glory of Jesus? He stumbles over the Gospel, stumbles over the concept of sin and his need for a Savior, stumbles over losing his life in this world to invest in life eternal. His stumbling and life of sin is, even now, being used mysteriously for others' good. If that person is my parent, their sin and unbelief is, at the very least, a living lesson for all who know them. If that person is my child, their stance against Jesus bears fruit in a parent's need for a faith that is cultivated in the wilderness. That is a beautiful thing that bears much fruit. And this all happens before the salvation of the one who rebelled!

Israel's stumble over Jesus meant riches for the world. The message of Jesus' death and resurrection spread like wildfire to any one ethnic group who would believe. My loved one's stumble over Jesus can focus a light on the salvation God offers and be just as contagious to those inside and outside the family. Perhaps the faith of just *one* new convert will bring the stumbling one to faith. Full circle. Full redemption.

I've seen it with my own eyes. I know it's true. Stir up the faith of any of us who doubt your power to redeem. Amen

JEALOUSY IS A POWERFUL CATALYST

Now I am speaking to you Gentiles. Inasmuch then as I am an apostle to the Gentiles, I magnify my ministry in order somehow to make my fellows Jews jealous, and thus save some of them. Romans 11:13-14

If I believe that my own flesh poses no threat to my spiritual condition anymore, then I just have to experience how powerful my feelings of jealousy can be. I can be offered something, turn it down because it fails to interest me in the slightest, but change my mind when someone nearby considers it a treasure. I'll be sorry I refused it.

Jealousy can actually work towards something positive, according to Paul. He hopes that a spotlight will be put upon his ministry to the Gentiles for the purpose of making the Jews take notice in order to arouse their jealousy. They had rejected Christ. He had come to them, called them His own, taught in their synagogues, healed many of their people, but in the end, they rejected him. All He offered, they refused. So, before His ascension back into heaven, Jesus sent His disciples to the ends of the earth and extended salvation to the Gentiles. When the Jews watched *them* embrace Jesus, watched *them* worship, even give their lives for the privilege of being His, jealousy began to simmer. This was the plan. God wanted, and still wants, the salvation of the Jews so badly that He's willing to use jealousy to bring them to embrace His Son.

Can jealousy work like that today? I can turn down a church position but then envy the one who *does* take it and prospers. I can watch others worship with passion and abandon, decide it's way too out of the box for me, but then struggle with jealousy over their free spirit. I can be spiritually lazy and take communion without emotion but then envy the ones who seem to tremble over the very word *'communion'*.

The first wake up call is that I still fail to understand the depth of my own sin. But God wants my heart so badly that He will even use my own jealousy of others to woo me. May I know a jealousy that saves!

Jealousy can make me want to hurt the ones who has what I want. May it only lead me to You, the One who is everything I want. Amen

BEYOND HUMAN POSSIBILITY

For if their (the Jews) rejection means the reconciliation of the world, what will their acceptance mean but life from the dead? Romans 11:15

Does it seem far-fetched to believe that the Jews can one day be reconciled to God out of their unbelieving state? Has their long history of antagonism toward Jesus painted a picture for us that is hopeless? Just because it's always been that way, do we have a hard time believing that this kind of transformation is possible? Why should the gathering of Israel seem inconceivable when it is God who is doing it? Is this too hard for him? *"With God, all things are possible."* **Matthew 19:26**

Women tell me all the time that their situation is hopeless and their problem un-solvable. *"It's always been this way,"* is their defense. The path of hopelessness is not the path for the believer!

Just because something has been broken, or someone has been alienated, or a marriage has been excruciating, is no grounds for unbelief. How can any of us pick up our face out of the dust and look up with eyes of faith? By standing on the promises of the Word of God and reviewing His track record.

The man at the pool of Bethesda had been crippled for 38 years. The Israelites had been slaves in Egypt for 400 years. The Jews have been blind to Jesus for 2000 years. Lazarus had been dead in a tomb for 4 days and had already started decomposing. These obstacles are nothing to God. One mere breath from His mouth puts flesh on skeletons. One command of Jesus brings a dead man out of the tomb.

Where do you smell death today? Where has it become a way of life; a comfortable mindset that embraces despair like an old friend? The Word of God is a sword that cuts through deception and unbelief. Repentance breaks the power of it over my life. Standing on the promises and character of God, out loud, will begin to infuse my soul with well-founded hope. The God who will one day bring a spiritually dead nation to new life is still invested in that which I have dismissed.

It's time to hear the call of Jesus on the other side of the tomb. *"Come out! Step into the light where resurrection power is the norm and where hopelessness is banished."*

Someone I love hasn't yet been fully transformed by your love. I'm waiting, but not without hope. I put their name in scripture and make these my prayers. I praise You. You are the God of the new-birth. Amen

LOVE DOES NOT GIVE UP

If the dough offered as firstfruits is holy, so is the whole lump, and if the root is holy, so are the branches.
Romans 11:16

The technicalities associated with a scriptural passage are important but I should not get lost in the minutia and miss the beauty of the larger meaning. All scripture is to cause me to worship God. This verse is no exception.

To be holy is to be set apart by God. Devoted and consecrated for His pleasure. Once God sees me, chooses me by His grace and sets me apart for Himself, I am considered holy – even if rebellious before my conversion. God's love does not waver and He is true to His promises. How unlike my love!

The firstfruits and lump refer to the first Jewish converts and the lump is the whole nation. The root is Abraham and the branches are all his descendants.

So what God doesn't want me to miss is this ~ Whom He loves, He loves. He does not give up no matter how long it takes and no matter how obstinate we are. Israel may be blind and rebellious for thousands of years but God still considers her *'His people'* and sees them as set apart for Himself. She is considered holy.

If God has made me a promise that someone I love will be saved ~ a father, a son, a friend ~ then their rebellion does not jeopardize that. The one He chooses, He chooses. I can fear that if this person whom I love keeps going down the path he is traveling, he will travel so far as to be out of God's mercy. God's promises can look ludicrous in the face of their present condition. My faith can shrink daily by what I see.

What is causing me to despair today? What loved one seems to be so far away from God that I am about to lose all hope? Let me ask. How long has their rebellion existed? Twenty years? Forty years? It's nothing compared to the thousands of years Israel has wandered. Time is nothing to God. His promises are 'now' and 'forever'. Just because the days and hours crawl for me doesn't mean He is bound by them.

I raise my eyes to a God I still cannot fathom. He is too good to be true. His love is so far out of my understanding. In this world, I hardly know what to do with such good news. Skepticism shouts in my ear. Faith, I must fight for. It is the fruit of wartime faith. I plant my feet in the Word, for behind it is the everlasting love of a holy God.

All glory and praise to you, O Lord, who keeps your
promises. Amen

OH, THERE'S TWO SIDES!

Note then the kindness and the severity of God: severity toward those who have fallen, but God's kindness to you, provided you continue in his kindness. Otherwise you too will be cut off. Romans 11:22

I had a dream last night. I was walking down the middle of a busy street. It was mobbed. Every person I passed had a hand-written label pinned on his or her jacket. On most of the tags was a detailed list but a few had empty tags with nothing written. In my dream, I asked the Lord about it. I came to understand that the labels with the long list were details of that person's sins against God. The longer they lived, the longer the list became. I saw evidence of that. Old people had a label reaching nearly to their knees. They were all walking aimlessly toward destruction.

I asked Him about the empty labels with no writing. *"These are the ones who have come to me, by faith, for the forgiveness of their sins. Their list of sins was nailed to my cross. There's nothing left on their list to forgive!"* That accounted for the joy on their faces as they passed me. They had purpose in their stride.

Two spiritual states. Two opposite destinies. Two polarized facial demeanors.

God has two sides. He is loving but He is also just. He is kind but He is also severe. Preach about a loving God and people will presume upon His kindness and end up in hell. Preach about a just God and people will distrust His love and become angry. Oh, for biblical balance.

I've stayed in hundreds of homes while on the road and experienced the dynamics. Some parents appeared overly permissive while others ruled with a firm hand. If there was little balance, the children's relationship with their mother and father was skewed. They disrespected the loving parents who provided no boundaries and presumed upon their good graces. Sinning was easy because they casually dismissed the notion that their parents would bring consequences to their rebellion. But they feared the rigid parents who expected perfection and withheld praise. Warmth and intimacy was non-existent.

In this age of grace, many presume upon God's love but they don't count on His holiness. The reality is this ~ we are, either the one with the long hang tag who will eventually pay eternally for the sins we've committed, or we are the ones who have trusted Christ and have experienced the exhilaration of Him wiping our history clean of sin. Every person alive will experience His kindness or His severity. Our witness must be urgent and accurate. God has two sides.

As Your child, remind me that I live under Your kindness, not Your severity. Deliver Your children from those who have skewed Your character. Amen

REVEALER OF MYSTERIES

Lest you be wise in your own sight, I do not want you to be unaware of this mystery, brothers: a partial hardening has come upon Israel, until the fullness of the Gentiles has come in. And in this way all Israel will be saved.
Romans 11:25-26a

When something happens that we fail to understand, we have a saying, *"It's a mystery!"* That usually means that there will _never_ be enlightenment. Like yesterday, a folder full of files just disappeared from my desktop. It contained notes to every seminar I teach; all my study notes for future seminars, and all the outlines for those who attend events. *"It's a mystery!"* And, they are, as of now, unrecoverable. (I stated, out loud, that their loss on paper meant little since every word and teaching given to me by God is in my heart, passionately simmering until I can deliver it. I am not without words just because the computer copies don't exist. I'm also trusting God for new oil!) Nonetheless, the folder's disappearance is a mystery. Was it warfare? Satan surely hates this ministry. But was it God? Perhaps

He's removing old props and plans to write something totally new on my heart.

'Mystery' in scripture doesn't mean that something is veiled. A mystery of the kingdom **is** veiled to the masses but **un**-veiled to the remnant who belong to God. They come to us as special revelations.

This is what Paul speaks about here. The same God who could raise a valley full of dry bones (spiritual unbelief of Israel) to life is the same God who will bring all Israel to faith in Christ in the end. The Spirit of God reveals these things to us, stirs up our faith, gives us spiritual eyesight, and we are able to live as though we have already seen it come to pass. We are certain of it even though it hasn't happened yet.

God is the revealer of mysteries. This makes great Christian fellowship. Two or three get together and tell stories of things God has been teaching them. Mysteries are unfolded and become plain through our sharing. Yet, if those outside of God's family hear such stories, they are confused and often turned off. We are the brunt of their jokes.

That's okay. The precious things He reveals to us are priceless jewels. *"The secret things belong to the Lord our God, but the things that are revealed belong to us and to our children forever, that we may do all the words of this law." Deut. 29:29*

My life would be empty without my spiritual journey with you. I love all the things You teach me. They thrill my soul! Thank you. Amen

A SWEEPING ACT OF UNFATHOMABLE LOVE!

"The Deliverer will come from Zion, he will banish ungodliness from Jacob; and this will be my covenant with them when I take away their sins." Romans 11:26b-27

Every child I know trembles when he hears the words, *"Just wait till your father comes home."* It is associated with anger and disappointment, as well as punishment and shame. Human parenting can be so far removed from the perfect parenting of our Heavenly Father. What is behind a 'deliverer coming from Zion to banish ungodliness?' A covenant.

Some covenants are made between two people. *"If you do this, I will do that."* This is not the covenant God makes with Abraham. In fact, he put Abraham in a deep sleep and God did all the talking. His covenant was one-sided. Not matter how obstinate or submissive the children of Israel were, or are, or will be, His covenant still stands because God promised it with His eyes fully open.

God exposes, dies for (through Christ), and forgives sin because He loves. If sin exists, there is a breach in the relationships He prizes above all else. The distance between the hearts of His people and His heart wounds Him deeply. He calls out into the night of men's souls with mournful cries to return to the One who loves them without condition.

Yes, this Love is outrageous. Who keeps a promise to a people who create mutiny and treat Him like an enemy? Only God. Who keeps a promise to a people who love their sin, the very sins a Father's Son gave His life for? Only God. Who comes to banish ungodliness without retribution? Only God. Who comes to banish ungodliness, then forgive and embrace? Only God.

Is it possible for human beings to make covenants with God? Ah yes. Jesus said, *"You shall not make false vows but vows but shall perform your vows to the Lord." Matt. 5:33* What happens if we don't keep our vows perfectly? We are forgiven. We break vows every day with the sin in our hearts. Nonetheless, it is good for me, in good faith, to make a vow to a Father who performs one act after another of unfathomable love. Even, *"I will love you forever with my life."* What happens on the days when I fail? I stand on today's scripture for I am part of spiritual Israel. *"The Deliverer came to banish ungodliness and take away my sin."*

I will love you forever with my life. Amen

ONCE GOD HAS SPOKEN

As regards the gospel, they are enemies for your sake. But as regards election, they are beloved for the sake of their forefathers. Romans 11:28

Paul lived in a time when he saw absolutely no proof that what he was writing (regarding the Jews collectively embracing the gospel) would come to pass. In fact, just the opposite. They were vehemently rejecting Christ and persecuting all who became disciples. Can you imagine telling the parents of a child who was murdered, *"Right now, the killer is your enemy. But one day he will be beloved by God, and by you."* How offensive and potentially explosive unless it was absolutely true.

God had once spoken. Abraham would be blessed and Israel would be His people. Nothing could shake that. Paul's certainty in his writing is due to His belief in the unchanging character of God. Even though it appeared God's promise was ludicrous, his faith didn't waver.

God has given each of us a promise that is specific to us and our story. It comes to us in prayer, built upon our time in the Word, and we know – that we know – that God has promised it. His word to us is life-saving but the fulfillment surely seems ludicrous. All evidence is stacked against it. For a time, our faith can remain strong but our enemy plants seeds of hopelessness in desperate circumstances. *"See, nothing is happening. God might have changed His mind. Maybe you've done something wrong and you've ruined things."* Lies come in a barrage of arrows. Without a fight on our part to stand on the Word and on the character of God, promises erode into dust. More Christians than not have sunk into places of despair.

Just as surely as Israel will experience a sweeping revival and embrace Christ as their Messiah, God will bring about that which He has promised to each of His children. Circumstances, and what appears improbable, are immaterial. Things change quickly when God decides it's time to move. One burning bush, one Damascus road experience, and an enemy is brought to His knees before an all-powerful God.

What has God promised you? Why are you fainting? Not only is God powerful enough to deliver, He must do so because He spoke it and He is holy and true. There is no such thing as a stray word.

And so, I review. Who are you? How have you kept your promises to your children down through the ages? No one is exempt from your faithfulness. I am standing in the cement of your character. Amen

THEY'RE STILL FOR ME!

The gifts and calling of God are irrevocable. Romans 11:29

Once God makes a promise, a covenant, it is irrevocable. The one upon whom God places His favor cannot 'un-earn' covenant love. *"But God, didn't you know that Abraham's descendants would commit gross sins against you? Didn't you know they would bow down to other gods? Didn't you know that they would throw their own children in the fire for sacrifices? Didn't you know they would hear You calling and choose to turn their backs?"*

Yes, He knew. His love remains to this day. Though He has experienced anger, even pronounced temporary judgment, His covenant still stands. Their calling is irrevocable.

While praying for you this morning, God showed me that some of you are reading these daily devotionals with one eye closed, head turned to the side, as if to lessen the impact. You don't dare believe this love is for you. No favor of God, no calling, no promise could possibly apply to you. You believe you've erred too badly, offended God beyond what a relationship can withstand.

Not true! Our sin is not the point. The power of Jesus' death *over* sin is everything. Nothing can separate us from the love of God in Christ.

Dare to believe. He has called You, has drawn You to Himself in love, and though you've backed up and turned yours eyes away, His arms are still extended. You don't need fear going home. *"I've missed you. Where have you been?"* might be the first thing you hear.

People punish me by withdrawing their love. Yours stands – no matter what. Oh what a Father You are. Amen

NO LONGER DISPOSABLE

For just as you were at one time disobedient to God but now have received mercy. . ..Romans 11:30

Mercy is cheap if I perceive it as something I barely need. Take a hardened criminal, he needs mercy, right? I only need a little in comparison. This is the deception in the church as we can easily think we're different from other people, other nations, other cultures. When I watch the news and see bands of gang members in the back of pickup trucks in Sudan, wielding weapons and machetes, I have no trouble seeing them as needing vast amounts of mercy. But am I like them? Do I need the same amount of mercy?

Mercy is only of infinite value when it's placed against the backdrop of sin and hopelessness. Until I see myself as utterly lost and condemned, then what Jesus did in giving His life for me will be a story that causes me to yawn in boredom. Who will feel the most ecstatic over being forgiven? The one who knows how deeply he has sinned and offended God. Who will embrace salvation with his whole heart? The one who has despaired of being justly condemned with no way out. The Pharisees made no admission of being lost. Therefore, Christ Jesus was of no value to them.

I'm not one who likes 'forwards' in emails. Rarely do I even read them. However, this was sent recently. The source is unknown. The story paints a moving picture of mercy that even our children can understand. I'm asking God to take the precious gift of mercy home to my heart in a more profound way today.

****

There once was a man named George Thomas, a pastor in a small Texas town. One Sunday morning he came to the Church building carrying a rusty, bent, old bird cage, and set it by the pulpit. Eyebrows were raised and, as if in response, the pastor began to speak ~

'I was walking through town yesterday when I saw a young boy coming toward me swinging this bird cage. On the bottom of the cage were three little wild birds, shivering with cold and fright.

I stopped the lad and asked, *"What do you have there, son?*

"Just some old birds," came the reply.

"What are you going to do with them?" I asked.

"Take 'em home and have fun with 'em," he answered. *"I'm gonna tease 'em and pull out their feathers to make 'em fight. I'm gonna have a real good time."*

"But you'll get tired of those birds sooner or later. What will you do then?"

"Oh, I got some cats," said the little boy. *"They like birds. I'll take 'em to them."*

The pastor was silent for a moment. *"How much do you want for those birds, son?"*

"Huh?! Why, you don't want them birds, mister. They're just plain old field birds. They don't sing. They ain't even pretty!"

"How much?" the pastor asked again.

The boy sized up the pastor as if he were crazy and said, *"$10?"*

The pastor reached in his pocket and took out a ten-dollar bill. He placed it in the boy's hand. In a flash, the boy was gone. The pastor picked up the cage and gently carried it to the end of the alley where there was a tree and a grassy spot. Setting the cage down, he opened the door, and by softly tapping the bars persuaded the birds out, setting them free. Well, that explained the empty birdcage on the pulpit, and then the pastor began to tell this story:

One day Satan and Jesus were having a conversation. Satan had just come from the Garden of Eden, and he was gloating and boasting. *"Yes, sir, I just caught a world full of people down there. I set a trap, used bait I knew they couldn't resist and I got them all!"*

"What are you going to do with them?" Jesus asked.

Satan replied, *"Oh, I'm going to have fun! I'm going to teach them how to marry and divorce each other, how to hate and abuse each other, how to embrace perverse things that will destroy them in the end. I'm going to teach them how to invent guns and bombs and kill each other. I'm really going to have fun!"*

"And what will you do when you are done with them?" Jesus asked.

"Oh, I'll kill them," Satan glared proudly.

"How much do you want for them?" Jesus asked.

"Oh, you don't want those people. They aren't any good to you. Why, you'll take them and they'll just hate you. They'll spit on you, curse you and kill you. You don't want those people!!"

"How much?" He asked again.

Satan looked at Jesus and sneered, *"All your blood, tears and your life."*

Jesus said, *"Done!"* Then He paid the price.'

The pastor picked up the cage and walked from the pulpit.

WHAT SPRINGS TO MY MIND

Oh, the depth of the riches and wisdom and knowledge of God! How unsearchable are his judgments and how inscrutable his ways! Romans 11:33

A.W. Tozer said, *"What comes into our minds when we think about God is the most important thing about us."* When Paul thought of God, he exclaimed about things like riches, wisdom, and knowledge. How close to that is my 'first thought' of God ~ the one that arises in private that no one else ever hears because I dare not speak it.

How I perceive God dictates the kind of relationship we share. Satan loves to encourage a distorted picture because he knows that if I believe it, the ability to trust anything God says will be shattered. Without trust, there is no love, security, beauty, and significance. At one time, my first thought of God brought words like 'distant', 'demanding', 'passive', and 'one who plays favorites'. My relationship with Him was cold as a result. He was warm; I was not.

If any of us today don't immediately think of God in terms of riches, wisdom, and knowledge ~ then we are being robbed. Correcting our vision must become our highest priority. The riches are too numerous to even list; starting with unconditional love, radical forgiveness, undeserved mercy, and un-ending graciousness. His wisdom is too vast to capture as well. Someone once defined wisdom as 'knowing what to do when the Bible sets no precedent.' God knows the answers to every delicate problem, relationally and practically. Whenever I am stumped, or curious, there is no end to what He delights to reveal. And knowledge? There is enough knowledge to last me for eternity. I will never approach the perimeter of boredom because the God of the Universe, the One who created it and holds it together, is a genius.

Thinking about God, is good for my mind, my soul, and my body. I was created to be captivated by Him and then to worship Him. When I do that, I am complete and happy. Oh, how I regret the vast numbers of days I rarely thought about Him at all. It's my loss. I've repented and now, I ask God daily to redeem the time. I cry out, *"Fill me to overflowing with all that I missed. Please, Lord!"* And on some days, like a recent Sunday in worship, I felt my spirit soar off the platform. On angel's wings indeed.

I was made for pleasure and I know where to find it. *"In your presence is fullness of joy, at your right hand are pleasures forevermore."* Psalm 16:11

My favorite habit? Thinking of you. My favorite vacation? You, me, and my Bible. You are at the center of my heart and soul. Amen

AM I SMALL ENOUGH?

For who has known the mind of the Lord, and who has been His counselor? Romans 11:34

"I am the Lord and there is none other," God would tell His children repeatedly. Why? Because they were not small enough. Their disobedience and worship of other gods exposed their arrogance. They had decided who was worthy of their worship, whom they would honor and obey. The God of the universe got the short end of the stick. Oh, how man elevates himself and how absolutely ludicrous.

William Beebe was a biologist, explorer, and author, and he was also a personal friend of Theodore Roosevelt. He used to visit Roosevelt at Sagamore Hill, his home near Oyster Bay, Long Island. He tells of a little game they used to play together. After an evening of talk, they would go outside onto the lawn and search the sky until they found the faint spot of light beyond the lower left corner of the great square of Pegasus. One of them would recite: *"That is the Spiral Galaxy in Andromeda. It is as large as the Milky Way. It is one of a hundred million galaxies. It consists of one hundred billion suns, each larger than our sun."* Then Roosevelt would grin at Beebe and say, *"Now I think we are small enough! Let's go to bed."*

If there is an issue about which I've decided not to obey, I am not small enough. If I tell God He is shortsighted, I am not small enough. If I tell God that He doesn't rule well and life will never be fair, I am not small enough. If I feel qualified, in any way, to make a judgment against God, I am not small enough. I am not even a grain of sand in the vast universe. He, who could move the Himalayan mountain range with a word, is the very one I accuse? No, I am not small enough.

The point for me is this ~ He is **large** enough but do I acknowledge it? Do I see myself small in comparison? Only then will I be humble. Only then will I feel safe. Only then will I trust sovereign grace in the midst of agonizing circumstances.

Job was troubled to the point of wishing he'd never been born but as soon as God reviewed His large-ness and asked Job a question about his small-ness, was Job's heart comforted. *"Where were you when I hung the stars?"* At that point, Job dared trust that his great trials had divine purpose. His childlike submission to God was well-placed. Now, we know the rest of the story. One day, our well-placed trust will also have divine perspective. My small faith is not blind. It has a history and a future.

I am small, oh, but You are not. You are infinitely tender with 'small'. I have never been safer. Amen

A SLAVE TO A DEBT

Or who has given a gift to him that he might be repaid?
Romans 11:35

If I try to repay someone for a gift they have given me, it offends them. Well, *if* they truly gave it without strings attached. Some give – in order to entrap. How well I know.

I was once enslaved to some people who insisted that they were owed an exorbitant amount of money. (I trusted them though there was no paper trail.) I lived to repay them and felt strangled by the debt as the years mounted. No matter how much money I handed them, I was made to feel like any payment, large or small, was insignificant.

I remember the day I was riding in the car with one of the people that I supposedly owed. In quiet desperation, I asked. . . .. *"How long it take for me to pay you back?"* I held my breath for the answer. Without flinching, I heard the word. . . *"Forever!"* All hope died in me and for the next ten years, I marked time until God delivered me from the relationship altogether. As it turned out, there was no debt. There was no love either. I stepped into freedom with a ton of wisdom in my hands; wisdom learned from my time with oppressors.

God gave a gift of grace to each of His children that we cannot possibly repay. He begs us not to even try, to just accept it and dance in the joy of being loved. But, such a gift makes the best of us squirm. We'd rather earn it, which is ludicrous. How many people distrust the news of the Gospel and, instead, want to work to earn their good standing with God. Their pride is offended that nothing they have, or might give, is good enough for God. Grace just can **not** be earned by the most impressive act of charity. Jesus paid my debt and to try to earn it __my__ way is to say that He died for nothing.

God does not give to entrap but to free. Paul called himself a 'bond-servant of Christ.' This had no negative stigma. How could it? The one whom he was forever indebted was safe to love, safe to need, and worthy of whatever allegiance to Christ would cost him.

"I owe You my life!" Oh, how different that feels than to be enslaved by men. It's light in my spirit. Amen

"AND, DON'T YOU EVER FORGET IT!"

Or who has given a gift to him that he might be repaid?
Romans 11:35

Yesterday's devotional brought so much mail! I'm not alone in having felt enslaved by a debt. Some of you shared that you are trying to pay back an emotional debt you never asked to assume. Others of you borrowed money from a friend or family member and you can't wait until you make your last payment. The unexpected relational toll has been way too expensive.

To give a gifts with no strings is rare. Our need to be larger than life can cause us to give to others with an expectation for ego stroking. We want to be the hero. The greater we sacrifice, the bigger the hero we get to be! What gets in the way though, is the recipient's unwillingness to cooperate with our emotional extortion.

God is not like us. And His gift is truly priceless.

When man gives a sacrificial gift, sometimes he never lets you forget it. When God gives a sacrificial gift, He gives us the freedom __to__ forget it but hopes we won't. He doesn't have an ego to feed.

- Man can punish when he perceives ingratitude by withdrawing his love when he doesn't get back what he thinks he deserves. God hopes we'll worship Him in return for the great gift of His Son but loves us even when we don't.

- Man can keep talking about his gift, keeping us on his hook for perpetual praise. God tells us that we owe no debt. Jesus paid it all.

I love the way God gives. Once I've tasted the freedom He offers me, I can see my enslavement to others. What would happen if I stop the cycle and refuse to enable their addiction to praise? Yes, they gave a gift. I humbly said *"thank you."* Beyond that, I should not be enslaved emotionally to someone who gives or withholds love depending on whether or not I will feed their narcissism. This is not of God and He will not share His glory with anyone.

You love our gratitude but not our servitude. I love the gift of Jesus but can't possibly repay you. I thank you with my life. Amen

CHAPTER 12

THE DESPERATE ACT OF BEGGING

I appeal to you therefore, brothers, by the mercies of God, to present your bodies as a living sacrifice, holy and acceptable to God, which is your spiritual worship. Romans 12:1

*I*n this next chapter, Paul is starting to teach us how to live as a believer of Jesus. Everything up until now has been foundational. He begins his teaching with the word *'urge'*. It really means *'plead'* or *'beg'*. This is a very strong way to start out, isn't it?

I'm trying to think if I have ever really begged someone for something. The thought has always been distasteful to me because of how I was raised. In fact, my sister and I were not allowed to dress up and go out on Halloween because we were told that to go to someone's door and ask for candy would be begging. It was nothing but pride that created such a rule. So rigid was the rule of begging that we thought twice before asking our parents for anything.

To beg is to put your heart on the line. The one who is being pleaded with has a lot of personal power at that point. They can refuse which leaves the one who pleaded pretty wounded and vulnerable.

I was shocked this morning to discover how many times Paul used the word *'urge'* throughout his writings. He pleaded with his converts on so many issues. Yet, Paul has been accused of having no heart! I don't think so.

Why would Paul have to plead with me to present my life as a living sacrifice to God? Wouldn't my gratitude over having been rescued from eternal condemnation cause me to give Him my life? It should. So, if I'm selfish with my life, if I see 'dying to live' as a repulsive prospect, the problem is really my understanding of God's mercy. No wonder Paul said, *"In view of God's mercy, present your bodies."*

For much of my life, I've lived pretty comfortably. Because of that, I will not easily get the message that I am a condemned woman, Hell-bound, without Jesus. Because my salvation involved a simple prayer, I didn't see the fires of Hell looming. I didn't see myself on the precipice of being cast there forever. I also didn't see the death of

Jesus firsthand; the bloody ordeal, the betrayal of someone perfect, and the love He gave to enemies. I can ascribe to the tenets of Christianity without ever entering into the truth of the story emotionally.

Without the Spirit of God showing me what mercy cost Jesus, I will not offer myself as a living sacrifice.

Talk to me about Your mercy until I see 'dying to self' as my heart's only response. Shake me up until I get it. Amen

METAMORPHOSIS

Do not be conformed to this world, but be transformed by the renewal of your mind, that by testing you may discern what is the will of God, what is good and acceptable and perfect. Romans 12:2

As a good Christian, I may act like I'm not conformed to this world but if people could see everything I'm thinking; they'd know that my actions are only putting on a good show. My thoughts are still trapping me, tormenting me, and deceiving me. I live in a constant battle and only because I know how I _should_ think and what I _should_ believe do I do the right thing. But here's the thing ~ Christianity, the real thing, is not about just modifying my behavior. God promises transformation of the mind; total renewal. No more putting on good behavior out of a need to look good or a need to assuage my guilt.

If I fail to engage in this renewal process and continue to think like the world thinks, who is in charge? Paul, himself, revealed the answer in another letter. .. *"In which you once walked, following the course of this world, following the prince of the power of the air." Eph.2:2* The author of the world's thinking is not the world. May I not be deceived! The author is Satan himself. I am allowing the enemy, my enemy and Jesus' enemy, to infiltrate my mind and dictate how I'm going to process life. No wonder my mind can be a series of traps, never bringing peace and hope.

What does God offer each of His children? Transformation. The word is the same as metamorphosis. And that word is the same for what happened to Jesus in the transfiguration. *"And He was transfigured before them and His face shone like the sun." Matt.17:2* He underwent a physical and spiritual transformation that defied anything human. This is the kind of spiritual surgery God promises me if I engage Him on a process of mind renewal.

How does it happen? How can I stop believing that others should like me? How can I stop believing that a family situation is hopeless? How can I stop fearing that I am unforgiven or being punished? 1. By recognizing that such thinking is of Satan, the one who authors the world's mindset. 2.) By recognizing that my mind is still darkened and why. 3.) By fully desiring and engaging in the renewal process through the Word of God. 4.) Realizing that all spiritual rebirth and metamorphosis happens as a result of the power of the Word plus the breath of God's Spirit bringing about change.

What is the result? Yes, transformation. But really, our own transfiguration! Is your mind revolting at that supposedly sacrilegious idea? Embrace the possibility. Here's the promise. *"And we all, with unveiled face, beholding the glory of the Lord, are being transformed into the same image from one degree of glory to another. For this comes from the Lord who is the Spirit. Therefore, having this ministry by the mercy of God, we do not lose heart." 2 Cor. 3:18-4:1*

> *Oh Jesus, is it true? That thinking like you allows others to behold Your glory? I want it. And it's by living in Your words and letting Your Spirit breathe over my mind and heart. Do it now with these verses, Lord. Amen*

THE MINDSET OF HUMILITY

For by the grace given to me I say to everyone among you not to think of himself more highly than he ought to think, but to think with sober judgment, each according to the measure of faith that God has assigned. Romans 12:3

When I am good at something and people admire my gift, conceit will most likely be birthed. Being able to do something that is unique and admirable is a powerful cocktail. Where is the line of thinking too much of myself? Am I allowed to be confident in what I do? Am I allowed to graciously accept a compliment? What is humility anyway?

These questions are ever in front of me. I have a public gift. I have had my share of standing ovations. I have seen hundreds of women come forward after teaching for an hour. I receive many emails from those who read books and devotionals telling me that God used my words to make a difference in their lives. Am I allowed to enjoy others praise?

Paul encourages me to think of myself with sober judgment. In other words, I take stock of my gifts, the ones that cause others to be so generous with their feedback. If I played the piano at 3 yrs. old, who gave the gift? If I have long fingers that can play technical passages, who made my hands? If I have the stamina to sustain a 36-year ministry, who gave me health? If my teaching is persuasive, who inspired the ideas and anointed my lips to speak?

To think of myself soberly is to come to a realization of the truth that God gives all things, even my very breath. To boast in myself is to pretend that I am the one who generates gifts. I am not. I will not steal the glory of my God. As soon as I accept the praise that belongs to God, I have crossed the line.

However, to defer all glory to God does not mean that I hang my head and live in a state of worthlessness. It does not mean that I should refuse all compliments and stifle the enthusiasm of the ones who want to express thanks. It is to live with an awareness that all that I have, all that I am, and all that I can do is a result of grace and favor. If I fully believe that, then self-exaltation is an impossibility.

On the flip side, I can fail to fully embrace God's gifts in me and declare that I'm really not all that good at anything. I can live with a nagging sense of insecurity. This is not humility. This is a form of pride. I am putting my low opinion of myself above God's calling. I insist that my view of myself is right and His is wrong by how I think, feel, and choose to live.

Humility ~ along with a confidence in who God made me to be ~ are actually the perfect pairing.

Oh Father, teach me more. Amen

I'M NOT REALLY OVER IT SOMETIMES!

Who are you to pass judgment on the servant of another? It is before his own master that he stands or falls. And he will be upheld, for the Lord is able to make him stand.
Romans 12:4

What God leads my conscience to do, or not do, is entirely specific to me. The problem comes when I feel that every other child of God should make the same choices. My father in law, the evangelist Jack Wyrtzen, came to Christ out of a culture of dance bands and nightclubs. He was a musician and played in a band. Every time he heard jazz, the sound took him back to the clubs he had left behind for Jesus. To him, jazz was a stumbling block. Jazz however, in and of itself, is a neutral thing. It is just music; an assembly of notes, rhythms, and instrumentation. How many churches have split over the issue of music styles when the real emphasis should be on the Spirit *behind* the music and whether the people who lead it have been anointed to do it. Talent and style of music are secondary issues.

In Paul's day, there were similar hot topics. Jesus' ministry was conducted almost exclusively within the Jewish community. Keeping kosher was an important part of Judaism. But Jesus stretched his fellow Jews out of their comfort zone when he and His disciples ate without washing their hands ceremonially. Jesus even sent His disciples into the town of Sychar (in Samaria) to buy food for lunch. A Jew would never touch food that a Samaritan had prepared. When the Pharisees erupted over Jesus and His group breaking the law, He answered them by attacking their legalism. *"You nullify the word of God by your tradition." Mark 7:13* Then He talked to them about their hearts, that it's what in the heart that makes a man clean or unclean. But we've always tried to make our Christianity about external things; what we do and don't do.

Having grown up in legalistic circles, there were many rules. Don't go to the theatre because someone seeing you exit won't know if you saw a PG or an R movie. Don't order a glass of wine at dinner because someone watching won't know if you drink excessively in the privacy of your own home. Don't even play the game of Rook in your own home because someone driving by might see you playing cards and assume they're _real_ playing cards. Of course, as a teenager and young adult, the only things I _wanted_ to do were the things that were denied. Human nature.

Am I over legalism? Nope. I still fight it. The rules have just changed. I can avoid those circles who are legalistic and want little to do with them. My bias has done a 180 degree turn. That's just as sinful. God is constantly dealing with me about this. He often sends me to legalistic churches to bring the healing message of grace to them. By going, He also brings the healing message of forgiveness to myself. To teach them, I must forgive them. To be effective, I must love them. Oh, I'm a work in progress and it's humbling how far I have to go sometimes. You can pray for me.

Legalism kills. Others killed my faith but I often still do it to others in new and creative ways. Show me. Forgive me. Change me. Amen

WHAT IS A CHURCH?

For as in one body we have many members, and the members do not all have the same function, so we, though many, are one body in Christ, and individually members one of another. Romans 12:4-5

"I'm going to church" we say to one another. What we really mean is, *"We're going to a building, one where a group of people meet."* The only biblical definition of church is 'the meeting of a group of people who have put their faith in Christ – a meeting where

the Spirit of God rests.' A church can meet in restaurant, the basement of a school, in a home, or in an institutional building with a steeple. In the last few years, the resurgence of house churches are becoming more commonplace in the U.S. That is a good thing since I can easily become close-minded to such an idea in Western culture.

One disturbing thing though was revealed in a recent USA Today survey. Of the 56 percent of Americans who attend church, 46 percent do so because "It is good for me", and 26 percent go because it is where they hope to find "peace of mind and spiritual well-being." Specific doctrine does not appear important to most. Biblical literacy and conviction has given way to whether or not "I feel good" when I go. The entertainment factor, the programs, and who else attends have become determining factors.

Another distortion of true church practice is how we believe that our denomination is what makes up the *true* church. Baptists tell Presbyterian jokes; Catholics tell Protestant jokes, etc.

Donald Grey Barnhouse tells how he once made slighting remarks about a denomination he considered to be on the fringe of genuine Christianity. A minister from this denomination was present and afterwards told Barnhouse how grieved he was at what he considered an unjust judgment. Barnhouse apologized, and it was agreed that he would meet for lunch with four or five ministers from this particular church.

When they got together, Barnhouse, who had suggested the luncheon, made the additional suggestion that during lunch they should discuss only the points on which they agreed. Afterwards, when they had finished, they could talk about their differences. They began to talk about Jesus Christ and what he meant to each of them. There was a measure of joy as each confessed that Jesus was born of a virgin, that he came to die for our sins and then rose again bodily. Each acknowledged Jesus Christ as Lord. They confessed that he had sent his Holy Spirit at Pentecost and that the Lord was living in each of his children by means of the Holy Spirit. They acknowledged the reality of the new birth and that they were looking forward to the return of Jesus Christ, after which they would be spending eternity together.

By this time the meal was drawing to a close. And when they turned to the matters that divided them, they found that they were secondary and they recognized that they were areas in which they could agree to disagree without denying that each was a believer.

So I ask myself some questions at the end here. 1.) Do I have a denominational prejudice? 2.) Am I part of a group of true believers where the Spirit rests? 3.) Am I nit-picking on peripheral issues? 4.) Am I able to feel joy when I meet other believers who are different than me? Jesus has a lot to teach me about the world-wide church and how it looked at Pentecost.

How it looked at Pentecost will be how it looks in heaven.
Prepare me to love all that now. Amen

SPIRITUAL GIFTS AND SPIRITUAL IGNORANCE

Having gifts that differ according to the grace given to us,
let us use them. . . Romans 12:6

Every single child of God is given at least one spiritual gift. I should not be exercising my gifts out of my own wisdom or as a lone ranger. I am to be part of a community where my gifts contribute to their well being and where their gifts contribute to mine. We make up the body of Christ. When one part doesn't function properly, there is a spiritual limp the whole group experiences.

As I talk with women, I find that so many have no idea what their spiritual gift is. Why is this? Because we have not been defined. We don't know who we are. Because of parental voids, we were not told how, and why, we are special. We have never experienced, as children, hearing how we are 'bent' by God's design. We grew up without a keen sense of self-awareness, without clear direction. We floundered into adulthood. We had no plans for ourselves and ended up following other's plans. People are not good taskmasters and we ended up disillusioned and suspicious.

None of us have to live in a parental void when God is our Father. He can penetrate the deafening silence of our childhoods with the clear direction of His Spirit. He is willing, and eager, to define us. The prayer, *"Show me who I am and how I'm wired. . .."* is answered with great detail.

Here is a link to a great spiritual gifts test. http://buildingchurch. net/g2s.htm Spending some time in prayer before taking it will sensitize us to the right answer. If we don't approach the test prayerfully, we will be prone to answer how we 'think we should answer' rather than by thinking freely with the Holy Spirit's help.

It's never been more critical for us to know who we are so that we can plug into our spiritual destiny. Every single gift, in every single saint, is needed in these last days. However, when I live each day like the last, numbed out to the call of God on my life, I miss the joy of doing what I was wired to do. There is nothing more exhilarating than knowing how God has gifted me, then hearing Him tell me when and how to use it. When I get the green light, my way is fueled with joy and confidence. God has already created an opportunity and left the spot open for me. Insignificance is never meant to touch any child of the kingdom.

Redeem the years. I lived in a vacuum and was lost as a person. Now, you are showing me the joy of living as You designed. There's no other way for me! Amen

I SPEAK FOR WHOM?

Having gifts that differ according to the grace given to us, let us use them: if prophecy, in proportion to our faith. . .
Romans 12:6

I can't believe it. The implications of being a prophet have washed over me this morning. A prophet is anyone who speaks the word of God. That would not be relegated to a few elite but to every child of God. So, that's me. In God's physical absence here on earth, I stand in for Him and speak on His behalf. What a sensational calling I enjoy and a sobering one, too.

The Greek word for prophet means 'one who stands in front of another person and speaks for him." Remember the story of Moses and Aaron? Moses fainted at the call of standing before Pharaoh and delivering the message God gave him. So, God allowed Aaron to speak for him. *"See, I have made you like God to Pharaoh, and your brother Aaron will be your prophet." Exodus 7:1*

Really, this could be re-phrased for any of us today who are speaking God's words into our life's situations. We are praying scripture over loved ones, speaking for God in church meetings, proclaiming kingdom principles inside a boardroom, and sharing the Gospel with a neighbor. *"See, I am making you like God to _____, and you are my prophet."*

If I had had a real burning bush experience, heard the voice of God calling me to be His prophet, how much differently would I view my purpose and significance? Probably a lot. But I must realize today that in God's perspective, I have been called like Moses. I am to bring the Gospel to those in my path and lead them from the slavery of sin. There should be no Pharaoh in their lives except the allegiance they give to their Lord and Master, Jesus Christ.

No wonder we are to consecrate our heart, our thoughts, and then our words to God. Reckless words reap huge consequences as I speak for God. He takes it seriously when I spout off without thinking, without prayer, and misrepresent who He is. If I've been careful before now and in awe of the privilege of being one of His spokesmen, my fuses have been blown today in a new way. I realize that when I speak for God, I've become His personal mouthpiece.

Only with fear, and trembling, and complete dependence on You leading me by the hand, Lord. Amen

LEADING THROUGH SERVING

Having gifts that differ according to the grace given to us, let us use them. . . if service, in our serving. Romans 12:6-7

I knew a period of time, four months in all, where Jesus washed my feet when I closed my eyes to pray. I saw Him stooped in front of me, sitting on a stool, washing my feet. He was in no hurry. Time stood still. He said nothing but just tenderly served me. The humility of His service and the power of His tenderness changed me profoundly. It has had ripple effects on my heart over the years; my willingness to forgive others being the biggest change.

The Son of Man did not come to be served, but to serve. Matt.20:28 The spiritual gift of serving is one that is so beautifully demonstrated through the acts of Jesus. He did it – even while silent.

Most leaders lead by making a lot of noise and standing out in front of others; beckoning them to follow. Serving as Jesus served doesn't look like that. If I'm going to serve as Christ did, I don't see myself at the top and others beneath me. I am their servant. I assess their needs and quietly minister to them.

William Booth, the founder of the Salvation Army, told his missionaries on the way to India: *"Go to the Indians as a brother, which you are, and show the love which none can doubt you feel. Eat, drink, and dress and live by his side. Speak his language, share his sorrow."*

Dietrich Bonhoeffer said, *"The church is herself only when she exists for humanity. She must take her part in the social life of the world, not lording it over men, but helping and serving them."*

I got a lump in my throat recently when I learned that our pastor served an elderly woman in our congregation by taking her sick cat to the vet. Ah yes, exactly the kind of service that leaves the aroma of Jesus.

I have to have a surrendered ego to serve others. To shut my mouth, forget the world's definition of leadership, and quietly share life with my brother or sister requires the grace of humility. Jesus will help me. He was tempted in every way as I am to seek a power that is too good to serve but the temptation didn't ensnare Him. He was meek, held His tongue except when His Father prompted Him to speak, and touched, fed, comforted, and healed. All without fanfare. When others would exalt Him to make Him king, He retreated.

Applause is the most confusing thing in my world. You have to sort this all out for me, Lord. Show me where, and how, to serve quietly. Amen

THE GIFT OF COURAGE

Having gifts that differ according to the grace given to us, let us use them. . . the one who exhorts, in his exhortation.
Romans 12:6, 8

Encouragers are hard to find. Discouragers are everywhere. One look, one word of criticism, and someone already fragile wants to throw up their hands and quit. Yet, when most of us think of the rare person who encourages, we tend to picture a person who compliments and gives positive feedback. That is such a weak translation of what Paul (and God) really meant for us to do for one another.

Oh, it's so much deeper. It means 'to give courage, console, counsel, and advocate.' Can I say that I know many of these kinds of people? And can I say that I am one?

I have to know someone well to give them comfort. I must know their life, their work, and enough about their family to understand where their sources of joy and pain exist. To know where to infuse spiritual courage, I have to be intuitive; knowing with just a look that they are not right on a given day. If they put on a good face, I will hopefully see through it and not let it slide. Ron and I teach a Sunday School class. Do we have a generic *"Good morning!"* and *"Good to see you!"* or are we engaging like Christ would be if He was the teacher?

The biblical bar is so high for how an encourager is defined that many churches are exposed for having only a few, or perhaps even none. If we're drowning in our own challenges and don't know how to live in the life of Christ, then we have no courage to give away. We can't give what we don't possess! We will be nothing more than parrots of clichés.

I am rich with encouragers. And because I have experienced the power of Jesus in their gifts to me, I love to encourage. I can't wait to meet women on the road, hear their stories, ask them where they struggle, and leave them with the strong words of Christ for where they faint. The promises of God, strategically spoken from one who lives prayerfully, are the lifelines others need.

Oh, make me more intuitive about people. Holy Spirit, speak to me about their heart, what their faces are saying. Our of your vast resources, let my speech pour out your love, counsel, and courage. Amen

WHEN I'M NOT A GIVER

Having gifts that differ according to the grace given to us, let us use them. . . The one who contributes, in generosity. . . Romans 12:6-8

There was an old man in the small town where I grew up who was quite wealthy. His life's goal was to amass a fortune and he didn't care how he did it. Was he driven by greed? In his case, no. Fear was his taskmaster. He lived through the depression with a mother and several siblings. Hungry, he had gone to work at seven years old to deliver papers in order to put some food on the table. He had taken a vow to never be poor and his entire life was shaped by those words.

In practice, he was stingy. If he gave you ten dollars, it was with strings attached. He expected repayment of some type; he was so afraid of having nothing in his hands.

Paul describes the Christian as one who is never skimpy. (One of the Greek implications of generous.) He loves to give and just can't help himself. He almost dances in celebration when the opportunity comes his way.

I think I know what you're thinking. *"I don't give like this. In fact, far from it. What's my problem?"*

Like the man who was afraid of having nothing, there are many reasons why I don't give generously. Fear of deprivation, fear of giving away something that I'm attached to, fear that it won't be received, fear that I will get nothing back. Greed is not always at the center of why a person withholds.

What is the cure? Ah, one I didn't expect to find this morning. *You will be enriched in every way to be generous in every way, which through us will produce thanksgiving to God. 2 Cor. 9:11* God promises, through Christ, to make us *so* rich that we'll give it away – confident that He will more than compensate. And when we give so recklessly, others will not understand it and be prone to give glory to God.

If I'm not a good giver, for whatever reason, it is only because I have not fully realized how much God has given me and how much I have yet to claim. How well do I know His promises? There are many resources from heaven's bank account that I've not drawn upon. How much have I received of His healing? He is not repelled by any need when I bring my broken heart to Him.

Only when I stop living as an orphan, looking to the earth to give me what I need and look to my Father whose arms are full of gifts, will I be overwhelmed by His generosity. I'll know I'm on the right track when I just have to share it with somebody. Until then, I've only just begun to realize what is mine in Christ.

I know some people who love to give. I think they love to do it more than I do. I'm looking hard at the reasons, Lord.
Amen

WHAT DID I SIGN UP FOR?

Having gifts that differ according to the grace given to us, let us use them. . . the one who leads, with zeal.
Romans 12:6, 8

If I am given something to manage and I've accepted the responsibility, I should do it well. The paperwork shouldn't sit on my desk, hidden under a stack of other things I'd rather do. When I don't turn things in on time, return phone calls, and administrate what I've agreed to organize, I leave a bad spiritual taste in other's mouths. If

I don't care, and I am Jesus' ambassador, then others conclude that *He* doesn't care either.

When Paul wrote these words, he was writing to people who lived under a different kind of local government. There were no hospitals, orphanages, or rescue missions. Extending compassion and mercy to those who needed it advanced the kingdom. People within the church were given responsibility to take care of people in their villages and cities, even cities like Rome. When their spiritual enterprise was well ordered, the love of Christ was on beautiful display and the flavor of the Gospel exploded.

God is not a God of confusion and whatever He does, He does well. If He redeems just one area of my life, there are always dozens of side-benefits. He gives even more than He promises because His nature is to bless.

What is on my plate today? Have I missed deadlines? Am I doing what has been promised but with an attitude of forced joy? Perhaps what I signed up for wasn't God's plan for me. I took the job because I felt pressured or because I have an issue with saying 'no'. This is a tough spot to be in because if God never called me to the work, then He hasn't given me His joy and energy for the task. I should finish the job and learn my lesson. A life lived prayerfully, only doing what my Father has designed for me, is to be able to tap into the resources He promises when I obey Him.

Bad work ethics associated with any man or woman of God is a tragedy. It shouldn't be. The tentacles to this are many. I look at my calendar. I ask the Lord to give me the ability to put holy order to what's ahead. If I'm on a church staff, I look at my church. Does it reflect good organization? Those who walk the halls can tell if we care; if our heart is in our work. Right now, our church here in Athens, GA is coming out of a deep sleep and a hard time in their personal history. Grateful now for the move of the Spirit, there is already talk of cleaning up Sunday School rooms, repainting, and allowing the new work of the Spirit in the hearts of people to be on full display in the esthetics of the building. Exactly!

Whatever I lead, may it be what God called me to lead. Whatever He called me to lead, let me stay on my knees until I have the zeal that makes others sense that the Spirit of God is with me. A good leader doesn't have to say much when He is anointed. Others just step onto the pathway behind him.

I used to have a calendar ~ full of things I dreaded. Thank you for taking them all away and teaching me how to live. Now, I love what I do and can't wait for each morning. Make me an excellent kingdom worker for Your glory!
Amen

MY CHURCH FACE

Let love be genuine. Abhor what is evil; hold fast to what is good. Romans 12:9

Genuine. Sincere. These should be the last words I see on a 3×5 card before getting out of my car and going out in public. The world is often a stage and 'nice' is the mask I wear as a Christian. Do others experience me as sincere?

Sincere is based on Latin words meaning 'without wax'. There was an ancient practice of using wax to hide cracks in inferior pottery so that it could be disguised as more valuable and sold for a higher price. A high-end piece of pottery had a stamp on it that said, *"Without wax"* to show that it had not been doctored. As a person, I want to be sincere, not just hiding my true nature and true feelings.

What would happen if our home church, for one month, decided to drop all masks and dispense with polite chitchat? No, "Good to see you! You doing okay?" What if every conversation was thoughtful, intentionally real? What if there was no pressure to say something to every person that walked by? What if there was no pressure to smile?

How many people at my church know what I love and what I hate? How many people know what, about them, I sincerely love and appreciate? God is love, certainly, but he also hates what is evil. (Proverbs 6:16-19) Among the things that God hates is religion that is merely formal. (Isaiah 1:12-15) When I am nice to the point of saccharin, I am not like God. This is not love but like Greek theater where I pull out one of many masks to act in my play. This replaces real church where genuine encouragement and genuine burden-bearing are the ways I relate to others.

Children are never fooled by insincerity. *"Good to see you,"* along with a pat on the head, will never draw a child to your lap. They dismiss you and know what's up. I've noticed that you always know where you stand with a child. They tell you what they like about you and also what they dislike. Gabe, my six-year-old grandson, was visiting me a day last week. I was posting my day's devotional on my blog. He saw my picture in the upper corner and exclaimed, *"Nana! You don't look so OLD in that picture!"* I laughed. I didn't hold it against him. I knew it was true and I know he loves me.

I'm convicted. I've lived on a stage for most of my life and I think it's infected my 'persona' more than I've admitted. I'm trying something new next Sunday. I'm letting my 'child' out more, removing some of the filters. Stay tuned.

You weren't polite, Jesus. But oh how you loved. And how you offended. Show me what a gracious truth-teller looks like. Amen

HONORING WHO DISHONORS ME

Love one another with brotherly affection. Outdo one another in showing honor. Romans 12:10

The 'one another' is another member of God's family. But let's face it, God's family doesn't always act like family. There are times I believe I must look out for myself because others around me aren't going to do it. It's hard to fathom that God would ask me to honor all brothers and sisters above myself. Aren't there conditions for this?

Apparently not. God honored me, was faithful to me, when I was not faithful to Him. God loved me when I didn't love Him. God preserved my spirit through treacherous times even though I wounded His Spirit. In this way, He showed me how to love, with action, the other members of His family that He loves. Even in their disobedience.

Recently, I saw a friend pray for someone who was extremely jealous of her. Tearfully, she asked God to bless her and reveal Himself to her. And He did. God rewards those who obey.

Every one of us have been slighted, passed over, ignored, criticized, belittled, and treated as one 'not precious' by someone in the family of God. You, like me, probably said under your breath, *"They're not much of a Christian!"* This morning, I must say that I'm not much of one at times either. Am I willing to honor those I'm not fond of with sincere encouragement, with prayers for God to touch their heart profoundly?

The best example of Jesus honoring those who dishonored Him was the scene at the cross. As He looked out in a haze of pain, He saw his own kinsmen who had betrayed Him. He saw the disciples who had deserted Him. He saw the faces of the Roman soldiers who hated Him but whom He loved anyway. His prayer of honor was this: *"Forgive them. They know not what they do."* And then He gave His life for their sins.

Whatever I do to honor any difficult person is miniscule in comparison to that. Remembering that will fuel my heart with the spiritual energy needed to imitate the One who is so good to me, still.

You've never dishonored me. You never stopped loving me and reaching out to me, even while I was wounding You.
Amen

SPIRITUAL STEAM

Do not be slothful in zeal, be fervent in spirit, serve the Lord. Romans 12:11

Fervent. To boil over. To have a spirit that is radiant. What causes that?

Sometimes I fervent because I feel it. Sometimes I appear to be fervent because I've learned to fake it. Sometimes I'm not fervent and am too *tired* to pretend. Spiritual steam, the kind that propels a train up a mountain is hard to know how to come by. Does reading more of my Bible give it to me?

I can learn something about WWII history, get excited, and then passionately share it. But that's one piece of history and the news will get old. Bible study (apart from the reality of Jesus revealing Himself to my heart) is this way as well. I can discover something in scripture, love what I find, but the series of facts will dissipate with time. When I'm hurting, interesting facts from the book of I Samuel won't give me spiritual fervor.

The steam needed for the long haul comes from something childlike. Love. When I'm tired from service, I need to go home to be loved. When I'm beaten up by life, I need to go home to be loved. When I'm physically weak from the pace of meeting so many needs, I need to go home to be loved. The strongest saint retreats, comes to his Father with childlike faith and says, *"Feed me, love me, hold me, and teach me."* These elementary expressions of need fuel the ones we would label as having mature faith. Unlike what we might believe, their stamina does not come from some intellectual study of Calvinism vs. Arminianism.

Deep weariness borders on total abdication. I teeter on the edge of just giving up. One small demand can send me over the edge. My body won't cooperate anymore with my drill-sergeant-self-talk. It revolts. My heart doesn't have one more internal speech to keep myself going. Quitting seems to be the only answer. I am afraid though that if I sink into an abyss of emotional and physical exhaustion, I won't ever get out. Oh, I have been there and I didn't know what was wrong or how to heal.

God showed me. Mature faith begins and ends with the recognition that my fuel is the love of God. 'Living life loved' is the fuel for the body. It feels wonderful. It's the fuel for the mind. It fosters the spiritual curiosity for study. It's the fuel for the heart. I can't stop thinking about the One who loves me like no other.

We will get tired. When we reach that point, let's go home.

Your love resurrected me from the pit. A two-year pit. I had given up, had no energy or joy, but I had not experienced

Your love. Thank you for the joy of serving You now with a fervent spirit. Amen

<u>NOT THREE THINGS – BUT ONE</u>

Rejoice in hope, be patient in tribulation, be constant in prayer. Romans 12:12

"Just what I need," you might say. *"Three more things to do when I'm hurting. I must rejoice, be patient, and remember to pray. Life is hard enough without putting more demands on me."*

To assume that God is putting demands on me is to miss the beauty and power of this verse. They aren't three separate things, but one constant chain of eternal energy and empowerment. Here's how.

Rejoice in hope. I will start the chain as prescribed. When things are hard and I'm ready to give up, I will stop and remember what's ahead for me. Eternal life with nothing but joy. Seeing Jesus and living in the presence of His love. Wholeness of heart with no more fractures from the wounds from others. If I stop to remember what's ahead I will automatically have what's next.

Patience in tribulation. *"I can make it because. . ..."* will be the natural outcome of having made a mental list of what's ahead for me. Knowing what's at the finish line helps me endure and get a new blast of wind under my sails. But what happens when the wind dies down and weariness threatens to overtake me? I'm automatically go to what's next.

Constantly go to God in prayer. *"Help me! I'm tired again. I don't know if I can go on. Encourage me, Lord."* And then He rises up to remind me of my hope in Him. New pictures of His power to redeem. New visions of heaven. New reminders of what abundant life look like. On the other side of His whispers of encouragement, I automatically go to what's next.

I can rejoice in hope. And the cycle of continues.

God's voice can be heard through the words of Paul. *"Start the chain!"* I know that when I do, it sets in motion my journey through the way of escape. Deep soul-weariness will begin to dissipate if I believe God that this is the pathway out of inertia.

So, I will rejoice. Rejoicing leads to a short supply of energy. When that wanes, I pray. Prayer leads to rejoicing. And so on.

What often seems like a burdensome command is only a mirage. When I step through the door of obedience, a new world of understanding opens up to me. I wonder why I couldn't see it before. I had totally misunderstood the whole point. Experience is such a great teacher.

How quick I am to think You are unreasonable in what You ask of me. Forgive me. I forgot that You are the One who promised abundant life. When others only see pain, they have no idea the how rich I am in Spirit. Amen

PURSUE IT? SERIOUSLY?

Contribute to the needs of the saints and seek to show hospitality. Romans 12:13

Get ready. The picture here is one who *pursues* the opportunity to show hospitality. I can too easily be passive, waiting for the need to arise and land at my front door. I'll wait to be asked.

Outgoing people can throw a great party and love having a crowd in their home. But that doesn't mean that they are exuding the love and presence of the Spirit. Their reasons for having people in their home can be as carnal as the reasons someone who is shy *doesn't* think they can do it or do it well.

What does it look like for a child of God to pursue hospitality? I must know the goal. It's showing the love of God in simple ways and that involves so much more than providing a meal or giving someone a place to sleep for the night. Those are just the means to an end.

The way I receive someone at the door sets the tone for the encounter. Genuine warmth, a listening ear, a prayer offered at the right time, staying prayerful while they're in my presence; these are the things which leave the aroma of Jesus and cause someone to know that their time in my home was somehow different. The meal I made and fussed over should not be the focus.

There are definitely those who have the spiritual gift of hospitality and those who don't. But none are exempt. I shouldn't believe that I need a large extravagant home, instead of a modest one, to show the love of Jesus to others. Recently, I stayed in a beautiful lakefront home but my beautiful room was beside the point. I shared a meal with a retired couple that loved Jesus deeply; knew how to listen, ask questions, and then jump into spiritual conversations that left you wishing you had many more hours to talk. At the end, we exchanged book titles, website addresses, even specific bible passages that we had referenced in our fellowship.

The point is: There is someone nearby who needs a touch from God. My husband, Ron, has a beautiful gift of helps/hospitality. Each time we drive down our street, we pass the home of an elderly woman who can hardly get out anymore. Her husband died a few years back and she is admittedly lonely. He will often say as we drive by, *"Can you imagine how long the hours are as she sits, night after night, in that house by herself?"* He has bleached the mildew off her home, maintains her car that she can't drive anymore, and suggests times that we might bring her meals. Last week, he even surprised her on her birthday with her favorite Kentucky Fried Chicken meal.

Each of us can be hospitable and pursue opportunities. God will show us whether our ideas are His ideas. But I can love someone, with His hands, whether I live in a mansion or a cabin. What they remember won't be the surroundings but how their heart felt when they sensed Jesus was in our conversation. Jesus made even introverts to be a people-persons. He will show us how and it will be a beautiful thing for each one of us and for the one who receives what God has led us to give.

Be the unseen, yet keenly felt, spiritual guest in whatever
You lead me to do. Amen

CAN I REJOICE ALONE?

Rejoice with those who rejoice, weep with those who weep.
Romans 12:15

To weep with someone who weeps is far easier than to celebrate with someone who rejoices. I believe that the one who weeps needs me and the one who rejoices doesn't. Feeling needed affirms my value. Watching another rejoice, and believing they will do so with or without me, can threaten my ego.

There's nothing lonelier than celebrating alone.

- Have you ever shared good news with someone who is jealous of you? You might have heard, *"Well, __that__ must be nice. I can't imagine that happening to me!"*
- Have you ever shared good news with someone who is distracted? They may never even look up from the paper or look away from the television. *"That's nice,"* they say.
- Have you ever shared good news with someone who was depressed? You probably tempered your joy in the face of their sadness.
- Have you ever shared good news with someone who needed to shrink the significance of your miracle? *"Be careful you don't put too much stock in that! It might not last."*

Oh, for those who will enter into another's joy. I can perceive that I'm not needed but the truth is, perhaps sharing their joy is more important to them than sharing their tears. While I should not make this scripture an either/or command, I feel led to remind myself this morning that there are those who are rejoicing alone. I can believe that they don't need me. They do! Their rejoicing *could* be turned to sorrow and bitterness as they wonder, *"Why isn't anyone happy for me?"* That always leads to, *"Why doesn't anyone love me?"*

So, take someone out to lunch to celebrate God's blessing. Bring them a cupcake and light a candle. Send a card. Make a telephone call. Hug them tightly and cry for joy. I can't assume others will flood them with these gestures. Just maybe they are alone. What should be a cause for a party might become the catalyst for their rejection. Whether they weep, or sing, I want them to know they're not alone.

If I withhold my joy from someone You have chosen to bless, I really have a problem with You. The next time I'm stingy, help me work this out in prayer. Amen

UNIFORM THINKING

Live in harmony with one another. Do not be haughty, but associate with the lowly. Never be wise in your own eyes.
Romans 12:16

Harmony doesn't mean keeping the peace and making compromises Jesus wouldn't make. He was Wisdom so He knew when to stand in truth and incur a holy division between right and wrong and when to bring factions together that were separated over non-essential issues.

To have the mind of Christ is to have His thinking on these very issues. He promises this holy wisdom to any of us who seek it. Most of our churches know division, quarreling, and standoffs over important and unimportant things. Leaders wring their hands and lose sleep over the choice of whether to bring harmony (whatever that looks like) or become resolute and let truth do its sifting.

This dilemma usually brings a cobweb of uncertainty. Should all the members of a church agree on **all** theological issues? No. The basic doctrines *are* non-negotiable. Peripheral issues however **should be** left to the convictions of each saint who seeks the Spirit for counsel. A healthy church holds fast to the tenets of the Gospel but encourages diversity on lifestyle, forms of worships, and other such issues.

I will tell you that I have seen many Christian organizations insist on uniform thinking – all the way around. They hire people, install board members, and clone themselves quite artfully. What they forfeit is freedom in the Spirit to change with the times. While the Gospel never changes, the mediums through which it communicates does.

Many of you who are reading this are gifted in administration. You are skilled, naturally, at bringing people together, finding common ground, in order to work together toward a goal. You are peacemakers. The challenge is to know when harmony is achieved at too great a price; truth was diluted and evil is blurred in order to hold hands.

Biblical harmony, the kind Paul encourages, is when I love Christ and listen to His Spirit, and you love Christ and listen to His Spirit, and find that our hearts are knitted together in His love and truth. Any other kind of harmony is quite fragile and ultimately short lasting.

I will guard the relationships where Your harmony exists. I will also stop trying to patch up what needs to be separated. Give me Your wisdom. Amen

BENT TOWARD ONE OR THE OTHER

If possible, so far as it depends on you, live peaceably with all. Romans 12:18

"If possible, live peaceably." That means that sometimes it's **not** possible. Other times though, it is and I should seek it.

I grew up in a church environment, and in a family, where peace at any price was practiced. All conflict was seen as bad. It created such discomfort that I watched my parents do whatever they needed to do to quickly recover harmony. They did this at the expense of themselves, their loved ones, and of truth.

Tragedy exists when I want peace more than I want truth! This has absolutely nothing to do with Paul's words today. The behavior of people around me may negate peace and, in fact, make peace impossible because they don't follow Christ. Truth cannot be sacrificed for peace. *James 3:17 "But the wisdom from above is first pure, then peaceable. . ."* Truth always comes first and must precede harmony. If I love Jesus, then I love everything He loves; honesty, justice, truth, and this may make peace unattainable. I live in a wicked world where evil exists and I should resist it at all costs.

The flip side however, is that I may be an angry person who loves to pick a fight. I have an argumentative spirit and love to play devil's advocate. This is not a fight for truth but a need to be right. My standards and expectations of others are out of line and I can insist on things that aren't realistic or holy. *Prov. 10:12 "Hatred stirs up strife, but love covers all offenses." Prov. 12:16 "The vexation of a fool is known at once, but the prudent ignores an insult."* If I love a good fight (which I don't), then those around me might enjoy the art of sparring. *"Prov. 17:14 "The beginning of strife is like letting out water, so quit before the quarrel breaks out."*

I am praying for you as you read this. If you are in a needed fight for holiness, then I pray that you won't listen to the enemy when he tells you that you are just a quarrelsome person. How Satan would love to have us twist these two pictures. For each of you who are quarrelsome, he'd love for you to believe that your crusade is a holy one.

For each of us who must sacrifice harmony for something *Jesus* would fight for, may God give us courage, stamina, and boldness with our tongue. For each of us who alienate others, either with a need to nit-pick or be right, may we lay down our arms and pray for humility and a peaceable spirit. Only God's Spirit can show us *which one* we are!

I'm bent toward being peaceable at all costs. You are making me bold but I have a long way to go. I give you my tongue today as You give me your passion for truth. Amen

A PERFECT MOMENT TO STRIKE BACK

Beloved, never avenge yourselves, but leave it to the wrath of God, for it is written, "Vengeance is mine, I will repay, says the Lord." Romans 12:19

Kids learn quickly how to take revenge. When someone plays a practical joke on them, they may pretend that it didn't faze them but watch out. When the jokester is long past the joke he played and forgets to watch his back, revenge is taken. The payback is usually worse, too. That's because revenge is in our bones. It is our natural response to being hurt.

I was the brunt of many practical jokes, really bullying, in junior high and high school. Drugs were planted in my locker. The same group of kids who planted the drugs would often wait for me to leave the building to find my bus. They would splash me from head to toe with mud or empty my book bag and throw all my papers in the air. By the time I retrieved them, I had missed the bus. I dreamed of revenge but didn't know how to act it out since I was only one person and they were more than a half dozen.

You've heard of someone taking advantage of you when there's 'blood in the water'. You know the phrase? Like a shark who is drawn to a scene where there is already something wounded. Many of us have been hurt in our moments of weakness. Abuse happened when we forgot to lock the door. Break-ins happened when we were home alone. Those who wished to inflict a wound just intuitively knew that they would be far more successful if they struck at our weakest moment. It was cruel but effective.

So when might we be tempted to take revenge? In *their* weakest moment. We take out our anger on an aging parent who can no longer defend themselves. We wait for that moment when our 'enemy' needs from us what they refused to give. It's the perfect setup and unless we are Spirit-led, it is too great a temptation.

David knew the power of a perfect opportunity. On two occasions, it appeared that God had delivered him into Saul's hands. A sleeping king was an easy target. But David came upon him, looked, was tempted, but trusted His God to rule. He walked away.

Sooner or later, our enemies grow old. Grow weak. Get sick. Lose a child. Suffer unemployment. My response in that moment is what will reveal the real essence of my faith and trust in God. Will I strike when they're down, when there's blood in the water? Or will I walk away from the opportunity and leave the matter in God's hands.

Cruelty was heaped upon cruelty when you walked the road to Calvary. You could have struck back and rallied the armies of heaven. And oh, your revenge! But You left the matter to Your Father and blessed those who cursed You. Only by Your grace can I do the same. Amen

THAT'S IT! I'M DONE IN!

Do not be overcome by evil, but overcome evil with good.
Romans 12:21

I admit it. In the past, I had a 'quitters' mentality. Something too hard? Give up. One too many disappointments? Become cynical. Numerous criticisms? Give way to self-doubt. Prolonged crisis? Become numb and grit it out till it was over. In all cases, I checked out. I chose to go away inside and disengage. I was overcome by evil.

For a while in Jesus' ministry, there was a honeymoon stage. As long as he healed, many hailed Him King. As long as He fed them, they followed. After a while though, His message grew too controversial. The Gospel of repentance burned in their hearts and it was no longer intoxicating to be in His presence. They left Him in droves. He was not overcome. His family called him insane. He was not overcome. His home town no longer welcomed Him. He was not overcome. Judas, the one He had chosen and loved, betrayed Him. He was not overcome. The crowd begged for His life over the life of a common thief. He was not overcome. He was savagely beaten, made to carry his own cross beam, and then nailed to it in agony. He was not overcome. His Father turned His back on Him as He wore the sins of the world. He was not overcome.

Jesus chose to stay engaged. He did not check out emotionally. He never abandoned the redemptive process. He persevered because He understood the plan and saw redemption in the darkest deeds of mankind. Not only was He not overcome, He returned their evil with good. He offered a salvation to every enemy that He had to die to extend. No exceptions.

What is it that overwhelms me today? Am I tempted to quit? What troubled relationship has me believing that I can no longer cope? Am I tempted to abandon it? Where am I scorned or despised? Am I thinking of going away and abandoning them all emotionally? If Jesus was not overcome, will He not help me stay centered in the plot line of His sovereignty? And if He overcame evil with good, will He not flood my soul with a love that is bigger than me in order to love others into the kingdom?

So many questions, Lord Jesus, but I vow to answer every one in the way You modeled life for me. Amen

CHAPTER 13

USING FACEBOOK, EMAILS, AND BLOGGING RIGHTEOUSLY

Let every person be subject to the governing authorities.
For there is no authority except from God, and those that
exist have been instituted by God. Romans 13:1

When those in authority over me are righteous, I thank God for them and have no trouble believing that they are God's choice for rule. But when leaders are unrighteous, even evil, what then? Are they God-appointed? Do I have to obey them? And, if so, how far should my obedience go? Is it ever right to wage a rebellion? God is clear that he puts rulers of this world in their positions.

1. Pharaoh ~ Paul quotes God as telling Pharaoh, "For this very purpose I have raised you up, that I might show my power in you, and that my name might be proclaimed in all the earth." Romans 9:17
2. Nebuchadnezzar ~ He thought he was superior to Jehovah because of the size of the kingdom he had amassed. Yet, God reminded him that "the Most High is sovereign over the kingdom of men and gives it to whom he will." Daniel 4
3. Pilate ~ Speaking to Jesus under arrest, he said "Don't you know that I have the power to free you or to crucify you?" Jesus answered, "You would have no authority over me at all unless it had not been given you from above." John 19:11

As a citizen to a government that is morally corrupt, I am called by God to obey and show respect to their authority. God has put them there. They are but puppets in the big scheme of things; playing a part in God's sovereign plan.

But, my obedience is not unlimited. When they disobey God and rule unrighteously, God leads me to speak up and declare truth. However, He does NOT call me to lead a rebellion and take up arms. My sword is the Word of God. While I may strain under ungodly leadership, whether nationally or locally, or within a company I work for, I am called to obey company rules, pay taxes, honor speed limits, and show respect to God-appointed leadership.

With Facebook, blogging, and the ability to forward emails to thousands of people at one time, disrespect and name-calling for those in authority are rampant. Christians can be the guiltiest. A dozen times a week, caricatures of our President flood into my inbox; cartoons that name-call, ridicule, and malign. This is not of God. While I may not like many things that the President stands for, I should speak respectfully about the views he takes that are in opposition to the purposes of God. I am called to treat him honorably. Emails _should_ abound that encourage my friends to pray for those in leadership.

What any of us say on Facebook, or in emails, should be the same things we would have no trouble saying to our Father in prayer. Yet, I can be one way in prayer and a renegade with my pen; a divided kingdom that forfeits the blessing of God. May it not be.

There are times I cannot obey those in authority over me. But that does not erase my respectful talk of them. Even with the sword of Your truth in my mouth, let me deliver Your words as Moses did. Humbly, plainly, void of venom.
Amen

TWO SIDES TO THE COIN – LITERALLY

Therefore whoever resists the authorities resists what God has appointed, and those who resist will incur judgment.
Romans 13:2

If I disobey authority, my Father will discipline me. Every time I spurn it, I illegitimize the chain of command God instituted to those around me. So are there legitimate limits to my allegiance, especially when leaders are evil?

Anybody ever ask you a tough spiritual question, one that seemed like a trap? Answer one-way and you're ensnared. Answer the other way and you're also ensnared. Is there a way of escape? There is.

Jesus' enemies came to Him with such a trick question. *"Is it lawful to pay taxes to Caesar or not?" (Matt.22:17)* If he said yes, he would potentially alienate his own people who were doubled over with the heavy burden of taxation. They felt enslaved to Rome. On the other side though, if Jesus said no, that they should spurn Rome by refusing to pay taxes, then these enemies could quote him to the authorities and have him arrested.

At this point, Jesus asked for a coin. When they produced one, he asked whose portrait was on it and whose inscription. Perhaps he held it out to them so they could see it. *"Caesar's,"* they answered.

"Give to Caesar what is Caesar's," Jesus said. Many believe that he then turned the coin over and exposed the back. On it would have been a picture of a Roman god or goddess. Jesus added, *". . .and to God what is God's." (Matt 22:21)*

In other words, no child of God should serve Roman gods at the expense of betraying the *true* God of Israel ~ so at the point where my heart's devotion to glorify God is threatened, my limit to obeying earthly authority is revealed. I am to be an honorable citizen – to the glory of God – and there are times I must not submit to ungodly demands – to the glory of God.

This biblical principle goes far beyond obedience to national and local government. I should honor authority in my workplace, not undermining those who lead poorly. I should honor the lines of authority in my church, not going around those who are 'technically in charge' to do what I think needs to be done.

I visited a friend recently in another part of the country. She was sharing with me how uncomfortable she was with a woman in her church. The two of them served on a committee together and my friend was pressured to defer to her. She was a strong personality. And, she had been in the church longer and knew the pastor well. She was notorious for making her own plans, then just doing them without asking for permission. So my friend asked her, *"Shouldn't the pastor know about this and shouldn't we wait for his permission?"* She dismissed my friend's concern with a wave of her hand. *"I can get him to do what I want. He'll be fine."* Such a reckless, subversive attitude toward authority, and spiritual authority at that, brings God's displeasure and negative consequences.

Knowing when to honor Caesar and when to honor His Father did not trap Jesus. He promises this wisdom to me – if I ask.

Give guidance to so many who read this in countries overseas who face the threat of persecution if they obey You. This is not light reading. Oh God, I hold them up to You for strength and wisdom. Amen

THE CONSCIENCE OF A FOUR YEAR OLD

Would you have no fear of the one who is in authority? Then do what is good, and you will receive his approval, for he is God's servant for your good. . . Therefore one must be in subjection, not only to avoid God's wrath but also for the sake of conscience. Romans 13:3-5

A few days ago my four-year-old grandson visited me for several hours. After a particularly trying moment where he tested the limits of my authority, I informed him that he _would_ obey me and decided he was old enough to begin to understand why. I sat in my office chair, pulled him up on my lap and said, *"The only way you will be happy is to obey whoever is in authority. God made you that way. Even Nana has people to obey, did you know that? Policemen tell me what to do. Even Jesus tells me what to do. And when I hear His voice, my heart should say, 'Yes, Lord!' Nana is just miserable if I don't obey Jesus. I love you, Andy, and I want you to have a happy heart. Obeying me right now is so important."*

I'm not sure he had a breakthrough moment. This will be the beginning of many discussions like this but it's a beginning. Ultimately, any of us in authority over children should handle it carefully for we are training them to grow up and say, *"Yes, Lord!"* to whatever He asks of them. We don't want them to have to learn submission through the hard road of rebellion and discipline. Whatever we don't teach them well, God will. The lessons will be harder at 35 then they would have been at Andy's age. Let's spare them that.

How tender is my conscience? I believe there is a test.

How easily do I ridicule authority? When those in power are mostly ungodly, I can become cynical, then disrespectful.

How easily do I malign my parents? *"But they live in such a way as to earn my disgust,"* I might argue. Disgust and sadness over their ungodliness are two different things. If they live foolishly, and in spiritual blindness, does my heart grieve or does it ridicule and disregard?

How easily do I take a casual attitude toward those in church authority? I may like certain elders and deacons but question the wisdom of why others were appointed. Each one, regardless of whether or not I believe they are spiritually equipped, has had their position conferred upon them. Showing honor means I have a level of respect for the office they hold. Speaking respectfully of them, and to them, is doing so to God.

How much do I value the wisdom of the elderly and protect their quality of their lives? Am I appalled by the growing disregard of youth against the aged? *"Get off the road, old man!"* is the prevailing attitude of this age. Meanwhile, many have stored up the riches of wisdom learned from a lifetime of living. Even those who have a ton of regrets have a lot to teach me. Do my arms surround them with care and tenderness? Does my attitude reveal that they are of value to me? That will come out in dozens of ways when I'm in public.

Sin sears my conscience. I know the biblical principle. But I can be short-sighted about what causes it; what God considers sinful. The next time I roll my eyes at someone in legitimate authority over me, I will be pulled up short to see how teachable I am to change. May God help me. My tender heart is at stake.

I want a teachable, tender spirit when I'm 80, Lord. Show me where I lost the pieces of my conscience. Amen

HIDING FROM RESPONSIBILITY

Pay to all what is owed to them: taxes to whom taxes are owed, revenue to whom revenue is owed, respect to whom respect is owed, honor to whom honor is owed. Romans 13:7

Why is it? If financial times are difficult and there have been several missed payments on a mortgage, the tendency is to hide from the company when they call? To *not* take their call might be understandable if I'm having a bad day, but to repeatedly ignore their attempts to reach me is not *'giving them what I owe'*. If I don't have the money, money is – at that point – beside the point. What I owe them is the respect and honor of communicating. Hiding insinuates that I'm turning a blind eye to my responsibility.

Hiding is a perfected art. I can even hide from God when He comes calling. If I have failed to honor Him with my life, when honor was owed, then He attempts to speak with me about it. I hide by avoiding silence! I drown out His still small voice with activity, music, television, and perhaps even drugs and alcohol. Sitting clear-headed in the stillness of a beautiful spring day is way too much of a threat.

Hiding comes from fear. I know because I spent many years hiding from all kinds of things – and people. I hid because I feared I was inadequate and worthless. If I had to face creditors, or enemies, or conflict, which could lead to rejection, I believed that I was setting myself up for a confirmation that I was really a loser.

Hiding is what our human nature does when we have not experienced the security of being loved by God. Jonah hid. Adam and Eve hid. Elijah hid. Moses hid. When God called, eventually they came. They grew up, obeyed, stood in the love of God and faced incredible obstacles.

So, of what phone call am I afraid? Let me **rehearse it ahead of time.** *"Lord, I am loved by you and nothing can shake that. Because I love you, I will be responsible. You are my strength and my salvation. Whom shall I fear? You are the strength of my life. Of whom shall I be afraid."* Then pick up the phone. Communicate the challenges and good faith effort to repay what is owed.

And if it's God who comes calling, sin and failure are for-given in the arms of a Father who never turns me away no matter how badly I've blown it. Shame. You came to heal it. Will I let you touch all of it? Amen

I UNDERSTAND MY TIMES

Besides this you know the time, that the hour has come for you to wake from sleep. For salvation is nearer to us now than when we first believed. Romans 13:11

Am I fully awake? Has God caused my spiritual senses to arise out of twilight sleep? Like one who drives a ten-hour trip, I can numb out and not recall the last four hours of the trip. Unaware of the scenery. Unaware of traffic. Just marking time and watching the mile markers change. *'You know the time'* has biblical history. Oh, how I can't afford to miss it. It's not about eschatology either.

In Matthew 16, the Jewish leaders came to Jesus and asked for a sign, a sign that would confirm who He was and that what He was saying was true. Jesus was firm that there were signs all around them but they refused to see them.

An even better understanding of this phrase comes from I Chronicles 12. When David was king at Hebron, a group of war-riors came to his aid. (The men of Issachar predominantly.) They are described as those *'who had understanding of the times and knew what Israel should do.'* Is there anything better than keeping company with those who are spiritually astute, who know the mind and heart of God and are able to interpret the times and events! I shouldn't have to rely on those who have a prophetic gifting to understand God's heart on a matter. Yes, they possess a keen sense of God's thinking on issues but that wisdom is available to all who seek Him and seek the truth.

'Wake me up!' is what I'm praying. I don't want to be like someone who is falling asleep; slowly ceasing to hear the creaking in the floors and the din of noise from the other room. I want to put off the mindset of the world, which is hard to do if I'm on their

journey of moral and spiritual decline. If Jesus were to step into my world today, read the headlines, watch the news, visit a local school, how would He react to the spiritual condition of my city, my church, my children, my home life, my marriage, and to me – most of all? Would He tell me to wake up or would He just hone my present skills and make me a more effective watchman on the wall? I don't want to assume it's the latter. I'm asking Him about it and making sure my own sin isn't numbing out my spiritual senses.

I bind my mind to your mind. Amen

CHANGING MY CLOTHES

The night is far gone; the day is at hand. So then let us cast off the works of darkness and put on the armor of light.
Romans 13:12

The night, referring to this evil age, has about run its course. It's not the time to faint nor sink into despair over evil. I can perceive Jesus on the horizon. The coming Light of the world is like a racehorse at the starting gate, just waiting for His Father to say, *"Son, it's time!"* Can you hear Him panting? Can you feel His heart beating faster? He's eager. He's ready.

The genocide of Darfur? Over. Persecution and martyrdom of God's children in the world? Over. Youth taking guns to school to exact revenge? Over. Corruption in government, in business, in church leadership? Over. The things that make me double over in pain and weep? Over.

Today is not just another day on the calendar. It's a day nearing the end of our age. It elicits a strong response. It's not the time to weigh a sinful choice against a righteous choice and think, *"Ok, I guess I'll choose God's way."* That's way too casual an approach. Paul said to 'cast off darkness'. That's a strong picture. I am to open my eyes wide, see the day in front of me and cast off anything associated with this evil age; its mindset, its values, its shady temptations. I throw each thing off like a heavy coat someone wants me to wear when it's 100 degrees outside. I can't get it off fast enough.

What do I put on? I wear what God wears. ***Isaiah 59:17 He put on righteousness as a breastplate, and a helmet of salvation on his head; he put on the garments of vengeance for clothing and was clad with zeal as a cloak.***

To wear the armor of light with zeal is to walk through my day with the eyes of Christ, enacting the laws of the kingdom upon my world, defending truth where Jesus would defend it. When He saw that the moneychangers and sellers of livestock had overrun the temple and corrupted it with its dishonest business practices, He drove them out with whips. What He said, *"Stop turning my Father's house into a marketplace,"* had been prophesied in Psalm 69. *"My zeal for your house, O Lord, burns in me like fire."*

That same zeal is promised to me. Apathy is cast off. Zeal is put on like a cloak. I press close to Jesus ear to hear my last marching orders. He's poised and ready to come back, but while He waits for God's final word, He's gives last minute instructions to His church.

So, I'm listening. I will wear Him; wear His light. Light warms and invites but light also repels. I expect both in my world today.

Don't let me be taken back by the sparks of wearing Light. It is the time for boldness. And don't let me be taken back by the grief of zeal. Time is short and Your compassion is pro-active. Through me, you stand on the edge of my Jerusalem and weep. Amen

REMEMBERING WHO I AM

But put on the Lord Jesus Christ, and make no provision for the flesh, to gratify its desires. Romans 13:14

I live in the 'now but not yet' as a Christian. I am seated with Christ in the heavenlies but I also live *here*. I was made holy at my conversion but I am told to *be* holy. Satan was defeated on the cross but He won't *act* like he's defeated until He is judged at the last day and thrown into the lake of fire. I was clothed with Christ when I made Him my Savior but Paul reminds me to *put on* Christ daily.

This is the battle. What is a spiritual reality must be chosen, embraced, and intentionally lived out every day. This morning, I remember who I am.

- I am adopted, not an orphan.
- I am free, not a slave.
- I am forgiven, not condemned.
- I am dead to sin, not trapped by former habits and sinful thought patterns.
- I wear His robes of righteousness, not tattered robes of shame.

I see the day ahead of me. I review my new status as a child of God and decide to live like it. Knowing I can't do it by myself, I call upon the Spirit of God inside to rise up and enable spiritual life. I ask Him to flood my desires with His desires. I ask Him for the grace to be who I am. I put on Christ like a cloak and it is not a heavy overcoat. It is lightweight. It fits perfectly. I feel ten feet tall when I wear Him.

Since I am a child of the *'narrow way'*, I know that I will stand out like a sore thumb. I won't be making the choices of the majority. I won't be thinking like the masses. I will be peculiar. I will confuse. I will draw criticism. And for that, the Spirit is ever close to comfort and encourage. I won't be tripped up by other's rejection. I expect it and won't abandon the way of the cross when false expectations attempt to entrap me. To *'put on Christ'* is to live His life; fraught with miracles, glory, but also scorn and rejection. Every step into the dark was redeemed on Calvary and glory awaits every child of God who lives for the *'not yet'*.

In spite of the challenges, wearing You is my deepest joy.
Amen

CHAPTER 14

WHAT IS A WEAK CHRISTIAN?

As for the one who is weak in faith, welcome him, but not to quarrel over opinions. One person believes he may eat anything, while the weak person eats only vegetables. Let not the one who eats despise the one who abstains, and let not the one who abstains pass judgment on the one who eats, for God has welcomed him. Romans 14:1-3

A weak believer is one who has strong opinions about a <u>secondary</u> issue. He sets out to argue about it with anyone who disagrees. It becomes the center of his focus. His quarrelsome approach destroys fellowship. Knowing a fight is coming, others nearby will brace themselves when they see the weaker brother approaching. The nature of his relationships within the church is argumentative.

How Christians treat each other is the subject of the next 35 verses. Paul thought it was extremely important and dedicated to dedicate a chapter and a half to the topic. Human nature hasn't changed much since the time he wrote this. We are still arguing about things that don't matter all that much in the kingdom.

Who is the weak believer? At times, all of us are. I feel strongly about some topics that, to others, might be peripheral. One reason might be because I've been hurt, or judged, by others in the past for my views. The comments still sting. The rejection can ever eat away at me if I let it. Because I can't let it go and feel a need to vindicate myself, I perpetuate the argument. I need to find peace with God and security in His love.

How do *I* handle someone else who is weak? Could be a family member who turns every get together into a quarrel. Dinners turn toxic as each around the table feels like a hostage to the one who is confrontational. Or, it could be someone at church. I've known those who admit going in and out a certain door to avoid someone who bends their ear about the same thing, year in and year out. Paul advises me to stop the arguing. I greet him warmly, in Christ, but am firm about my unwillingness to discuss his hot topic. I encourage him, lovingly, to agree to disagree.

Insecure people try to surround themselves with people who agree with them on every issue. Churches and ministries can be staffed by clones. This is not healthy. The greatest thing pastors, leaders, and Christian parents can do is raise up those under them who are free to think differently. Is Christ large enough in me to love someone who believes differently than me about topics I feel strongly about? This is a test of my faith and my maturity.

Are there arguments I need to stop? Give me courage. Are there arguments my pastor needs to silence? Give him courage. Amen

WAY TO WRECK A SUNDAY!

One person esteems one day as better than another, while another esteems all days alike. Each one should be fully convinced in his own mind. The one who observes the day, observes it in honor of the Lord. Romans 14:5-6

The same legalistic churches and groups that had rules about dancing, card playing, and movies during my childhood also had rules about the Sabbath. Sunday was a day for nothing other than total quiet. For a kid, it meant ~'*no fun!*' Other families played games, went swimming in the summer, ice-skating in the winter, and went outside to play ball with their fathers. On Sundays, we brought home company for dinner after church, then sat in our living room and visited for several hours. The guests left middle of the afternoon and then everyone went to bed for long naps. I sure couldn't wait for Sundays! And what did my sister and I do while our parents visited with company in the living room? Sat on the floor of the hall and rolled a ball back and forth. Are we having fun yet?

Should there be a Sabbath day? Yes, but the Pharisees held on to the ritual of the Sabbath, and all its rules, to such an extent that it led to harmful legalism. This was a huge point of contention between the Jewish leaders and Jesus. Neither he, nor his disciples, held to strict ideas of how the Sabbath should be kept. They were criticized for their unorthodox behavior. The Pharisees hated Jesus for challenging them on this topic, something they considered sacred. Jesus said, *"The Sabbath was made for man, not man for the Sabbath. So the Son of Man is Lord even of the Sabbath."* Mark 2:27

Our family believes that one day should be set apart as a day that is different from the other six. It is God's day. We anticipate the power of our encounter with God – even Saturday night – and begin praying that He will speak to us on Sunday. Sunday is a day for our family to eat together, play games, go the lake and enjoy God's creation, and most of the time, sit on the back porch and swing with our grandchildren. No rules. Just joy because it's God's day.

As for the enforced naps of my childhood? I wouldn't mind one now but I won't do it on Sunday while the rest of my family twiddles their thumbs in the next room wishing I'd wake up so we could have some real fun. As for rolling the ball down the hall for entertainment? No one beyond the age of a two should be asked to consider that!

My Father in heaven knows that I love the Sabbath. He's redeemed it because He replaced the rules with the joy of relationship. I love the fellowship with believers, the worship of our congregation, the intimacy of our Sunday School class, the way He speaks through an anointed time of teaching, and the priceless afternoons with our family. Not to mention the benefits of soul rest on the rest of my week.

When I was rigid about the Sabbath, I was rigid about most everything. Thank you for delivering me from pointless rules. Enjoying You is my Sabbath. Amen

I'M GETTING TO HIM!

For none of us lives to himself, and none of us dies to himself. Romans 14:7

This scripture is true. First, because the Spirit of God declared it through Paul. Secondly, because it relates to the myriad of ways I interact, or fail to interact, with other people. I can believe that if I'm a recluse, I won't affect others. I'll argue that I am protecting them from myself. While I may be sparing them of my negative influence, I am withholding something else that could be of value. Even the vacuum has an impact.

Words live. *"Death and life are in the power of the tongue." Proverbs 18:21* If I call my child stupid, he will absorb the label and potentially struggle for life until someone tells him the truth. If I call another's giftedness out of the dark and define it for him, I free him to discover his uniqueness in the family of God. My words have life-shaping ramifications.

Emotions live. A sullen face repels my children and makes strangers in public shrink from me. An angry demeanor frightens others. A depressed countenance causes others to worry about us. A period of grieving invites others to join me in my tears. Even though any of these emotions might have been expressed without words, it affects others profoundly. *"When you sit down to eat with a ruler, observe carefully what is before you. . ." Proverbs 23:1* I can not let myself be enamored by someone's status and believe that the honor of their invitation will only be a positive thing. Who they are, what they feel, what they have concealed; these all affect my entire being. Emotions have life-shaping ramifications.

Actions live. If I forgive when most others wouldn't, people are stunned and consider the Gospel. If I am full of loving-kindness in a world of narcissists, the recipient is left with a lump in his throat. If I take out my anger at the driver of the car behind me, I potentially ruin his day. If I privately sin, habitually, and think it's isolated, I carry around the demonic baggage of my stronghold and pollute the fellowship of friends and family. If I withdraw completely from those in my church, I deprive them of the unique ways God is expressed through my story. *"I do not conceal your love and your truth from the great assembly." Psalm 40:10* Actions have life-shaping ramifications.

A life lived in the power of God brings the kingdom to earth. That is cataclysmic.

Potential. My eyes are open to the ways Your Spirit works through me. Amen

THERE IS NO 'WAS ALIVE'!

For to this end Christ died and lived again that he might be Lord both of the dead and of the living. Romans 14:9

Both my parents are in heaven. Both of my husband's parents are in heaven, too. In speaking of them and recalling favorite memories, it's easy to say, *"When my mother was alive, she did such and such."* The truth is, my mother's life never ended and there is no *'was'*. She is alive. She is God's daughter and though her body died, her soul never skipped a beat. It left her bodily shell and flew to Jesus. How well I remember my mother's face, moments after she died at age 64, and it was so obvious that the essence of her had left. I was looking at an empty container.

The Sadducees of Jesus' day tried to trap Jesus with a question about a physical resurrection from the dead. They believed it to be foolish. Jesus told them they were wrong for two reasons: 1.)They didn't know their scriptures very well. And, 2.)They didn't comprehend the power of God. He quoted Exodus 3:6. *"I am the God of your father, the God of Abraham, the God of Isaac, and the God of Jacob."* The *"I Am"* is in the present tense, telling all those who study the scriptures that those who die in Christ are still alive.

For any of you who are getting ready to say a temporary goodbye to someone you love, it might appear that they are going to the great unknown. They are not. The God of the Universe takes His children home, off of foreign duty. The same One who provided for them as ambassadors on alien soil, with orders to rule the earth, is the same One who rules the heavens and carries them safely to His arms. They, and we, are safe in life and in death. They, and we, are alive in life and in death.

I can't see them just as I can't see You. But I know You're there. I ascribe, again, that You have all power over life and death. I can't comprehend it but I rest in it. I ache for my own home-going. Amen

TRUSTING THAT TIME WILL STAND STILL

Why do you pass judgment on your brother? Or you, why do you despise your brother? For we will all stand before the judgment seat of God; for it is written, "As I live, says the Lord, every knee shall bow to me, and every tongue shall confess to God." Romans 14:10-11

Every powerful encounter I have had with Christ, one where He was speaking to me, had one element that remained constant. It seemed like time stood still. It seemed suspended. A powerful five-minute encounter seemed like hours. And a several hour encounter seemed like it could have been a whole day. When I recorded my last music project on CD, the one with piano, flutes, and recorder, I named it SUSPENDED IN THE SPIRIT. I prayed that the music would 'suspend' each one who listened to the music to heaven's time; one where God speaks and the moments are timeless and poignant.

Why talk about that with these scriptures? Judgments are passed on others because I am caught in the frustration of earth's time. I've heard nasty words spoken or seen unfair actions taken against me. I either lash out in response or mutter unkind words under my breath. Either way, I speak as if my words were needed to make final judgments.

Here's the thing ~ Whatever I say is a temporary judgment and it is not my place to make it. I will stand before Christ one day and be accountable for my nasty retort and the one who wronged me will *also* give an account for what he/she did. Every knee will bow.

Who is frustrating me today and wounding me on a personal level? Who is hurting the body of Christ in a way that makes me simmer in anger? Where am I expending needless energy because

I've forgotten that 'just around the corner', there will be nothing but time. Events that seem to run wild and out of control here will be reviewed in very slow motion when Jesus looks at them. Because I live by faith, I look ahead to that day and rest. I take a deep breath. Not only will my brother bow before His Lord and re-visit how he lived, I will do the same. How tragic if all my 'judgments' were re-played, all in a row, from heaven's recorder! How long would that take?

Everything I say under my breath, I have said it as far as heaven is concerned. It has been recorded. So let my 'mutterings' be the whispers of a bride who praises her Bridegroom and rehearses His goodness to her. I can trust Him to protect me, defend me, and make all things right.

You rule and I trust You. Set a watch on my tongue. Amen

WHO AM I IN THE EQUATION?

Therefore let us not pass judgment on one another any longer, but rather decide never to put a stumbling block or hindrance in the way of a brother. Romans 14:13

When my faith was young and fragile, I was easily disillusioned when I saw flaws in someone I looked up to. My spirit felt the crash as they came tumbling off the pedestal I had put them on. If the offense, in my eyes, was serious enough, I would wonder if they were even Christians. This is what those who are weak in the faith do when they pass judgment.

Those who are stronger in Christ and are seasoned followers of the Spirit have far more latitude. They understand more about true liberty within the parameters of God's moral law. Because of that, it's easy for them to look at the weaker Christian, become exasperated, and call them childish.

James Boice describes this best. *"The weak are not to judge the strong by considering them unspiritual, and the strong are not to judge the weak by considering them immature."*

If I am a young Christian, I am looking for the 'do's and don'ts' of scripture. I want God to make everything clear for me. I am a toddler – looking to a Daddy to tell me what to touch or not touch, what to embrace and what to avoid. I need clear and concise commands to show me how to walk.

If I am an older Christian, I settle on a principle like, *"Whatever you do, do all for the glory of God."* With the help of the Spirit and a conscience alive to Him, I work out its interpretation. How I choose to live within the parameters of that verse will be different than my friend.

In light of that, I am to accommodate the weaker brother. His faith doesn't have much elastic. He can't understand the meat of the Word and shouldn't be judged for that. If, in my Christian liberty, I would make him stumble by engaging in something I feel is okay for me, I protect his faith by adjusting my behavior. I take care of him. He is a toddler and adults should not expect toddlers to understand adult things.

The rub is this ~ When seasoned Christians *act* like toddlers and impose legalistic rules on the church, the way becomes foggy. And if I've been a victim of their abuse, I will clutch my new-found Christian liberty and resent having to adjust it for anyone. That is not an excuse but a reality.

Only time with Jesus, only basking in His grace, will heal the ravaged soul that has been battered by the Pharisees; the ones who claimed to see but were so often blind.

Personalize the equation. Show me who I am – in these hot issues. Give me your heart for my brother. Amen

IS HE ARGUMENTATIVE OR SPIRITUALLY WEAK?

For if your brother is grieved by what you eat, you are no longer walking in love. By what you eat, do not destroy the one for whom Christ died. Romans 14:15

Having been acquainted with numerous Christian environments that wanted to legislate nearly every part of life, I must say that I am still trying to understand this passage. Admittedly, if I listened to everyone who had an opinion about every peripheral issue of my life, I'd be frozen in place. So many have something to say about **everything**. Having lived in a fishbowl of some notoriety, your life is often studied by others. With study comes criticism. Some is ludicrous, some is ignorant due to lack of information, and some is probably justified. Sifting through it, and sorting out the hurt feelings that come from others' comments, is difficult.

So, am I to adjust my behavior to every person who say they are offended by me? Or, does Paul mean something different here? Legalism will always be with us. So will honest seekers who stumble.

I believe, for me, the answer lies in considering the one I am offending. If the spirit of legalism is at work, ruling this person's life, seeking to encroach upon the true spirit of liberty Jesus died to extend to His children, then I am not obligated to comply. I want to extend the graces of Christ Jesus to others so why would I take on a yoke that Jesus died to free me from?

But, if I encounter someone who is honestly seeking Jesus, one who loves the Word and is growing in his faith, but also one who stumbles over a particular thing I'm doing, I should consider his fragile faith and change my behavior. I am not to destroy what God is building.

For any of us who have walked out of legalism into the spacious place of grace, this can seem like a step backwards. Am I not walking again in the bondage I left behind? It **feels** like that but it is **not** like that. Look, I can't sort this out without prayer and looking for the nod of my Savior over whether another's issue with me is a valid one. If it is, Jesus will give me the grace to consider my brother even though it will take some time for my emotions, damaged by past experience, to catch up. Legalism will always be a tender spot for any of us who have been beaten up under its umbrella.

Who can sort it out? Only Your Spirit. I'm glad You're in me, teaching me, making hard things clear. Thank you for the grace to obey when my feelings betray me. Amen

WHY WOULD OTHERS BELIEVE I'M A CHRISTIAN?

For the kingdom of God is not a matter of eating and drinking but of righteousness and peace and joy in the Holy Spirit. Romans 14:17

I'm holding my breath while writing this. I'm realizing that an unbeliever may call me a Christian for all the wrong reasons. And if they do, legalism (the thing which has hurt me and the thing I despise) is still a part of me. So how do others perceive me?

- Am I known for what I don't do?
- Am I known for being out of touch with what's happening in the world?
- Am I known for being disgusted by our times and intolerant of those captive to sin?
- Do I look so peculiar by the way I dress and wear my hair that I become a joke to anyone in the mainstream?
- Am I perceived as someone who is 'against' a litany of things?

These should not be the things that define my Christianity. Paul gives a different list. It's not a long one. There are only three things on it.

1. Righteousness is my theme. Not self-righteousness but the exhilarating message that Jesus offered to wash me clean of all of my sins. I have a clean slate. I am not plagued by my past. His beautiful robe of righteousness is around my shoulders and my sin no longer defines me. He died for everything I've ever done as if He were the one who committed it.
2. Peace is my theme. Not peacemaking as in running from all conflict. Peace with God is the message I bring to those in self-hatred, self-condemnation, and inner torment. For each person who is afraid to be alone with himself; afraid of the silence, afraid of hearing God in prayer, the message that

Jesus is my peace is one that I bring to him, by example. Do others enjoy resting in my shade or do I bring conflict?

3. Joy is my theme. The Spirit of God is large in my life. I have allowed Him to transform me by believing that I'm forgiven and that I have peace with God. Gratitude and joy are the result.

What am I known for? *"Yes, she's a Christian because. . .."* The themes of my life will be what others recite when attempting to answer that question. How deeply I've been forgiven, how relieved I am that my relationship with God is peaceful, and how joyful I am over both of those things are the VERY things that make anyone's faith contagious. When my witness begins with, *"I love Jesus so much because. . ."* then I'm on the right track. The rest of it won't sound like I'm running for office.

Boasting of You. That's it entirely. Amen

THE TIMBERS OF WHAT WE'RE BUILDING

So then let us pursue what makes for peace and for mutual upbuilding. Romans 14:19

Not a mistake that Paul uses the phrase 'building up' for what happens when I love other believers as Jesus would love them. Not only are they built up on the inside but also the church at large is being built.

Ultimately, Paul wants me to understand that I am involved in the building process. And building is not haphazard. A successful project is only realized when there is a blueprint. Intentionally sticking with the design is what ensures success. Each piece of steel, each timber, each footing, must be crafted with care according to the Architect's plan.

I am part of our worship team at our church, a fantastic group of singers and musicians. Just last night I was thinking about the growth of our church and the slowly escalating move of the Spirit. This is what I saw being played out. The bass player is undergoing rigorous cancer treatments. He arrived not feeling well. We surrounded him and prayed for him. Another has a son who is toying with occult involvement. Again, time for gathering around him to pray. There was a song that required a solo. No one had an agenda to have to **be** the soloist. Actually, someone in the band who had never sung a solo before was asked to consider doing it. At then end of the evening, we all loved each other more than when we came. When we spoke with one another about the worship, there were tears of gratitude for our mutual experience of Christ and the edges of revival we are seeing on the horizon.

The music program in the church can easily be the Achilles' heel for a congregation. Musicians are under great attack, they are more sensitive – good and bad, their egos are easily threatened, and their training and skill level invites arrogance and insecurity. When actions or words are derived from any of **these** realities, the church is dis-assembled rather than built up. The Architect's design is spurned and thrown to the wind.

As I interact with other believers today, whether by email, Facebook, Twitter or in person, will my timbers be timbers that build according to God's plan or will my critical tongue and hellish agenda provide the sledgehammer that tears down a wall that God built? Every action is loaded with potential.

It's beautiful when we're building according to Your plans.
Spread the fever through me. Amen

WHEN IN DOUBT, DON'T DO IT

But whoever has doubts is condemned if he eats, because
the eating is not from faith. For whatever does not proceed
from faith is sin. Romans 14:23

Timidity, something that has plagued me for much of my life, is to live unsure of who you are and what you're called to do. While those two areas are comprehensive, what's even more crippling is to live with everyday uncertainties. Am I going to the right church? Am I serving in the right capacities in my church? And for some, have I married the right person? Have I taken the right job? Every decision, big and small, is made without _faith_ that it is the right decision. I am not a person of kingdom influence because I'm always hiding in the shadows, timid and unsure of myself. Ultimately, this is a spiritual problem. A strong father/child relationship with God is what gives anyone confidence and purpose.

I consider the times I begin a conversation with *"I've been thinking a while about saying something to* _____ *about* _____*."* It's dangerous to go forward with a potentially serious conversation on shaky ground.

Or, *"I've been thinking about making a job change." "I've been thinking about starting a new venture."* I have lived much of my life on the whims of human ideas without waiting for God to speak and confirm.

It's taken me over fifty years to realize that if I'm in doubt, don't move! If I'm in doubt, don't speak! God has promised to lead me and take me by the hand. He is not a Father of confusion. He is not unkind, withholding direction but then expecting me to move with self-doubt. If I'm unsure about whether to move forward with an idea, I know I must spend more time in prayer. I wait for the answer – confirmed by God's still small voice, or a scripture He leads me to, and/or a word from someone else who knows nothing about my dilemma but speaks a confirming word out of the blue. God is always trying to communicate with me, in more ways than I _believe_ He can speak, but I'm not tuned in and listening.

My experience is this ~ God is gracious to confirm things two, three, even four ways so that I can live by faith. I may have a strong kingdom idea but implementing it at the right time, at the right place, with the right people, takes prayer. Timidity is erased in the prayer closet.

I don't want the fallout of making the wrong decision. I don't want to start something prematurely. I don't want to say something I'll regret. I follow Your pillar of fire and Your whisper in the wind. Amen

CHAPTER 15

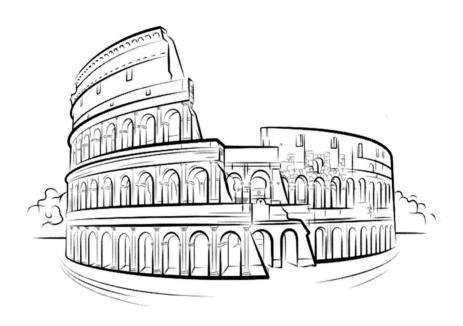

A SKIRT, HOSE, AND A STRAND OF PEARLS

We who are strong have an obligation to bear with the failings of the weak, and not to please ourselves. Romans 15:1

*C*onverted Jews and Gentiles were having such a hard time getting along that Paul has to keep writing to them, urging them to love each other. He is asking the strong to be tolerant of the limited understanding of the weak. He is also asking the weak to embrace the strong – whom they believe to be in error. What does that look like? I'll give you a personal example. First a little history.

It took our whole family a long time to move out of legalism. That was our history. We bore the pain of those who live under its umbrella; joylessness, discouragement, false guilt, and living defeated by others judgment. The way out was long and painful. To embrace new brothers and sisters in the body of Christ, those who had been portrayed as living in gross error, called for courage and a shift in spiritual paradigms. Most of the 'lifestyle issues' that had previously been labeled sinful, over time, became entirely neutral. Grace, in place of judgment, became the banner over our home.

The challenge came when I was called to re-visit the places and people who were still trapped by legalism. I will confess that my attitude stunk. I didn't want to go. Disgust, that only covered hurt, still reigned in my heart. God had to work with me by calling me to travel, embrace, and teach those who live like those in my past.

Recently, I was invited to speak to a church to speak at their annual women's conference. It was very conservative. The rules were stated up front. They only approved of one version of the Bible. The dress code was also mandatory. I decided, before praying about it, to turn down the invitation. Honestly, my flesh was groaning at the thought of it. But, God moved in my heart and told me to go. I changed all my scripture references, both in my notes, their handouts, and in PowerPoint, to the version of the Bible they required. I put together an outfit for the event; found a skirt in the back of my closet, dug for a string of pearls in the bottom of my jewelry box, and also realized I'd have to wrestle with a pair of hose and some shoes with a heel. When I came out of the bathroom dressed the morning of the conference, Elizabeth – my close friend and co-worker in this ministry said, *"Who are you?"*

Humor aside, God blessed that day. I loved the women and they were so appreciative (and acknowledged) the adaptations I had made to accommodate their invitation. We were united in our desire to see women come to Christ, love the Word, and live for His glory. On the major things, we could agree and celebrate. And, that was the whole point.

Legalism will always be tender subject for me. But you're working on me to love like You love. Amen

PICK A SIDE!

But Christ did not please himself, but as it is written, "The reproaches of those who reproached you fell on me."
Romans 15:3

"Whose side are you on anyway?" I remember the pressure. I remember the question? Bullies in my 6th grade class picked on the underdog in my class. He had done nothing wrong. I felt the pain of the afflicted and stuck my neck out to say, *"Stop hurting him."* With that, the bullies demanded that I pledge allegiance to one side or the other. I did and would have paid that day if it had not been for the end of recess and teachers standing in the gap.

In lieu of pleasure and ease, Jesus picked sides and stood with His Father. He paid for that choice with His life and He gave His disciples a heads up. *"If they hated me, they will hate you."*

Is a broader picture painted of the bias against me if I align with Christ? It is. The 'reproach' quote from this verse in Romans comes from one of the great Messianic psalms of the Old Testament. Psalm 69. If I read it with Jesus in mind, this foretells His suffering in detail.

- He was slandered by his enemies. (Ps. 69:4)
- He was estranged from his own brothers. (Ps. 69:8)

- He was the subject of gossip and ridicule. (Ps. 69:11)
- He was criticized by rulers. (Ps. 69:12)
- He was the subject of obscene songs by drunkards. (Ps. 69:12)

If I am suffering any of the above, it could be because of association. By picking sides, I acquired instant enemies, spiritual and fleshly. I can forget that. When disliked and discriminated against, I often take it personally. Mostly likely, it is not. God's enemies lash out to hurt God by hurting His kids!

I am not alive to please myself. I was born to pick sides, to speak as a sword and cooperate with God in the great meta-narrative of the Bible, the plotline of redemption. It is my privilege. It is my destiny. It is the pathway of glory and suffering. It is the way of the cross and the crown.

Today, I remember the way of Christ. I align my expectations accordingly.

I choose You. Again. Afresh. Amen

WHAT I MUST DO IF I'M GOING TO MAKE IT

For whatever was written in former days was written for our instruction, that through endurance and through the encouragement of the Scriptures, we might have hope.
Romans 15:4

Scripture is more a heart thing than it is food for the intellect. Yet, because of my early mentors, I approached God's Word as if it were for my thoughts only. Meanwhile, my heart languished and I wondered if I could go on.

While I am currently not in a place of hopelessness, I realize that you *may* be. Life has temporarily come apart. You are exhausted and out of the fight to survive. You are waiting for someone to come along and impart supernatural strength. There is no one offering it to you. There **_can_** be no one to offer enough of what you need. So what must a man or woman do to make it?

We must not read the first line of Paul's words and stop. The scriptures were written to supply what the heart needs to make it and thrive. Courage and perseverance are the outgrowth of living in the stories, instruction, and promises of scripture.

How does it work? When I'm running on empty; physically, spiritually, and emotionally, I come to Jesus and cry out for help. I ask Him to open my heart to His Word. I ask Him to do, supernaturally, what must be done so that His strength will override my weakness, so that His words will override my self-talk, so that His promises will override my helplessness. Then, prayerfully, I ask God to take me to the scriptures that are to be mine for that day. They may be the next few verses in the book that I'm currently studying or reading. Or, He may whisper the name of another book entirely. If I ask, He leads me to water.

I stay on a verse until I feel something! If I don't feel hope stirring and the faint embers of an extinguished fire burning again, I stay put. I confess my sin of unbelief and keep asking the Spirit to give me life where there is none. I know He will do it. He lives inside of me – so how can He not respond as I meditate on His very words? He **_will_** react emotionally to His own words.

Jesus did not leave any of us as orphans. When He left this earth, He knew we would feel abandoned. So, He assured us that He would come to us in a better form. He wouldn't just be available externally, to share a meal with or travel with from one town to another. He would come to live internally. No limits to our intimacy. No limits to accessibility. And when I engage with the Letter He has written to me, He responds viscerally. I can feel it. I get up from my knees and my favorite chair with a new sense of strength.

So, let me assure you. You **_can_** make it. If you are God's, He is fully invested in you. The Word you need is near you.

Daily strength. It's not a cliché. It's whispered promises between lovers. Amen

HARMONY – WHAT IS IT?

May the God of endurance and encouragement grant you
to live in such harmony with one another, in accord with
Christ Jesus, that together you may with one voice glorify
the God and Father of our Lord Jesus Christ.
Romans 15:5-6

Before Jesus was arrested, he prayed at length over His disciples. What He emphasized the most was their need for unity. Harmony and unity. Jesus knew what we would experience. Relationships can get tiresome. Relationships can get strained. Relationships can grow argumentative. Paul prayed that endurance and encouragement would fuel harmony. And how many reasons there are to pull away from each other!

I can disagree with someone's leadership style and let frustration separate us. I can struggle with someone's opinion at the conference table. I can be put off by someone's personality. I can disagree with how another is using their spiritual gift. I can strain under someone's abrasiveness and try to avoid them.

Real families try to survive the strain of relationships. So do church families. But when it comes time to raise our hands in worship together, unity can, and must, be there. We agree on one thing ~ that we love Jesus, that He is glorious, and that we will give our lives for Him if it comes to that.

The Roman church saw many divisions become insignificant when the Roman boot of oppression came down against them. When a diverse group of believers stood boldly in the center of a Roman arena and waited for the lions to devour them, petty differences were suddenly insignificant! They praised, embraced, sang, and waited for heaven together. Their hope in Christ knitted them together.

Many church leaders down through the ages have demanded harmony ~ but a kind of harmony Paul (and Jesus) did **not** advocate. Simply put – we are to unite to glorify God, the Father of Jesus Christ. For the matters pertaining to daily life, God promises to help us endure.

Where I am weary, put out, put off – give me fuel for mutual worship of You. Amen

WHEN A WELCOME IS RUINED

Therefore welcome one another as Christ has welcomed you, for the glory of God. Romans 15:7

Why would I not want to welcome someone today into my home, into my fellowship? While there may be a temporary reason like weariness, there is a much deeper reason when I can't welcome someone over a long period of time. Chances are, they have hurt me by something they did or said *or* they offended me by their beliefs and lifestyle choices.

A lukewarm welcome feels terrible, doesn't it? No welcome at all stings for a long time and the memory of it sits interminably in our soul.

Jesus' welcome of me is beautiful. It has a history of longing. He knew me before I was ever conceived, knew I'd be born with the sin of Adam and lost without the intervention of a Savior. Because He longed for me to be His, He planned His coming to earth. He was called 'The Lamb' from before the foundation of the world; so old was the plan to make a way for me to be welcomed into His family.

He welcomed me even though I was His enemy. He welcomed me even though my list of personal offenses against Him was long. He welcomed me by paying for my ransom with His own death. Nothing, absolutely nothing, threatens His open embrace.

When I walk the halls of church, I am always tempted to welcome some more than others. Some, I like more than others. But is this the criterion of Jesus? If I'm in fellowship with people long enough, I will get hurt. When I see them, I'll be tempted to mutter under my breath, *"I remember what you did!"* That taints my ability to welcome them.

The underlying theme of today's scripture is forgiveness. I knew it as soon as I read it. Forgiveness is a lifestyle. When I'm offended, I lift the person who committed it to Jesus and leave them, and the offense, with Him. I'm not qualified to take His seat and play judge and jury. Otherwise, I hold others at arms length and fail to welcome them. At that point, God is mocked – not glorified. The world watches and they rightly assume that I am not like the God I say I love.

Forgive. Embrace. Breathe the life of the cross. God is lifted high and adored when warm welcomes, though undeserved by human standards, are extended. Gracious responses to offenders give off the aroma of a gracious God who forgives sin.

When my hug is tentative, I will be aware. Amen

BLIND TO GOD'S PLANS

And again Isaiah says, "The root of Jesse will come, even he who arises to rule the Gentiles; in him will the Gentiles hope." Romans 15:12

The first announcement that there would be a Savior to the world came in Genesis. The Psalms are full of revelation that **all** nations will praise the Lord. Psalm 117 is the shortest Psalm in the Bible, only two verses long, but it has one of the broadest outlooks. The nations of the world are worshiping God because of His love and His faithfulness.

Paul's quote in today's scripture comes from Isaiah 11. Through the line of King David (Jesse was his father), a king will come and bring universal blessing. This will be the messianic age when lions and lambs will live together without the urge to kill and without the fear of being prey.

If God's plan was to include all nations in His plan for salvation, how did the Jews miss it? They had the Torah and had memorized it. Yet, their bias against God sharing His blessings outside their borders were expressed strongly down through the centuries.

It makes me wonder today what I'm missing. Is my Gospel inclusive? It is easy to be standoffish with those I don't understand, with those whose culture is so unlike my own. I am repelled by their violence, their practices, and shake my head in disbelief when I see their stories portrayed on the evening news. They are so far from God and the gap seems insurmountable. Yet, God is revealing Himself to modern-day Sauls; to those who kill Christians and to those whose passion is to destroy every vestige of Christianity. He appears to them in dreams, in visions, and they wake up exclaiming, *"Lord Jesus!"* Do I rejoice over such stories? Am I surprised over the power of God?

God is the Savior of any who want Him, of any to whom He grants the power to believe. It may be a Rabbi of a rural town in Israel. It may be an Imam in Pakistan. It may be a Chinese government official who, at this very moment, arrests pastors in his village. And it may be American teenagers who, at this moment, are so infected with the darkness of our age that their spiritual condition appears hopeless. God's plan to be the God of __all__ peoples prevails. My heart must adjust accordingly – humbly – to rejoice in such unbiased love. And my heart must hope in a God powerful enough to touch the one *__I consider most unlikely__* to believe.

Give me global eyes and a global heart. Amen

CAN I PRAY FOR YOU?

May the God of hope fill you with all joy and peace in believing, so that by the power of the Holy Spirit you may abound in hope. Romans 15:13

This sounds like the end of Romans. Paul expresses a beautiful hope and prayer. It is packed with everything anyone might ever need. While His prayer moves my heart and I could write about it, the Spirit of God prompted me to pray these scripture over each of you today. I hope it connects. I hope it lights the flame of hope in your heart. I hope you are stronger and resolved at the end of it. It is a privilege to love and pray for you.

Lord, You can see Your child. She's reading this and needing You to break through the barriers to her faith. She's tired, ready to cave in. Afraid to hope. Afraid to feel the pain of waiting for you. The ability to endure no longer exists.

She hoped in someone for something she needed and hope was smashed. She has no joy and no peace in believing that You are true to Your promises. She has not felt the power of the Holy Spirit in a long time.

First, I ask that You deliver her from evil. Send Your angels to wherever she is right now and fight against what she cannot see. Defeat her enemies and put a blood covering over her. Restrict all enemies from speaking to her and moving against her. In the authority of Christ Jesus, I cancel their plans to lie, steal, kill and destroy her faith.

I bind her mind to Yours. Be large in her, Holy Spirit. Every prayer that has been spoken over her, bring to full budding and blossom. Every scripture that she has planted in her heart, bring out of the deep and put it within her heart's grasp. As she opens Your Word today, remove the veil from her eyes to see the power of Your love, the power of Your authority, and the power of Your hand to be the source of all that she needs. Bring such powerful revelation as she reads that a journal page cannot contain her insights.

Through Your Word, and through the God-moments that You will ordain today for her, grow her faith and her hope. Transform the flickering flame of her faith into a blaze of glory. Infuse her heart with fresh faith and the ability to stand in the cement of Your love and believe You! You are not distant. You are not passive. You are a God of intervention and no one who has ever trusted in You has ever been put to shame.

Break through the fog. Reveal Yourself to her so that she may see Your glory and live. The kingdom is here now and near her.

Seal this by the power of the Spirit and it is by the name of Jesus Christ, Son of God, Savior of the world, and King of Kings, that I pray these things. Amen

RELEASED TO BECOME GOOD

I myself am satisfied about you my brothers, that you your-
selves are full of goodness, filled with all knowledge and
able to instruct one another. Romans 15:14

"She's such a good person!" What does that mean? In circumstances when most would _not_ be good, she is good.

Paul didn't write Romans to a disobedient and carnal church. It
might appear that way when I consider the depth of his message on
law and grace. He was really writing to a church that had embraced
Christ deeply. He reveals that he calls them good – inferring that
their faith in the Gospel had translated to a goodness born of the
Spirit.

So what's going on when I am stingy, unforgiving, vindictive,
pessimistic, controlling, and hopeless about the future? I have not
embraced the full impact of the Gospel in my heart. Stressful circumstances don't offer me an excuse from being good. The message
of the Gospel of Christ and the power of the cross supersede any bad
day and any set of crushing circumstances.

Imagine someone who has been locked up in solitary confinement for 35 years, but then gets an unexpected pardon. One day he
walks out of a dark jail cell into the vast sunshine – free to go where
he wants. What is his posture from that day forward? Pinching himself that he is free. Grateful every morning that he can awake to
the sounds of the birds singing. I am that person. Once condemned,
imprisoned forever and separated from Christ, I was set free by His
death to forever live in the Light. If I have grasped that, I will dance
over the choices available to me today to truly live out from under
the life sentence of sin. Radical generosity will be the result.

Once guilty, I am now forgiven. Once unloved, I am now cherished. Once hopeless, I am now held firmly by the God of hope.
Once one who demanded fairness from others, I am now excited
to give others a taste of the grace I have received. Once plagued by
insecurity and unaware of myself, I am now defined by my Creator
and free to be a unique, authentic creation.

Joy and goodness are released at the cross. If I am technically a believer but goodness is far from me, the message of the Gospel has not fully impacted my heart. Only the Spirit of God can take it there and melt my heart of stone.

Don't let me forget my deliverance and pardon. Amen

HOARDING THE TREASURE

But on some points I have written to you very boldly by way of reminder, because of the grace given me by God to be a minister of Christ Jesus to the Gentiles in the priestly service of the gospel of God, so that the offering of the Gentiles may be acceptable, sanctified by the Holy Spirit.
Romans 15:15-16

When I'm sitting on a discovery of wealth, what do I do? Do I call and tell everyone I know about my find so that it can be shared? Or, do I save it all for myself?

That's how Israel felt when the love and favor of God went outside their borders. They felt God's love was theirs exclusively. They resented the fact that His grace and mercy knew no boundaries. Though they had been chosen to be God's people, they were also commissioned, as far back as the early Old Testament, to be a nation of priests to those outside of Israel. *". . .But you shall be called the priests of the Lord; they shall speak of you as the ministers of our God. . ." Is. 61:6* No wonder Paul reminded the Roman church that he, as a Jew, was a priest to the Gentiles.

Love like the kind God gives is what my heart has always been seeking. Can't I just bask in it and enjoy it without an obligation to make sure others find it too? God offers me a place to belong, the kind of place I've always been seeking. Can't I make myself at home in His heart without sharing the space with others? The more I've been deprived here, the more I will wrap my arms tightly around Jesus and want exclusivity. But personal obsession is not the heart of the Gospel. I receive to give. I am healed to heal others. I am loved to love. And in the mystery of becoming a priest and pouring myself out for others, God pours out His favor on me and that feels exclusive.

Though I am a priest, my relationship with God is unique, as is yours. He relates to each of us in ways that no other person can fully understand. Just as you and I might know some of the same people, each of us has a relationship with them that is unique to our heart and to our personal history.

Jesus is mine and He is everyone's. He loves me completely and He loves everyone. I can and should be a priest. There is no risk. I don't need to hoard Him. It is safe for me to share the good news.

For any who feel a need to enjoy you exclusively, heal us.
Amen

OVER WHAT CAN I BE PROUD?

In Christ Jesus, then, I have reason to be proud of my work
for God. Romans 15:17

If you heard your pastor say that he was proud of the job he was doing, would that be a red flag? Probably, the answer is yes. A toxic kind of pride is so rampant that when we hear the word 'proud', it has negative connotations. Paul says that he is proud of his work. What's up?

1.) Paul is at the end of his life. He is reviewing his ministry. Just after writing Romans, he will be arrested and die as a martyr. As he looks back, he is proud of what he sees. But only because what he sees was done 'in Christ.'

I think of a child who has been asked to clean his room. When he's finished, he comes and gets his mother to show her. He stands proudly in the doorway and proclaims, *"And I did it all by myself!"* This is the problem in ministry. I can call myself to noble things, label it a 'holy calling', and because I have some natural gifts, I can do it *'by myself'*. I have not had to live *'in Christ'*. The results are really wood, hay, and stubble. Paul is proud of his work because there is no way he could have faced imprisonment, beatings, floggings, confrontations by emperors, and angry mobs without the love, grace, and spiritual dynamite provided by the Spirit of God.

2.) This leads to the next point. Paul is proud of his work but to most, it appeared that He failed. He didn't usually win over crowds. He spoke; they stormed him in anger. He preached; he was imprisoned and beaten. If I measure success by receptivity, then I should doubt Paul's calling and ministry.

The more we travel toward end times, the more difficult it is to find receptive audiences. Recent talk among well known pastors reveal a suspicion that only 30% of most congregations are actually believers. Biblical teaching grates and only the minority really embraces Jesus.

On the other side of the cross, only thirty gathered in the upper room. Where were the masses? Weeded out by persecution.

Here are the bottom lines for me this morning. 1.) If I live through my connection to Jesus, then I can say that I am proud of my work. And, 2.) My work is a success if it only wins a few. If most are repelled, I follow in the footsteps of Jesus and the likes of Paul.

I used to be depressed over things I should have celebrated.
Keep re-writing all my paradigms according to your values.
Amen

WHEN I CAN'T SEE THE SEEDS OF CHANGE

. . .I make it my ambition to preach the gospel, not where
Christ has already been named, lest I build on someone
else's foundation. Romans 15:20

Some, like Paul, are called to plant seeds, to take the Gospel to remote parts of the earth. Others are like Apollos, coming along behind to water what's been planted. We who are called to water other's seeds are the majority.

I heard from a mother yesterday who is heartbroken that her adult son is so far from Christ. She is reading the prayer every day over him that God led me to write about a week ago. She is not alone in her grief. Every one of us love people in whom the seed was planted long ago but who are showing no signs of following Christ. We can easily despair and lose hope. I've been there recently.

But seeds are just that. Seeds. Out of sight. Beneath the soil. They are there, just not visible, and need watering. If I despair and abandon the process of spiritual gardening, I won't hasten the work of God in their lives.

God promises that if I speak the Word of God into the lives of people and into desperate situations in my life, it will not return void. (This is what it is to rule my garden.) I have spiritual dynamite in my hands in the form of the Word of God but if I never speak it or pray it, I never see my garden flourish. When I see nothing but brown soil, it is not the time to quit! It is the time to till, cultivate, and use my mouth to, either plant, or water what is there.

"Is not my Word like fire, declares the Lord, and like a hammer that breaks the rock in pieces?" Jer. 23:29 Hearts of stone are broken, warmed, reshaped and transformed into flesh only one way. Through the speaking of the Word.

Lord Jesus, forgive me for unbelief. Who am I to declare anyone a hopeless cause? The Word of God has been planted in their lives. They have scripture hidden away in their hearts. They have been prayed over and loved in Your name. But I don't see any evidence that the seeds are there today. In faith, I water. I abandon the illusion that I am speechless. Lead me to three verses of scripture that I can stand in for my loved one. I will write them out, insert their name, and pray these verses out loud. I make 'speaking Your Word' a way of life. It will be the norm, not the exception. As I water the seeds with Your Word, transform the landscape of their garden. According to Your mercy and Your power, bring vistas of green where there is only a brown wilderness. I wait for You with tears and faith. Amen

HOW A MINISTRY SURVIVES

. . .Since I have longed for many years to come to you, I
hope to see you in passing as I go to Spain, and to be helped
on my journey there by you. Romans 15:23-24

Those who lead ministries are dependent on God's people to
provide for what they need. Paul made it clear that He was coming
to Rome not only because he longed to see <u>them</u> but to ask them to
provide for whatever he needed to travel to Spain. His needs would
include food, money, fares for travel, and traveling companions.

There is a balance when leading a ministry. I know missionaries
who feel entitled. They have no trouble walking through homes,
where they are guests, and ask for furniture and objects they admire.
They offend their hosts and leave a bad taste for missions. The
implication is, *"I have given up everything to follow Christ and*
you haven't! Support me!"

Seeing this abuse, it is easy for me, as a leader of a ministry, to
downplay the needs of **Daughters of Promise**. I am reminded today
that this is an overcorrection and a mistake. I will be making some
changes. Not only does this ministry operate on the gifts of God's
sons and daughters, but it could greatly benefit from provisions that
are not monetary; donated skills, equipment, etc.

If you also labor for the kingdom, you should not hesitate to
make your needs known. We are a team, not lone rangers. Paul never
would have reached Spain before coming one last time to Rome,
where he was martyred, if the church had not rallied to get him
there. We might re-label his endeavors *"The Outreach of Roman*
Church" instead of *"Paul's Missionary Journeys."*

Make sure I ask for what I need without apology. Amen

OVERHAUL OF A MINDSET

At present, however, I am going to Jerusalem bringing
aid to the saints. For Macedonia and Achaia have been

pleased to make some contribution for the poor among the saints at Jerusalem. Romans 15:25-26

When charitable giving is the topic of a Sunday morning, I can tune out because I believe that I am already generous. My mindset is skewed due to the fact that I am innately selfish. Unless I am like Jesus, willing to give up everything for an enemy, I know little of generosity.

Those in Macedonia and Achaia were non-Jews from wealthy urban areas in the Roman Empire. Their mindset was that Rome taxes the weak in order to fund the empire. Many of the Gentiles enjoyed their wealthy status at the expense of the Jews throughout Judea. To give back to them charitably, instead of take, was an upside-down idea. Jesus does that well. He turns everything on its end, making our head spin, reinforcing the reality that kingdom thinking is the opposite of everything we've believed to be true.

Who might be the last person I would consider giving to today? Perhaps my mindset has closed off my spiritual hearing. Could Jesus ask me to give something costly to someone I have, historically, been at odds with? He might. The question is this ~ can I hear Him if He asks?

New life in Christ re-writes old paradigms. I feel compassion for those whom I've hated. I give when it's undeserved. I make peace with those who have been borne the brunt of generational biases within my family. The wealthy Gentile believers within the Roman Empire allowed a transformation of their affections for the sake of the Gospel. They sent Paul back to Jerusalem, not with news of higher taxes, but with generous financial gifts. With his arrival came the aroma of a Christ-like they had only begun to understand.

I'm in Kindergarten. Show me what generosity looks like.
Amen

'YOU WON'T BELIEVE WHAT'S HAPPENED TO ME!'

I know that when I come to you I will come in the fullness of the blessing of Christ. Romans 15:29

The word 'blessing' has been thrown around so much in our Christian culture that it may as well be a common word like shoe or house. Yet, what it really means is ~ something miraculous has happened to me. I should use then word when I follow it up with, *"You won't believe what's happened to me!"* Paul is going to come to Rome in the fullness of blessing. What does that look like for him or for me? Blessing is based on unbelievable realities. I've chosen three.

1. "The Spirit himself bears witness with our spirit that we are children of God and if children, then heirs." Rom. 8:16-17 What is the announcement? *"You won't believe what's happened to me. I've just inherited a fortune and become an heir, equal in wealth to what God gave Jesus Christ. When I die, it's mine. My heart is bursting. I'm blessed."*

2. "All are yours. You are Christ's and Christ is God's." I Cor. 3:22-23 What is the announcement? *"You won't believe what's happened to me. Christ, yes Christ, has claimed me to be His. And because I'm His, His Father wants me too. I'm blessed!"*

3. "Blessed be the God and Father of our Lord Jesus Christ, who has blessed us in Christ with every spiritual blessing in the heavenly places." Eph. 1:3 What is the announcement? *"You won't believe what's happened to me. God loves me and is looking for ways to give gifts to me that I couldn't possibly buy, nor have I earned. It's just too good to be true and I had to share the news with you."*

The wonderful thing about being blessed is that my blessing can't be stolen. It's mine no matter how well or how poorly my day is going. It's mine no matter how badly I mess up. The love is dependable, constant, and secure. Why don't I walk around in fullness of heart? Probably because at some level, I don't really believe it. I'm living in the cursed state of this world and the brokenness of past relationships. May it not be.

I'm looking up. Everything I want is already in You. Amen

MORE THAN A MENTION

I appeal to you, brothers, by our Lord Jesus Christ and by the love of the Spirit, to strive together with me in your prayers to God on my behalf, that I may be delivered from the unbelievers in Judea and that my service for Jerusalem may be acceptable to the saints. . . Romans 15:30-31

Some of you are struggling for your lives whether spiritually, emotionally or physically. You know that you desperately need prayer but where are those who will cover your needs in a way that is more than just a quick mention? Where are the ones who will get on their face before God to listen to the Spirit on your behalf, to invest time and energy and be spiritually intuitive as to your needs? Who will cover your situation from every possible angle? They are few. And they are always the ones who believe in the power of God and the power of answered prayer.

Someone who is having surgery today needs a more strategic prayer than this ~ *"Lord, be with him in surgery today and be in control. Amen"* This is pretty lame, lazy, and shortsighted. Yet, this is what our prayer meetings sound like, isn't it? Those who pray for someone facing surgery need to be thorough. What about praying for the surgeon to have a sound night's sleep the night before? What about praying for the operating room to be filled with God's glory and a host of angels? What about praying that any plans of the enemy to sabotage would be thwarted by the victory Jesus won for us on Calvary? What about praying that Jesus would be in control of every incision and movement of the surgeon's hands? What about safe passage under anesthesia? What about a blanket of grace to cover the patient?

Paul nailed it when he asked his readers to *'strive'* in prayer. It's work. It's investment. But he needed it. He knew he might face an angry mob. His life was at stake. And he knew that the church is often equally dangerous. The message of the Gospel can fall on unreceptive hearts.

For whomever I pray today, may God help me perceive the needs as He sees them. Someone's life may depend on it. Praying without ceasing is often to cover the <u>same</u> situation from one new angle after another – as God gives insight.

Make me a kingdom strategist. Amen

REFRESHING

So that by God's will I may come to you with joy and be refreshed in your company. Romans 15:32

The word 'refresh' is found 17 times in scripture. In most of them, the spirit of one person is being refreshed in the company of another. That got me thinking. What really happens when I am refreshed? Who is it that refreshes me? And most importantly, am I a person who refreshes others? Do I leave them feeling stronger or weaker?

I jotted down names of people who refresh me when I'm in desperate need of it. What is it about each one? Each is:

- Someone who is deeply at rest in the Lord.
- Someone who is unshaken by life.
- Someone who has had their needs met in Christ and can listen well without self-distraction.
- Someone whose heart is full of the scriptures and it comes out of their mouth at just the right time.
- Someone who inspires faith, not blind optimism.

- Someone who whispers courage based on God's presence and promises.
- Someone who prays for me, by name, with intuition and discernment.

I know it's possible to be refreshed by someone who is kind and positive. Perhaps they're not even a believer but their personality and attitude toward life are contagious. But when I need more than a pep-talk and someone to speak God's words into my life for perspective and strength, I won't get it from a cheery disposition. Without Christ, there is __no__ foundation to their strength. Their encouragement has no substance.

Paul knew that if He went to Rome to be with the Roman believers, he would be refreshed. Weariness and discouragement would be replaced by hope and renewal. If I don't have others in my life who refresh, I need to ask God why and possibly make changes about those with whom I fellowship. Jesus sent his disciples out in pairs ~ so important was the spiritual refreshment that happens between two who love Jesus.

Make me more like my list. Amen

CHAPTER 16

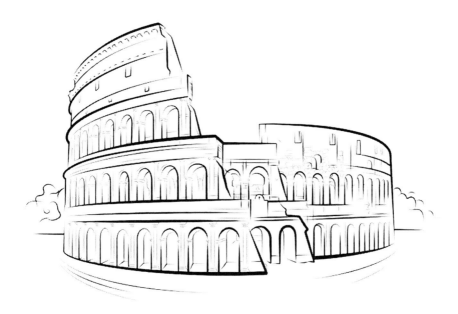

IS IT REALLY INSIGNIFICANT?

I commend to you our sister Phoebe, a servant of the church at Cenchreae, that you may welcome her in the Lord in a way worthy of the saints, and help her in whatever she may need from you, for she has been a patron of many and of myself as well. Romans 16:1

A ex-murderer wrote a letter to a church in Rome. A woman who was moved by his faith contributed extensively to his ministry and felt called to serve him. When he needed someone to deliver his letter, she took on the burden of carrying it to the Roman church.

Travel for women was dangerous. Most likely, she had others traveling with her but Paul doesn't mention them. Phoebe stood out.

She had no idea the power of the letter she carried on that trip. The theological history of the church was in that letter. The Reformation was in her satchel. She couldn't know, of course. Nor do we, when we choose to obey God in what we believe is insignificant.

This weekend, my husband and I joined a group from our church on a trip to Atlanta to see a live theater production of C.S. Lewis', **The Screwtape Letters**. A fictitious work on what happens in hell when higher demons train younger recruits to destroy a Christian, Lewis admits to writing this work from personal experience. He knew well how cunningly and strategically the enemy works in a Christian's life. What was so self-revealing and risky to publish continues to speak to the church long after his death.

When God compels me to speak, or go, or serve, I never know what it means long-term. A simple message may seem insignificant but I can never know that. Who would have thought that some scratching on parchment in the baggage of a well-to-do woman traveling to Rome would shake up the church and history would forever be re-written! The domino effect of my own obedience potentially has the same ramifications.

I knew who Paul was – but not Phoebe. But I'd never know him if it weren't for her. Burn the message of simple obedience in my heart. Amen

THRIVING IN CHANGE

Greet Priscilla and Aquila, my fellow workers in Christ
Jesus, who risked their necks for my life. Romans 16:3-4

In a day when so many have lost their jobs and businesses and
are trying to get any kind of employment to make ends meet (even
something that has nothing to do with their field of education), it is
easy to believe that life is over. Watching their homes go into fore-
closure, moving across state lines to live with parents and relatives,
these undermine feelings of stability.

It is always comforting to know the stories of those who have
gone before us. Priscilla and Aquila, invaluable in their work for the
kingdom, lived on the run. Stability was not measured by predict-
ability but by learning to rest in a God who would use them and
provide for them no matter where they went.

Originally from Pontus, they settled in Rome. Not there long,
they were forced to leave when the Emperor Claudius expelled Jews
from the city. Did they leave everything behind? Was it a fast and
traumatic exit?

They went to Corinth and set out to make a living there. Aquila
became a tent maker and that's where he met Paul. Instead of set-
tling in Corinth for life, Aquila and his wife left with Paul when he
left. Together, they went to Ephesus to begin life, yet again, in a new
place. But Paul got into trouble there when a mob, led by those in
the 'idol making industry', rioted against him. Again, Aquila and
Priscilla stood with him and left everything to move back to Rome.

In Rome, they established a house church and continued to disciple believers and give their lives for the kingdom. Pontus, Rome,
Corinth, Ephesus, and back to Rome. Many changes – some chosen
– some not.

No matter what life brings regarding employment, housing, and
where we are forced to live, kingdom life can still thrive. Our iden-
tities are not written by earth but by the One to whom we belong.
Even as sojourners, our mouths still work to spread a Gospel that
lives long after us. May God help each of us re-define what stability

means. Change is not our enemy. False expectations, however, have driven many to despair.

Aquila, my brother, Priscilla, my sister ~ among the cloud of witnesses praying for us as uncertainty threatens. I remember their story. Amen

SEEING JESUS UNDER PRESSURE

Greet Rufus, chosen in the Lord; also his mother, who has been a mother to me as well. Romans 16:13

Rufus was the son of Simon of Cyrene. This is the same Simon who carried Jesus' cross through the streets – to the hill of Golgatha – when Jesus was too weak to do it himself. Simon was a Jew and would have grown up despising the Romans who oppressed them. To be commanded by Roman soldiers to carry the cross of a condemned man must have been bitter. He had to comply without a fight.

But on that journey, Simon saw Jesus under the greatest pressure of his life. There was no swearing. No vows to get even. Even in agony, Jesus was full of grace. There is no way to view a man's darkest moments and not get a sense of 'who and what' he is really made of. There is a saying, *"Who a man is under pressure is who a man is."* Can you imagine what Simon saw, what he heard, and how he was changed? Did he stay to watch the crucifixion? Did those hours at the foot of the cross draw Him to Christ?

Simon became a believer and passed on his faith to his sons. The stories he passed on to them at mealtime, at bedtime, were most likely tearful accounts of the most important walk of his life.

What I share of Christ, in tears, is what impacts others the most. No one cares what I know until they see that I am deeply moved by it. Preaching to my audience is the next best thing to sharing personal stories. No wonder Charles Wesley said, *"I learned more about theology from my mother than from all the theologians in England."*

Oh Lord, help me not to be a know it all. Just a storyteller.
Amen

WHO WOULD I MENTION?

Priscilla, Aquila, Epaenetus, Mary, Anronicus and Junia,
Ampliatus, Urbanus, Stachys, Apelles, Aristobulus, Herodion,
Narcissus, Tryphaena Tryphosa, Persis, Rufus, Asyncritus,
Phlegon, Hermes, Patrobas, Hermas, Julie, Nereus, Olympas.
People Paul remembered in the last chapter of Romans.

I'm nearly at the end of Romans. What a journey over this past year. As I start reading the last 5-6 verses, I realize these are the last words of Paul's to the Roman church. He won't see them again and he has invested so much of himself into the birth, and growth, of their church. He did it to his peril as he was beaten and imprisoned. Though Paul has often gotten a bad rap as being non-relational, his closing words are all about people and relationships.

If I were about to die or to be taken away in chains, what kind of a goodbye list would I make? This morning I daydreamed. I imagined that I will send a good friend on a journey to visit the people who have impacted my life the most profoundly. *"Tell _____ that I thank him for showing me the face of Christ through his kind spirit." "Tell _____ that I thank her for choosing Christ when she could have easily abandoned her faith because of her life story."*

So, apart from this public devotional, for time's sake I'm toying to make a list of 10 people. Who is it that has invested in me? Who has made a difference in my life that, at this moment, is completely unaware of their impact? I haven't started it yet – but perhaps as I do – I'll want to send some notes today to express my thanks. None of us knows if we'll get another chance.

And an additional question would be this? Whose list would I be on? Is my faith that captivating?

Above all, I am filled with gratitude as I see faces cross mind. Amen

POSTSCRIPT

I appeal to you, brothers, to watch out for those who cause divisions and create obstacles contrary to the doctrine that you have been taught; avoid them. For such persons do not serve our Lord Christ, but their own appetites, and by smooth talk and flattery they deceive the hearts of the naïve. Romans 16:17-18

I've had long phone conversations with friends over the years. Just as it appears it's time to hang up, one of us says, *"Oh, one more thing!"* That 'one more thing' might have been frivolous but most of the time it was something important.

I remember one occasion when I was visiting a friend. We had said our goodbyes. I was in my car, backing out of the driveway, when in the rear view mirror I saw her running down her driveway after me. *"There's something I've been too scared to tell you the whole time you've been here but I can't let you drive away without speaking it."* I pulled in, parked, and we sat in the car to talk another hour.

This is tone of the important p.s. in Paul's long letter. He has said his goodbyes. He has reviewed faces, carved out last words, and just as he's ready to say farewell, he stops to change gears entirely. What is so important? The matter of bad doctrine seeping into their midst.

What's so dangerous about that! Isn't it usually over minor issues? That's naïve if that's what I believe. Here's the thing. The Word of God is the Word of Jesus. Anything that is added or distorted is *no longer* the words of Jesus. Whose words are they? Who would want to twist, distort, minimize, and mislead? Our enemy. He is subtle and works through the sinful appetites of men through their cravings for power, control, respect, or wealth. Adjust a small preposition in a sentence and the whole meaning changes.

Paul is parental. He sees the faces of these loved ones and is suddenly afraid for the potential that exists for bad doctrine; the kind that might begin small and lead them away from their secure position as a much-loved son or daughter of God. Peter was also parental and warned his loved ones of the same thing. *"Be on your guard so that you may not be carried away by the error of lawless men and fall from your secure position."* What is the security he speaks of? Knowing who my God is and knowing that I can trust Him no matter what. Bad doctrine always erodes trust and causes me to back up.

And important postscript to any conversation.

One bad doctrine, Lord. Like – You could disown me and I could lose my salvation – and I'll live in fear. So, please set off alarms so that I am not fooled in this age of deception.
Amen

MAKING RIGHT JUDGMENTS

Your obedience is known to all, so that I rejoice over you, but I want you to be wise as to what is good and innocent and what is evil. Romans 16:19

Do mature Christians need to be concerned about being deceived? Aren't they grounded enough in the Word to be past such a threat? Apparently not. And if any of us believe we are, we live dangerously.

As long as I live here on earth, I can be fooled. Good and evil aren't always obvious. The author of evil is so good at deceiving that he can make what is sinister appear holy.

What is wisdom? Warren Wiersbe defines it as 'knowing what to do when there is no biblical precedent.' Satan is always in the cobwebs. He weaves webs around the outlines of our Christian lives and mixes in his own brand of what appears to be holy. His options are never dark-colored but glittering and full of light.

He might tell me to stand up for righteousness and discipline a child when grace is called for.

He might tell me to take on a role in the church that I am really not called to do. He is the author of burnout.

He might bring a wolf in sheep's clothing to my church; one whose family looks stellar and whose outward appearance deceives.

Wisdom is having God's mind on all things pertaining to my life. Here's the crucial point. No matter how mature I may be in my faith, I do not have the perfect mind of God. I can't make judgment calls on my own.

Ah, but Wisdom lives *in* me! I can bind my mind to His, make all things a matter of prayer, ask Him to rise up and speak to me about what is good and what is evil, ask Him to wave red flags when someone or something isn't right. When I lack wisdom, He promises to give it.

The Spirit is the One who promises to define what's in the shadows.

I've made judgment calls on my own and paid dearly. I thought I assessed things clearly. Never again. I need You at every moment to unveil 'what is'. Amen

JESUS SHOWED ME HOW

The God of peace will soon crush Satan under your feet. The grace of our Lord Jesus Christ be with you.
Romans 16:20

How does God crush Satan under my feet? Now, that is a visual! I crush the serpent's head the same way Jesus did. This act of subjection was predicted in Genesis. *"You (Jesus) shall crush his head and he shall bruise your heel."* Gen. 3:15 While Jesus declared that he came to destroy the works of the devil, and he did this through signs and wonders, the actual crushing of Satan's head didn't happen until the cross. Jesus had to give His life as the perfect Lamb in order for Satan's power to be broken.

Paul says that I have a similar opportunity to crush Satan under *my* feet. How does this happen? Just as Jesus gave up all rights to his life and came to do His Father's will, and Satan was crushed, this act of subjection is repeated again and again through me and every child of God. When I give up all rights to *my* life and choose righteousness over sin, Satan is crushed.

Ultimately, Satan must use people to get his work done. He needs bodies he can control. As long as I take his bait, I give him free reign on the earth.

And ultimately, God uses people to get his work done too. He needs bodies His Spirit can control. As long as I take His orders, Jesus lives His life through me, yet again, and crushes the enemy beneath my feet.

So – today I follow Jesus and accomplish powerful warfare in three ways. 1.) I live a life of constant communion with my Father. 2.) I speak the Word into every kingdom clash. 3.) I make righteous choices with the grace that God offers me. Ah, the cumulative effect of an army on the move, all obedient, all prayerful, all speaking the words of God upon the earth puts Satan in his place. Today, I will not waver.

The grace that kept Jesus all the way to the cross is mine. How can I know defeat if I rely on you? Defeat evil through my life today. Amen

THE ENDING TO ROMANS

Now to him who is able to strengthen you according to my gospel and the preaching of Jesus Christ, according to the revelation of the mystery that was kept secret for long but has now been disclosed and through the prophetic writings has been made known to all nations, according to the command of the eternal God to bring about the obedience of faith – to the only wise God be glory forevermore through Jesus Christ! Amen

It's the end of Romans. How do you feel? Have you been changed?

I remember the day, sitting on the edge of my bed in a hotel room in Minneapolis, that God spoke to me and impressed upon me to study and teach Romans. I was trembling, literally, with the prospect of such an undertaking. That was two years ago. Two hundred and forty devotionals later, you'll never know how many mornings I feared that I would never grasp the meaning of the verse in front of me. My testimony today is this ~ The Holy Spirit loves to teach and is faithful to anyone who seeks to be moved by the most difficult scriptures.

In the end, Paul's last words are about the sources of strength. He will need it for the violent end of his life and ministry. And he knows we will need it too. We have been sent out to live as sheep amongst wolves.

Are you fearful of the wolves? Are you out of physical strength? Out of emotional stamina? Are you intellectually tormented, wondering if what you believe is really true?

Paul sends us to three places to get strength.

1. Review the Gospel. Go back through the Romans devotionals (perhaps you've saved a handful) and allow yourself to be stirred up by what you previously highlighted.
2. Review Jesus' words. What if I asked you to tell me your favorite Bible story about Jesus? What would it be? Why do the words move you? Explain them in a paragraph like you would to a child.

Finally, go digging in Isaiah, Jeremiah, or Micah. Taste their despair over their times but also their hope in the Savior to come. Feel the wonder of Jesus' arrival on the earth and be wide-eyed that you are alive in a time when you have the scriptures in front you and are able to see, both the prophecy, and the fulfillment. You have seen the mystery revealed.

Romans has given me substance and a weight to my faith. In the center of it is Jesus Christ, stunning in all of His glory, reminding me that the Gospel is a feast on so many theological and experiential dimensions. Even at the end of a book like Romans, I know I've only scratched the surface.

I hope you will journey with me to the next chapter of my life ~ whatever that may be.

To You be all glory, honor, and praise. Amen

CPSIA information can be obtained at www.ICGtesting.com
Printed in the USA
LVOW132013280313

326466LV00002B/5/P